Bernard Mandevil.
of Publick Stews´

A
Modeſt DEFENCE

OF

Publick STEWS:

OR, AN

E S S A Y

UPON

W H O R I N G,

As it is now practis'd in theſe Kingdoms.

Nimirum propter Continentiam Incontinentia neceſſaria eſt, incendium ut ignibus extinguitur.
Seneca.

Omne adeo genus in terris, hominumq; ferarumq;
Et genus aquoreum, pecudes, pictaq; volucres,
In furias, ignemq; ruunt. Virg. Georg. 3.

Written by a LAYMAN.

LONDON;
Printed by A. MOORE near St. PAUL'S.
M.DCC.XXIV.

Title page of the 1724B edition, a corrected version of 1724A.
Beinecke Rare Book and Manuscript Library, Yale University.

Bernard Mandeville's "A Modest Defence of Publick Stews"

Prostitution and Its Discontents in Early Georgian England

Edited with an Introduction by
Irwin Primer

First published in 2006 by
PALGRAVE MACMILLAN™
175 Fifth Avenue, New York, N.Y. 10010 and
Houndmills, Basingstoke, Hampshire, England RG21 6XS
Companies and representatives throughout the world.

PALGRAVE MACMILLAN is the global academic imprint of the Palgrave Macmillan division of St. Martin's Press, LLC and of Palgrave Macmillan Ltd. Macmillan® is a registered trademark in the United States, United Kingdom and other countries. Palgrave is a registered trademark in the European Union and other countries.

ISBN 1–4039–7166–6

Library of Congress Cataloging-in-Publication Data is available from the Library of Congress.

A catalogue record for this book is available from the British Library.

Design by Newgen Imaging Systems (P) Ltd., Chennai, India.

First edition: March 2006

10 9 8 7 6 5 4 3 2 1

Printed in the United States of America.

ISBN 978-1–4039–7166–8

CONTENTS

ACKNOWLEDGMENTS

I wish to thank the following persons who provided me with useful information or critical comments relating to the texts in this edition: Andrea Branchi, Andrew Brown, James A. Brundage, Dario Castiglione, Maurice Charney, Estelle Cohen, Faramerz Dabhoiwala, Edmund L. Epstein, Barbara Fisher, Frank Felsenstein, M.M. Goldsmith, Tim Hitchcock, Malcolm Jack, Arne Jansen, Ruth Mazo Karras, Inger Leemans, James E. May, Maximillian Novak, Martin Price, Charles W.A. Prior, Richard E. Quaintance, Manuel Schonhorn, J. Martin Stafford, Philip Stewart, Randolph Trumbach, Mary K. Weigand, and Martha K. Zebrowski. David C. Greetham imparted valuable advice when I consulted him on editorial and textual matters. Warren Mayer and Murray Karstadt of the Computer Center at Rutgers in Newark provided valuable aid in software applications and word processing. I am also indebted to Lynn Mullins (Director of Rutgers' Dana Library) and to the library's staff including Ka-Neng Au, Natalie Borisovets, and Dorothy Grauer for attending to the many requests relating to this edition. Both Miriam Mandelbaum (Curator of Rare Books at the New York Academy of Medicine Library) and Deborah J. Leslie (Head of Cataloging at the Folger Shakespeare Library) provided useful bibliographical information. Paul Axel-Lute at the Rutgers Law School Library in Newark was helpful in locating information about prostitution and the law in medieval and early modern Britain. Other librarians who responded to my queries with useful replies are Nina Bozak (Tulane), Joel B. Silver (Lilly Library, Indiana University), Katherine E.S. Donahue (Biomedical Library, UCLA), Taran Schindler (Beinecke Library, Yale), and Juliet McLaren (English Short Title Catalogue, University of California at Riverside). My largest debt, however, is to my wife Blossom R. Primer who read and commented upon my typescript at various earlier stages.

Introduction

A Modest Defence of Publick Stews (1724), one of the most influential publications on prostitution in its century, gained instant notoriety through its argument in behalf of state-regulated brothels. It is usually mentioned in histories of prostitution, and no dissertation or book-length account of its presumed author, Bernard Mandeville, fails to mention it.[1] Since Mandeville is not as well known as his contemporaries Daniel Defoe and Jonathan Swift, a brief survey of his career may be useful to those who know little or nothing about him.

After receiving his M.D. at Leyden University in 1691, Dutch-born Bernard Mandeville (1670–1733) may have traveled to Italy and France. He emigrated to London in the early 1690s, became very proficient in English and married an Englishwoman in 1699 with whom he had two children. His fame proceeds not from his medical writings or practice, but from various works that he published on social, political, and religious issues. His early doggerel poem *The Grumbling Hive, or, Knaves Turn'd Honest* (1705) became the core of his masterpiece, *The Fable of the Bees: Or, Private Vices, Publick Benefits* (1714–1729), the later additions being notes or "Remarks" on selected lines of his poem together with further essays. He argued throughout that the vices of private persons contribute to the benefit of the whole society. Opposing the common moral judgment that it is better to be frugal than to consume expensive products, he recommended luxury consumption. He defended free trade, but he also thought that the value of England's exports should exceed that of her imports. Consequently he came to be viewed as an apologist for both laissez-faire and mercantilism. He regarded individual human actions as motivated primarily by self-love and self-interest, and he believed that human reason is weak in comparison with the force of the passions that dictate our behavior. His ideas influenced the thought of David Hume, Adam Smith, Jean-Jacques Rousseau, Voltaire, and other voices of the European Enlightenment. Following Locke and Bayle, he also wrote in defense of religious toleration.

---

[1] Because Mandeville's name was withheld (appearing nowhere in his book), our naming him as its author merely signifies that he is the likeliest person to have written this work. See the essay "Authorship" in the Commentaries for further discussion.

He was a lively satirist who enjoyed exposing hypocrisy, excessive pride, and other vices, but he generally avoided attacking living individuals and did not care to engage in protracted controversies.

★   ★   ★

In 1973 *A Modest Defence of Publick Stews* was reprinted with an introduction by Richard I. Cook that has remained authoritative for the last three decades. During that time the women's movement generated heated debates on pornography and prostitution, and research into the history of sexuality continued to expand. From time to time writers on these subjects have quoted or cited Mandeville's book on whoring in order to support their arguments or expositions, but in so doing they have always simplified this very ambiguous and complex work.

For examples of whoring and prostitution in English literature before 1749, the year in which John Cleland's *Memoirs of a Woman of Pleasure* appeared, readers familiar with that period are far more likely to name not Bernard Mandeville, but his more famous contemporary Daniel Defoe, simply because of the wide popularity of Defoe's whore fictions *Moll Flanders* (1721) and *The Fortunate Mistress, or, Roxana* (1724). Nowhere in these two works or in any other writings does Defoe praise or defend prostitution. He mitigates Moll's guilt by having her undergo a moral reformation late in her career, a pattern that he did not repeat for Roxana. Mandeville's pamphlet significantly differs from these novels and from all other fictional accounts of whores or prostitutes in that he never dwells on the personality or adventures of any individual whores. Instead we find him (or his speaker) dealing with prostitution as a dangerous social problem that needs to be remedied by some inventive sociopolitical planning and firm execution.[2] Almost always scholars who have discussed the plan offered by Mandeville have failed to realize that it is embedded in a work of remarkable literary energy. It is a complex work of literary art with deep roots in the traditions of European literature and philosophy, and it deserves to be studied and appreciated as such. Its "content" or "message" remains important, but the entire pamphlet has been much underestimated precisely because it has been regarded as a simpler work than it really is.

---

[2] The terms "whore" and "prostitute" were sometimes synonyms but the prostitute received payment for sex while a whore would be any woman who violated the rules of modesty and chastity. It is important to know that Mandeville rarely used the term "prostitute." Furthermore, as Dabhoiwala remarks in his article "The pattern of sexual immorality . . ." (87), "Contemporary attempts to distinguish prostitution as a type of behaviour were not identical with our own. They focused mainly on motivation, rather than on promiscuity and payment. . . . Both at law and in general discourse . . . a 'whore' was any woman who had sexual relations outside marriage, irrespective of her promiscuity, social position or remuneration; just as a 'bawdy house' was simply any place—a home, tavern or lodging-house—where men and women met to commit sexual immorality."

One reason for its relative neglect up to now is that it has always been viewed as a counter-cultural work; it advances a proposal that generally offends public morality. Some readers will call this work pornographic, even if it is not as culpable as works of hard porn. What may disturb other readers is not the whiff of pornography that floats through this work but the possibility that its author might really have wished to see his proposal for state-controlled prostitution become a living reality. This or any other proposal to establish a national system of regulated brothels will always be opposed by a large army of antiprostitution forces including not only radical feminists but also many libertarians, religious groups, and others opposed to prostitution of any sort. Many practicing prostitutes themselves would reject the author's proposal for regulated prostitution as an infringement upon their freedom to choose their customers and determine their own prices.

Thus various groups whose values may be sharply opposed will agree in rejecting this author's proposal, whether on moral, political, religious, or economic grounds. It is always a mistake, however, to confuse his proposal with his entire work, some parts of which may possibly undermine that very proposal. Can we be certain that Mandeville fully and unequivocally supported his own project for regulated brothels? The key to understanding this text is the realization that it is much more than the source material or eighteenth-century "content" that sociologists and historians have extracted from it. Whether *A Modest Defence of Publick Stews*[3] will come to be appreciated as a lively and carefully crafted piece of literary prose remains to be seen.

In this work Mandeville anticipated various issues on prostitution and pornography that have been vigorously debated over the last three decades, yet it has rarely been named in these debates. One of the reasons for this neglect is that the tone of his essay is not consistently serious but often spills over into witty remarks, sexual puns, and other kinds of bawdy humor. It is hardly an ideal source for serious reflections and arguments about prostitution, where the stakes seem so high.

Though it elicited very few published rejoinders when it first appeared, it continued to be reprinted some half-dozen times until 1745.[4] Because it is sexually explicit it was open to prosecution for obscenity and lewdness, but both author and publisher escaped criminal charges by remaining anonymous. As we shall now see, *A Modest Defence* has an interesting

---

[3] Readers who are puzzled by the word "stews" in this context need to be informed that, in Martha Carlin's words, "A stewhouse was, technically, a bathhouse (from Old French *estuve*, 'stove'), but many public bathhouses also served as places of prostitution, so that by Langland's and Chaucer's day stews always had a disreputable connotation. There is no evidence that the Bankside stewhouses [in Southwark, across the Thames from London] had bathing facilities at all; they were probably simply brothels." Carlin, *Medieval Southwark*, 211.

[4] A reprint of the 1727 French translation, *Vénus la Populaire*, appeared in 1796. See the Bibliography for a list of the early editions of *A Modest Defence*.

history of its own, taking us back into some of Mandeville's previous writings and into the early modern literature on sexuality.

★   ★   ★

Apart from his will and a few short letters, no manuscripts in Mandeville's hand have survived. For this reason the genesis of each of his works can be known only from the printed record and from external historical contexts. Most accounts of the origin of *A Modest Defence* state or imply the obvious—that he wrote this book because he objected to the activities of the Societies for the Reformation of Manners (hereafter abbreviated to SRMs). And so he did, but that alone does not convey the precise course of events that led to its composition.

Mandeville satirized would-be reformers as early as 1705 in his doggerel poem *The Grumbling Hive*, the kernel of his later *Fable of the Bees*. In 1714, among the various prose "Remarks" or annotations he added to this poem, he also included "Remark (H.)," in which he demonstrates the seeming paradox that parties opposed to one another (for instance, virtuous women and prostitutes) actually do support or assist each other in various ways. Or, to cite the conclusion of "Remark (H.)," "Chastity may be supported by Incontinence, and the best of Virtues want the Assistance of the worst of Vices." Through such instances Mandeville was demonstrating the interdependence of diverse social groups that his hypothetical wise politicians manipulate in order to produce social harmony (*Fable*, ed. Kaye, I, 24–25). This message would have irritated most clergymen and other defenders of public morality, but apparently they were not sufficiently outraged by anything in the *Fable*'s first edition (1714) that might have caused them to take punitive measures against it.

On the other hand, after adding his notorious "Essay on Charity and Charity-Schools" to his *Fable of the Bees* in 1723, the outrage did emerge, for in that year the Grand Jury of Middlesex "presented" his *Fable* together with some essays by John Trenchard and Thomas Gordon.[5] All three authors were charged with blasphemy, denial of God's providence (which for some was tantamount to atheism), and anticlericalism. The charge that these authors attacked religion and virtue and urged that vices such as luxury, avarice, and pride were "necessary to *Publick Welfare*" probably referred to Mandeville in particular. And to cap their list of vices, these Jurors pointed to prostitution and fornication:

> Nay, the very *Stews* themselves have had strained Apologies and forced Encomiums made in their Favour and produced in

---

[5] The Presentment of the Grand Jury of Middlesex was published in *The Evening Post* on July 11, 1723. Mandeville reproduced it for the convenience of his readers in "A Vindication of the Book," the last separate piece of prose in the third edition of his *Fable* (1723). The political composition of the members of this particular Grand Jury in 1723 and its significance are brilliantly detailed by W.A. Speck in his article, "Bernard Mandeville and the Middlesex Grand Jury." See also, Curtis and Speck, "The Societies for the Reformation of Manners. . . ."

Print, with Design, we conceive, to debauch the Nation.   (*Fable*, ed. Kaye, I, 385)

Before the end of 1723 Mandeville responded briefly in *A Vindication of the Book, from the Aspersions Contain'd in a Presentment of the Grand Jury of Middlesex*, which he soon placed at the end of the next edition of his *Fable*. At a certain point in this *Vindication* he moves from a general defense of his *Fable* to a rebuttal of the specific charge concerning his treatment of the stews in "Remark (H.)":

> The Encomiums upon Stews complained of in the Presentment are no where in the Book. What might give a Handle to this Charge, must be a Political Dissertation concerning the best method to guard and preserve Women of Honour and Virtue from the Insults of dissolute Men, whose Passions often are ungovernable. . . .   (*Fable*, ed. Kaye, I, 405)

He continues with a review of "Remark (H.)," protesting that his description of the Amsterdam brothels was meant to instill "a Disgust and Aversion against them," and that nothing in this Remark "can either offend the chastest Ear, or sully the Imagination of the most vicious. . . ." Besides, he adds, his *Fable* was written not for the common people but for "the few that can think abstractly, and have their Minds elevated above the Vulgar" (I, 405–407). The dominant note here is indeed "vindication," which also implies that he is delivering an *apologia* or personal defense of his writings. By 1724, the year following his "Vindication," he decided to adopt a different approach by widening his attack on the reformers, turning from the supporters of the Charity Schools to his next target, the members of the Societies for the Reformation of Manners (the SRMs) and their supporters.[6] He was also, no doubt, capitalizing on his recently earned public notoriety.

Beginning in 1690 and gradually spreading to other towns, the SRMs zealously sought out and reported any persons supposedly guilty of petty crimes and common vices such as drunkenness, disorderly behavior, profanation of the sabbath, swearing, and of course "strolling" or streetwalking for purposes of prostitution. They maintained that prostitution was criminal as well as sinful and immoral, and that prostitutes merited the punishments such as "carting" and whipping that were routinely inflicted upon them. They claimed to be upholding Christian values, but their methods, especially their use of paid informers and their collusion with constables, were widely criticized. They were also accused of profiting from the arrests that they instigated. One of their chief targets was the lower-class whore

---

[6] Samuel J. Rogal notes that the targets of Mandeville's satire in *A Modest Defence* are not only the members of the SRMs but also the jurors in the Grand Jury who hoped to have him tried for various crimes against the State and the Church. See his article "The Selling of Sex. . . ."

(generally a streetwalker) who, lacking the protection of a powerful male, could not pay the fine for her latest infraction.[7]

By no means did the SRMs have the universal support of the nation's clergy, though some well-known Church of England preachers did speak on their behalf. Some prominent High Churchmen, including the embattled Dr. Henry Sacheverell, disapproved of them because they included Dissenters among their members. After 1738, a few years following the death of their leader the Reverend Thomas Bray, their organization ceased to be active. Their own measure of their success seems to have been the lists of arrests and prosecutions published annually, usually prefaced by a sermon delivered at their annual meeting by a prominent clergyman. Anyone who dared to defend and condone prostitution—which is what the author of *A Modest Defence* appeared to be doing—thereby incurred the enmity and hatred of the "gentlemen" of these societies.

If scholars have disagreed on the significance and value of Mandeville's defense of prostitution, they have always agreed that its satire is directed primarily against the members of the SRMs. But never, it appears, did he name one leader or representative of those societies, though he did satirize one of their eminent clerical supporters, Bishop Burnet, at the end of his mock Dedication. It is possible to see *A Modest Defence* as another offshoot of his foundation poem, *The Grumbling Hive*, insofar as both works satirize the reformers in his milieu. One in particular whom he would have attacked was the Reverend Jeremy Collier, the author of *A Short View of the Immorality and Profaneness of the English Stage* (1698). Collier's denunciations of licentious or indecent passages in the works of Otway, Congreve, Dryden, Wycherley, and other dramatists stirred up a lively controversy and had a visible effect in elevating the moral tone of most stage plays in the eighteenth century. Collier's title phrase "immorality and profaneness" reappeared in essays and sermons by other reformers well into the 1720s. It seems obvious, when one knows the contents of *A Modest Defence*, that Mandeville, in daring to argue for the social utility of prostitution, was deliberately cultivating "immorality and profaneness" in order to ridicule and annoy the reformers.[8]

In his "Preface" (p. *xv*) Mandeville alludes to the sermon delivered to the SRMs on January 6, 1723 by no less a figure than Edmund Gibson, "Lord Bishop of London." For prudential reasons he avoids naming Gibson directly, but the irony with which he treats Gibson's attack on the evils of the popular masquerades tells us clearly to which ideological camp he belongs. It would be difficult to claim that this sermon alone was the immediate occasion of Mandeville's *A Modest Defence*, but it was surely one of the irritants that led him to write it. (He could have been working on his essay for months or possibly years before coming upon Gibson's

---

[7] For discussions of the Societies for Reformation of Manners, see the works by Bahlman, Bristow, Burtt, Gregg, Shoemaker and Speck listed in the Bibliography.

[8] Mandeville does in fact allude to Collier without naming him, when he criticizes Collier's essay on duelling later on, in 1729. See *Fable*, ed. Kaye, II, 93.

sermon.) In any event, he seems to have been more interested in the annual report of the SRMs appended to Gibson's sermon than in the bishop's sermon itself. According to the statistics presented in this report to the SRMs, 86,000 offenders "have been lately punish'd" and 400,000 religious books were distributed—but to no avail, Mandeville argues, because "Lewdness still so much prevails."

Since, as he believes, this lewdness cannot be removed, he unapologetically asserts that the best solution to the problem of satisfying male lust is to construct and operate new stews for that purpose. The notion that this scheme represents the lesser of two evils is anticipated in his previous works but is used here to support a specific proposal. He knew that he was compounding the charges against him by openly advocating a system of prostitution as the best way to satisfy male desire, and he must have felt in advance that he had sufficient protection through his patron the Lord Chancellor, before proceeding to make a proposal that would offend so many devoted to upholding civility and morality. No longer was he engaged merely in apologetic vindication: what he now offered to those who had accused him of impiety and immorality was a direct attack on their standards of public virtue and morality. If the legislators were to enact his proposal for public stews, they would be sanctioning precisely the immoral sexuality that the reformers were trying to prevent or to punish.

★ ★ ★

One of the reasons why *A Modest Defence* received relatively little attention in print for two centuries was that much of its content could not be discussed publicly or in polite circles. Eventually booksellers and librarians came to classify it as erotica, and when it was no longer in print it remained a collector's rarity. In the earlier decades of the twentieth century Havelock Ellis regarded it as a pioneering document in the study of human sexuality.[9] F.B. Kaye, whose edition of the *Fable of the Bees* remains unsurpassed,[10] was convinced that Mandeville wrote this pseudonymous book but he did not attempt to study it in greater depth.

In the best twentieth-century analysis of *A Modest Defence*, Richard I. Cook noted various literary devices employed by Mandeville, including parodies of a "naively optimistic reformer" and of a Mercantilist social engineer more interested in the wealth and power of the state than in the welfare of its individuals.[11] Cook commendably sensed the literariness of

---

[9] Havelock Ellis, *Studies in the Psychology of Sex* (New York: Random House, 1936 [1906]), IV, 249, 285, 364.

[10] *The Fable of the Bees: Or, Private Vices, Publick Benefits* 2 vols (Oxford: Clarendon Press, 1924).

[11] See Cook's introduction to the 1973 reprint of *A Modest Defence of Publick Stews* (1724). For an expanded version of Cook's introduction, see " 'The Great Leviathan of Leachery': Mandeville's *Modest Defence of Publick Stews* (1724)" in *Mandeville Studies*, 1975. For more on Cook's place in the critical history of *A Modest Defence*, see the section on twentieth-century discussions of this work in the Commentaries.

Mandeville's pamphlet. He also correctly perceived that Mandeville was not seriously concerned about gaining popular support for his proposal, yet a number of later commentators blandly ignored this insight and dealt with the content of *A Modest Defence* as if it were nothing more than a serious plan to reform prostitution. This is evident in the following paragraph by the eminent historian Lawrence Stone:

> In 1724 Bernard de Mandeville launched a vigorous protest against the Society for the Suppression of Vice, which was then very busy trying to close down brothels and to drive prostitutes off the streets.[12] He argued that the consequent private and unregulated prostitution was a menace to society. It led to the spread of venereal disease; it caused extravagant consumption patterns among the patrons; it tempted the girls to murder their bastard infants; and it encouraged men to tempt married women to adultery or to seduce and later abandon innocent girls, who then became common prostitutes. His solution was the establishment of publicly licensed and medically supervised brothels under state control, with different classes of girls and houses catering for different social groups, the cost varying from two shillings and sixpence to one guinea. Needless to say, his plea fell on deaf ears, and all the evils to which he drew attention became more and more common and serious as the eighteenth century progressed.[13]

It is obvious from this brief summary that Stone regarded *A Modest Defence* as nothing more than a work of limited sociological and historical import. On the whole, this is how most readers, including Havelock Ellis, have dealt with it. Stanley D. Nash, compiler of a bibliography on prostitution, saw this situation somewhat differently: "Although it is clearly written in a humorous and satirical style, several literary critics have contended that the ideas proposed in this work were meant to be taken seriously."[14]

The truth of the matter is that in addition to its status as a document of sociological and historical interest, it is also a literary tour de force and a complex work of rhetorical showmanship. One of the keys to its meaning and design lies in that pair of polar opposites inherited from Greco-Roman literature: jest and earnest. Other terms now used to express the same set of contradictory qualities are "the jocoserious" and "the seriocomic."[15] Many

[12] The society that Stone names was formed toward the end of the eighteenth century. He mistakes that society for the Societies for the Reformation of Manners, which flourished from the 1690s to 1738.

[13] Lawrence Stone, *The Family, Sex and Marriage in England (1500–1800)*, p. 617.

[14] Stanley D. Nash, *Prostitutin in Great Britain, 1485–1901: An Annotated Bibliography*, p. 63.

[15] The seriocomic has a long literary history, extending at least as far back as the Cynic philosopher Menippus, who is best remembered as a recurrent character in the comic dialogues of the late Greek author Lucian. The literary style or specific literary strategy associated with him is the seriocomic; in transliterated Greek, the "spoudogeloion." The genre of "Menippean satire," known almost exclusively through the works of Lucian, has been studied in detail by Northrop Frye and others. At least one scholar has associated Mandeville's satiric practice with the Menippean tradition: see George Hind, "Mandeville's *Fable of the Bees* as Menippean Satire."

of the passages in this book, especially those in which Mandeville describes the evil effects of prostitution such as venereal diseases and the humiliations suffered by whores in his time, are meant seriously. Yet throughout we also find bawdy insinuations and other threads of laughter that threaten to disrupt the sobriety of his plan for reforming prostitution.

The speaker is quite self-conscious about intermixing jest and earnest, and in his "Preface" he ludicrously justifies this practice by employing a figure of speech involving food, eating and digestion: "*a dry Argument has occasion for the larding of Gaiety to make it the better relish and go down.*" Basically the same opposition is used in the opening sentence of the book's main essay where he remarks that

> THERE is nothing more idle, or shows a greater Affectation of Wit, than the modern Custom of treating the most grave Subjects with Burlesque and Ridicule.

The Dedication and the "Preface" together suggest that Mandeville seems incapable of discussing human sexuality without laughter or at least a sly smile. This is not to say that he cannot be serious or grave at other times. These issues are closely involved with questions of genre or literary kinds.

Of the three overlapping literary kinds that govern this work— satire, paradox, and the classical oration—satire is what we encounter first because it pervades his ironic dedication to the members of the SRMs. Mandeville satirizes these reformers by exposing their cruelty to prostitutes and the total failure of their efforts to stamp out that vice wherever it was practiced. In order to combat these policers of morals, he deliberately maintains a flow of discourse that includes not only direct argumentation but also references to male and female sexual organs (with a detailed description of their uses), much sexual wordplay, and a stream of images and ideas involving fornication. The immodesty of this naked language and sexual imagery becomes a satiric gesture, a weapon of defiance against those who would repress the irrepressible. However, though we can detect veins of satire here and there, we hesitate to conclude that the work is a satire from beginning to end. Unlike Defoe's *Shortest-Way with the Dissenters* or Swift's *A Modest Proposal*, it seems not to be consistently satirical throughout.[16]

Paradox, a figure of thought in Aristotelean rhetoric, was often exploited by satirists such as Erasmus, Rabelais, and Swift. Sometimes an entire work

---

[16] In his valuable reinterpretation of Mandeville's writings, Edward Hundert characterizes his "scheme for the licensing of prostitutes" as "wholly unsatirical," which suggests to us that he thinks Mandeville was quite serious in proposing his "scheme" for regulating prostitution. Earlier in his book, however, Hundert observes that Mandeville in *A Modest Defence* "adopted an obviously Swiftian pose," a phrase that suggests unflagging or uninterrupted satire from beginning to end, as in *Gulliver's Travels*, *A Tale of a Tub*, *The Battle of the Books* and *A Modest Proposal*. Hundert correctly perceives both the satiric and the unsatiric (or "earnest") dimensions in *A Modest Defence*, but he avoids considering them together, leaving the problem unresolved. See Hundert, *The Enlightenment's Fable*, pp. 121 and 217.

is structured by paradox or else suffused with it. I have not discovered a central or unifying paradox that governs the whole of Mandeville's pamphlet—unless it is the paradox in his first epigraph, attributed erroneously to Seneca—but from the title page forward it appears that paradox contributes much to the form and spirit of this work.

Our dictionaries inform us that a paradox is a statement that is either apparently or actually self-contradictory. In Shakespeare's time a paradox was understood to be a statement contrary to received opinion or to current beliefs and expectations. One of the best-known paradoxes in the Renaissance period was the Copernican hypothesis which denied that the earth is the center of the universe. To the end of the seventeenth century book-length collections of paradoxes, both sacred and profane, testified to the popularity of this vogue. One of the most popular collections, the *Paradossi* of Ortensio Landi, included such chestnuts as "poverty is better than riches," "it is better to be in prison than at liberty" and "it is better to be ugly than beautiful." It is impossible to say exactly how old these paradoxes are, but they are certainly visible in Cicero's *Paradoxa Stoicorum*, or Stoic Paradoxes. While the English taste for paradox peaked in the seventeenth century, it did not suddenly die out.[17] Mandeville, who certainly encountered the paradox tradition while studying at the University of Leiden (if not earlier), became one of its most successful continuators after he arrived in England in the early 1690s.

Further evidence of continuing interest in paradox appears in scattered essays of his time, and occasionally one finds an attempt to theorize about it, as in this extract from *The Ladies Diary* (1715):

> A PARADOX is a seeming Falsity, but a real Truth; it is that which to unthinking Persons seems absurd, or impossible; but to a thoughtful Man is plain and evident; the main drift whereof is to whet the Appetite of an Inquisitive Learner, and to set him upon thinking. Although (says an ingenious Author) the Soul of Man is a Cogitating Being, and its Thoughts so nimble as to surround the Universe it self in a trice; yet so unthoughtful, and strangely immur'd in Sence, are the generality of Persons, that they need some startling noise, to rouse and awake them.[18]

Among the Mandevillean paradoxes that conform to this definition is his famous subtitle "private vices, publick benefits" and his view that luxury consumption, not frugality (which is a "mean starving virtue"), is the best

---

[17] The classic study of paradox in early modern literature is Rosalie Colie's *Paradoxia Epidemica*. Colie thought that the vogue of paradox among English writers was virtually over by the end of the seventeenth century. Another perceptive study of paradox in French writers of the pre-classical period (generally, the sixteenth century) is Barbara C. Bowen's *The Age of Bluff: Paradox & Ambiguity in Rabelais & Montaigne*. For the paradoxical encomium in Mandeville's era, see Henry Knight Miller, "The Paradoxical Encomium."

[18] *The Ladies Diary* (London, 1715), p. 19.

path to increasing the wealth and welfare of society. At the end of "Remark (H.)" in his *Fable* he tells us that "I think I may justly conclude (what was the seeming Paradox I went about to prove) that Chastity may be supported by Incontinence, and the best of Virtues want the Assistance of the worst of Vices."

Ten years later Mandeville resumed this thread, with an emphasis upon incontinence, in *A Modest Defence of Publick Stews*. We encounter paradox as soon as we set eyes on its title page. After all, how "modest" can a "modest defense" or apology for houses of prostitution be? The few who took the trouble to respond to Mandeville's short book believed that his defense of public stews, far from being modest, was actually outrageous. And when our eye moves down from the title to the next passage, the first of the two Latin epigraphs on the title page, we find that "incontinence is necessary for the sake of continence [and] a conflagration is extinguished by fire," echoing the conclusion of "Remark (H.)."[19] The two paradoxes in this epigraph ingeniously anticipate Mandeville's arguments that exposing young men to sexual experiences in public brothels will ultimately produce better marriages, and the older claim revived by Mandeville that prostitution (incontinence) is necessary for the preservation of the chastity and honor (implying continence) of most other women.

Paradox and irony pervade the entire work. Mandeville readily admits that prostitution is a social evil, but he also sees it as a necessary outlet for the superfluity of sexual energy in young men. Hence one can think of this social evil as in some sense a transaction that is also beneficial to society insofar as it shields the honor and modesty of virtuous women while it removes the "peccant humour" implicit in male sexuality. In his *Fable of the Bees* Mandeville had earlier asserted that private vices (such as prostitution) were, or could become, public benefits. Among the benefits produced by prostitution in that earlier context are the circulation of money and the expansion of commerce and trade resulting from the purchases of luxurious clothing, food, drink, and lodgings. One year before the appearance of *A Modest Defence* Mandeville added the following passage to his *Fable of the Bees*:

> A Highwayman having met with a considerable Booty, gives a poor common Harlot, he fancies, Ten Pounds to new-rig her from Top to Toe; is there a spruce Mercer so conscientious that he will refuse to sell her a Thread Sattin, tho' he knew who she was? She must have Shoes and Stockings, Gloves, the Stay and Mantua-maker, the Sempstress, the Linen-Draper, all must get something by her, and a hundred different Tradesmen dependent on those she laid her Money out with, may touch Part of it before a Month is at an end.   (*Fable*, ed. Kaye, I, 88)

---

[19] In his Italian translation of *A Modest Defence* (1989), Dario Castiglione points out another paradoxical element connected with the first epigraph: it was penned not by Seneca but by the Church Father Tertullian. Whether it was Mandeville or another writer who deliberately attributed the first epigraph to the pagan Seneca instead of the Christian Tertullian, is not known.

In *A Modest Defence*, however, Mandeville no longer emphasizes the paradox of the economic benefits of prostitution but takes a different approach, dividing prostitution in general into the bad old variety (the private whoring still current in his society) and the new better kind, the state-regulated stews of some improbable future.[20] The dream of future amelioration serves to underline starkly the catalogue of ills that bedevil the system of whoring current in his time.

The contradictions and paradoxes abound. In one passage of *A Modest Defence* a whore is touted as a fine woman whose embraces provide healthier relief for sexual urges in males than sodomy (which he deplores) and masturbation, which he calls a rape upon one's own body. In another passage, silently lifted from *Paradise Lost*, he uses Milton's language to describe the embraces of a whore as "loveless" and "joyless." In some passages he seems to sympathize with the fallen women seduced or driven into prostitution by their poverty and hunger, and he criticizes the harshness of the punishments inflicted upon them. Yet, sympathetic as he is, he still seems to support a social practice that keeps many women in a state of abjection and subjugation. Wearing the mask of the imperturbable wise lawmaker, he affirms that since prostitution will survive despite any efforts to halt it, the best approach would be to place it under state control with medical supervision.

The deepest paradox in this work, however, occurs not in any single passage but in the pervasive underlying ambiguity of the whole: is it essentially an elaborate joke or jest from beginning to end? Or, apart from any humor or jesting, is it a serious critique of current mismanagement of the means to satisfy recurring and irrepressible human lust? It appears to be neither one nor the other exclusively, but rather a combination of jest and earnest, and difficulties arise when the reader is uncertain about which label to assign to an ambiguous passage.

Though we observe satire and paradox coursing through this work, these categories do not identify its genre. One literary group or genre to which it belongs is well known: Mandeville follows in the path of Defoe's *An Essay upon Projects* (1697) and other schemes for public improvement recorded in essay form.[21] An important difference between *A Modest Defence* and the proposals offered by other "projectors" is its polemical or

---

[20] For further discussion of economic ideas in this work, see the section on economics in the Commentaries that follow the primary texts.

[21] Projects for social improvement are visible or implied in utopian writings from Plato's *Republic* onward and culminating, for the sixteenth century, in Sir Thomas More's *Utopia*. Scientific experiments and projects for social improvement were encouraged in the seventeenth century by the philosophical writings of Sir Francis Bacon, among others, and multiplied in print after the founding of the Royal Society of London in 1662, shortly after the Restoration of King Charles II to the throne. Many earlier projects and experiments appeared ludicrous to some literary minds, producing satirical and burlesque renditions of the ethos of the projectors. The most memorable satire on the Royal Society and projectors appears in the third voyage, the voyage to Laputa, in Swift's *Gulliver's Travels* (1726).

argumentative edge. In satirizing a known group, the SRMs, and also some Church of England dignitaries, it reveals characteristics of a debate. As a plan for future improvements in society it also treads near the extensive genre of utopian writing cultivated in Europe at least since the time of Plato, but it falls short of being utopian insofar as it makes compromises with existing evils in society. There are probably other genres suggested or touched upon in this work, but its structure suggests one that has not yet been named, the classical oration. Viewing this work in the context of classical rhetoric will permit us to comprehend better how Mandeville organized his materials and managed his argument.

Virtually all commentators on *A Modest Defence* have been unaware that in this pamphlet Mandeville closely followed the pattern of a classical oration and indeed was acutely conscious of the precepts of rhetoric in composing the entire work. He focuses our attention upon rhetoric by using that term four different times in this work and by proceeding according to the well-known ancient rules of rhetorical composition. While in those four passages "rhetoric" generally means persuasion, that term also conveys the sense of verbal display and elaborate patterns of discourse. One is reminded that Queen Gertrude, annoyed with Polonius's verbosity, demands that he deliver "More matter, with less art."[22] Readers who share Gertrude's impatience with Polonius's rhetorical capers may possibly dislike the same kind of rhetorical posturing that Mandeville sometimes uses in his *A Modest Defence*, as in this passage:

> But I need not waste any Rhetorick upon so evident a Truth [that modern young men are no less sensitive to sexual stimulation than Socrates was at an advanced age]; for plain and clear Propositions, like Windows painted, are only the more Obscure the more they are adorn'd.   (p. ix)

Enjoying his paradox, Mandeville uses rhetorical art to affirm that he does not need rhetoric to convince us about an obvious fact. In employing rhetoric as a weapon against rhetoric, he implies that his entire oration may be a form of play, a jeu d'esprit. Yet it also contains some "plain and clear Propositions"[23] which would constitute the "earnest" part of his pamphlet. One effect of the relatively few passages of rhetorical display in this essay is to retard temporarily the progress of his exposition and argument.

We should regard *A Modest Defence* as a classical oration because, even though it is not overtly offered as such, it nevertheless contains all of the conventional arrangement and divisions of the whole that writers and speakers over the centuries have found in the rhetorics of Aristotle, Quintilian, Cicero and the anonymous treatise *Rhetorica Ad Herennium*,

---

[22] *Hamlet*, II, ii, 95.

[23] This phrase reminds us of Descartes's "clear and distinct ideas," a concept widely discussed when Mandeville was studying philosophy in his school years.

dating from Cicero's time.[24] Classical rhetoric posits three major types of discourse: the forensic, involving issues of guilt and innocence in a trial; the deliberative, dealing with many kinds of opposing issues; and the epideictic, in which praise or blame is bestowed upon persons and by extension upon other objects. *A Modest Defence* is easily assignable to the deliberative group, but it also has touches of the epideictic. As the author of the *Rhetorica Ad Herennium* informs us, "Deliberative speeches are either of the kind in which the question concerns a choice between two courses of action, or of the kind in which a choice among several is considered."[25] In this pamphlet, which is an argument from its beginning to its conclusion, Mandeville considers two lines of action: the repressive measures favored by the SRMs, and his alternative quasi-utopian proposal. Not surprisingly he devotes most of his pages to building his case for state-regulated stews.

According to the *Rhetorica Ad Herennium*, the general aim of a deliberative discourse is advantage, which "in political deliberation has two aspects: Security and Honour" (Loeb edition, 161). Since Mandeville's proposal is designed to remove the dangers of unregulated prostitution, it is clear that he favors security (in this case, safe sex) over honor. Though he also uses the old argument that the stews must be tolerated in order to safeguard the honor of virtuous matrons and virgins, preserving their honor does not appear to be his primary goal. He seems to be more concerned to preserve the stews (depicted as a necessary evil) for the convenience and delectation of adult males. In this case, security trumps honor.

Handbooks and outlines of rhetoric commonly list five major parts of rhetoric (as found, for instance, in Cicero's *Orator*): invention, arrangement, style, memory, and delivery. Because a full rhetorical analysis of Mandeville's piece would require the space of a monograph, I shall arbitrarily examine only a few of the features that reveal his continuing reliance upon principles of rhetoric. Under "arrangement" it was usual to divide the classical discourse into six or seven consecutive parts: (1) the proemium or exordium, (2) narratio, (3) explicatio or definitio, (4) partitio or divisio, (5) confirmatio or amplificatio, (6) confutatio or refutatio, and (7) peroratio.[26]

---

[24] The only critic, so far as I know, who speaks of Mandeville's "attention to the strict principles of classical rhetoric" is Samuel J. Rogal, in his essay "The Selling of Sex. . . ." But Rogal (p. 149) dismisses Mandeville's rhetoric by observing that "the result is perhaps too lengthy, made bulky by historical illustrations, anticipated counter-arguments, digressions and repetitions that—while they may serve to solidify and then substantiate Mandeville's thesis— never really cast any fresh light upon the problem." A ponderous judgment indeed! Rogal apparently did not notice or did not care to point out how much fun Mandeville was having in manipulating "the strict principles of classical rhetoric" for comic or ironic effects. But even without those comic effects, I would contend that Mandeville's uses of classical rhetoric are intrinsically interesting and deserve to be studied in greater detail.

[25] *Rhetorica ad Herennium*, Loeb Classical Library edition, 157.

[26] According to Richard A. Lanham's *Handlist of Rhetorical Terms*, p. 112, the *Rhetorica Ad Herennium* combines numbers three and four in this list.

Following the *exordium* or introduction in which opposing courses of action are presented and the "gentlemen" of the SRMs are satirized, Mandeville takes us into the next part of his classical discourse, the *narratio*, which begins where his main essay opens, following the Dedication and Preface. He soon enunciates his three-part proposition:

> That publick Whoring is neither so criminal in itself, nor so detrimental to the *Society*, as private Whoring; and that the encouraging of publick Whoring, by erecting *Stews*, will not only prevent most of the ill Consequences of this Vice, but even lessen the Quantity of Whoring in general, and reduce it to the narrowest Bounds which it can possibly be contain'd in.   (p. 2)

The *narratio* continues with a discussion of a half-dozen of the "ill Consequences" of private whoring, the most serious of which is venereal disease. It is noteworthy that his proposition contains the beginnings of the next stage in the conventional pattern of a classical oration, the *divisio* or *partitio*. This occurs as soon as he distinguishes between public and private whoring, with the intention, as we later realize, of justifying some form of whoring for his society. This distinction is the centerpiece of his proposal insofar as it separates the "old" (i.e., current) condition of unregulated private whoring from the newly- proposed system of state-regulated whoring. His description of the "new" system with its hierarchy of whores and their graded remuneration is what most impresses his readers. Subordinate examples of *partitio* appear later when he distinguishes between males who remain chaste until marriage and those ostensibly more fortunate ones who learn about women and sex through premarital whoring. In discussing the sexuality of women he divides them into four groups, from the frigid to the most libidinous. Other partitions and subdivisions occur throughout.

Following *divisio* or *partitio* the next stage is *confirmatio* or proof, the large middle section of his essay in which he musters all of his assumptions, facts, and persuasive skills to "prove" or validate the claims that he makes in support of his proposal. He announces the start of this section on page 8, beginning with a definition of "publick whoring." We soon find him defending the inevitability of a woman's continuing to follow prostitution (p. 9) on these grounds: once the woman has yielded her "treasure" to a man or has been forcibly deprived of it, it is impossible for her to find honorable employment even if she attempts to do so, because public opinion will brand her as a whore forever after. That being the case, argues Mandeville, it is obviously more prudent and advantageous for the fallen woman to be employed in his projected public stews (the lesser of two evils) than to be open to all the risks and misfortunes attendant upon private whoring. In another "proof" to support his scheme he argues that it is more advantageous to society to have successful marriages than marriages that break apart, and the way to achieve lasting marriages is to be sure that the new husband is realistic, experienced, and knowledgeable about women and sex, rather than inexperienced, idealistic, and hence more prone to disillusionment after the first glow of amorous union.

Yet another argument contributing to his "proof" maintains that "it shows a certain Baseness of Mind" to attempt to debauch a young virgin and thereby force her into "leading the Life of a *Publick Courtezan*," when the same sexual gratification might easily be obtained by resorting to the proposed state-run brothels. The materials comprising the "proof" section extend even to the comparisons and similitudes "invented" or found by the author and to the quotations and authorities he cites. Altogether the author spends about fifty of his main essay's seventy-eight pages in developing his "proofs," before reaching the next stage of a classical oration, the *confutatio*, on page 66. In his *confutatio*, which involves the anticipation of objections together with the speaker's responses to them, Mandeville returns to his satiric attack upon the "gentlemen" of the SRMs and the clergy who support them:

> After what has been said, it may, perhaps, appear somewhat odd to talk of Religious Objections, as if either Christianity or Morality could possibly object against a Scheme, which is entirely calculated for the Welfare and Happiness of Mankind.   (66)

The major thrust of his ironic *confutatio* is that whatever absolute commandments or prohibitions Christians and moralists may cite to discredit the practice of prostitution, the fact remains that practical decisions about the control or elimination of prostitution rest with the legislators, and if their statutes employ questionable means to achieve "a greater Quantity of Good," then the use of those means (the stews, in Mandeville's proposal) will thus be justified.[27]

Continuing his exercise of foreseeing objections and answering them, he introduces a line of patently fallacious reasoning:

> Since the Sin of the Intention [to engage in whoring] is entirely out of the *Legislature*'s Power, the utmost they can do, with regard to this Sin, is to prevent it being aggravated by actual Commission.
>
> But the *Publick Stews*, as we have already prov'd, will prevent as much as possible this actual Commission.   (70–71)

In the first of these two sentences he makes the legislature resemble the SRMs by dwelling on their power to prevent the "actual Commission" of the sin of whoring. But the second sentence implies that if his proposal for public stews is implemented by the nation's legislators, there will be no need for them to rely on forcible prevention. Here again we see him indulging his

---

[27] Modern philosophers (including Bernard Williams) have published much on this problem in ethics under the heading of Consequentialism, a relatively recent name for a very old idea in the history of philosophy.

taste for playful paradox, for we are led to ask, how can the establishment of new public stews (at least one hundred houses with twenty whores per house) reduce the quantity of whoring "as much as possible"? Would they not tend to increase and encourage fornication in males so inclined?

Anticipating this very question Mandeville proceeds to refute the charge "that the authorizing of *Publick Stews* is a Publick Encouragement for People to Whore" (71). This assertion he stoutly denies by mustering a number of arguments, including the waggish one that the men "are already as bad as they can be," and hence the only thing that might drive them into marriage is complete satiety. As for the women, no modest woman will rush to the public stews to lose her maidenhead, and the licensing of public brothels will limit rather than expand the quantity of whoring in general. Furthermore, with support of verses by Ovid and Martial, he argues that restraining the males will only increase male desire, not cure it.

In his conclusion or *peroratio* Mandeville reviews some of the major edicts and statutes relating to prostitution in England from the late medieval period to the middle of the sixteenth century when the public stews were finally closed down. He speaks nostalgically of the tolerated stews as they existed before being outlawed in 1546. From that year onward all whoring in England was "private" whoring, and the uncontrolled sex industry, in his view, went from bad to worse, and is "now" as bad as it can possibly be. Admittedly this historical survey appears not to conform to the common expectations for a peroration, namely, a summary of the argument together with an emotional appeal to the audience. Mandeville's summary precedes the historical sketch, but this historical coda itself contains an emotional appeal insofar as it demonstrates a nostalgic longing for the openly tolerated stews that were a source of church revenues until the middle of the sixteenth century, when they were banned and criminalized.

Though it appears that Mandeville quite deliberately constructed his essay on the pattern of a classical oration, it is important to keep in mind that various passages suggest a tongue-in-cheek performance. In his opening sentence he deplores "the Modern Custom of treating the most grave subjects with Burlesque and Ridicule." However, the reader finds out soon enough that he fully intended to mix gravity or high seriousness with low burlesque. Thus his oration is also a mock-oration. His whole assemblage of quotations, examples, comparisons, syllogisms, and other literary and philosophical embellishments belongs to old-fashioned or "school" rhetoric, a performance designed to entertain as well as instruct.[28]

---

[28] In classical rhetoric quotations were used not only to introduce authorities but also to serve as embellishment and ornamentation. Among the figures named and sometimes cited by Mandeville are Seneca, Zeno of Citium, Chrysippus, Socrates, Plato, Aristotle, Arcesilaus, Demetrius Phalereus, Erillus, Epicurus, Metrodorus, Diogenes Laertius, Martial, Horace, Virgil, Ovid, Juvenal, Plutarch, Ariosto, Montaigne, Shakespeare, Samuel Daniel, John Stow, Cervantes, Samuel Butler, Bishops Burnet and Gibson, and Dr. Samuel Clarke—with many allusions to Mandeville's own earlier writings. In addition to these authors and thinkers, he mentions Numa and Lycurgus, Pope Sixtus V, John Felton, the Duke of Buckingham, Cato, Richard the

A Modest Defence has certain affinities with that much more famous mock-oration, Erasmus's *The Praise of Folly*, the best-known example of the paradoxical encomium in early modern literature. *A Modest Defence* has some affinities with this particular genre but does not meet its requirements because Mandeville, instead of praising prostitution, regards it rather as a necessary evil and the lesser of two evils. In Erasmus's masterpiece it is Folly who speaks, not Erasmus, and it is the reader's task to decipher Erasmus's true message. In Mandeville's *A Modest Defence* we find the same strategy at work, because we sense at times that we are hearing not his voice but that of some invented persona, and we are challenged to discover what message and intentions the author had in writing it. Both Mandeville and his countryman Erasmus included much levity in these works, and both expected their educated readers to find the serious truths that they intermixed with their humor and laughter.[29] Both were very well aware of Horace's famous rhetorical question, "ridentem dicere verum / quid vetat?"—what prevents one from speaking the truth with a smile?[30] This notion pervades *A Modest Defence* and applies to many passages in *The Fable of the Bees*, with the result that George Bluet in 1725, A.O. Lovejoy in 1922, and Roy Porter in 1988 all admitted that it is difficult to know when Mandeville is joking and when he is serious.

Scholars have generally sought only what they regarded as the content or "true" matter of Mandeville's book, and in so doing they have read and seen only the "earnest" half of his complex utterance while ignoring the possibility that his jesting might also be an important part of his meaning, which it certainly is. Eager to extract the essential message of his work, they seem to agree that the kernel of *A Modest Defence* is his proposal that the government erect and supervise new public stews. They tend to bypass ambiguous or troublesome remarks that might possibly undercut the serious intent of his statements.

What, for instance, are we to make of the afterthought with which he concludes his account of the hierarchical organization of the proposed stews?

Note, That three Claps shall be reckon'd equivalent to one Pox.   (p. 15)

Is it possible to refrain from smiling at this parody of medical thinking or social planning? Can a man or woman who has contracted gonorrhea

---

Second, Wat Tyler, William Walworth, John of Northampton, Henry VI, Charles VIII, Henry VII, Henry VIII, Bishop Gardiner, and Martin Bucer. This collection of notables is meant to add luster to Mandeville's pamphlet. Most of them are expendable in the sense that they are not required for the advancement of his primary argument, and hence they can be said to serve a decorative function as well as contributing to the copiousness of this highly concentrated work.

[29] On Mandeville and Erasmus, see my essay "Erasmus and Bernard Mandeville: A Reconsideration," 313–335. More about the persona in Mandeville and Erasmus will be found in the commentary on marriage, below.

[30] Horace, *Satires* I. 1. 24–25. This famous line was engraved in the title page of the first edition of the duc de La Rochefoucauld's *Maximes* (1665), a work that Mandeville admired and quoted from in his *Fable of the Bees*.

believe that it is only one-third as bad as a case of syphilis? Is a prostitute who has been infected with the clap for a third time just as dangerous as her co-worker who has been infected with the pox only once? Is it possible to believe that Mandeville was entirely serious when he composed this sentence? I put these questions because this "note," tacked on as an afterthought, seems to be a huge anticlimax to the presentation of his grand scheme.

Mandeville may have had his tongue in his cheek as he penned this brief sentence, but so far as we can tell from the printed record most readers have taken his proposal as sincerely meant. Assuming that he did offer it as an earnest proposal designed to be implemented in practice, his readers would then have the task of deciding to what extent they can accept it and its underlying assumptions. He argues, as we have seen, that establishing his system of regulated public brothels will reduce the quantity of whoring in general. But common sense tells us that if the new system of prostitution founded upon rational deliberation should indeed turn out to be more affordable, more convenient, and safer than the old practice of "private whoring," more men, not fewer, would resort to prostitutes for sexual satisfaction.[31] Bluet was probably right in predicting that Mandeville's proposed stews would endanger the institution of marriage rather than support it. If some of Mandeville's arguments in support of the public stews seem to be deliberately flawed (as I have argued), how can we know where the jest or jocularity breaks off and where a statement is made in "earnest" and is seriously meant? Did he really believe his version of the "reformed rake" theory, that males who frequented the stews would eventually decide to marry and make better husbands than those who did not, and that the marriages of inexperienced chaste males would tend more often to break up? Perhaps. But the possibility remains that he was deliberately using some specious arguments to support his case for national public brothels. That is, he was undermining the very case that he was trying to make.

At this point we need to ask, why would the author deliberately defend his proposal with weak or flimsy arguments? Did he himself not take his proposal seriously? And what in fact was he really *defending* in his *Modest Defence*? It would be inaccurate to reply that he was defending the public stews because he actually deplored those that were known to exist in his time and place. What he really defends in this work is an unrealized plan

---

[31] The impact of this easier and safer access to prostitutes on the institution of marriage is a necessary part of the argument. Like many before him and since, Mandeville argued that the purity of faithful wives would be protected by the availability of prostitutes as conduits or "sewers" for the excess sexual energy of young males. Others, including George Bluet, argued that easy access to prostitutes could only affect marriage adversely by removing one of the major reasons for marrying in the first place. There is another reason for supporting state-regulated prostitution that Mandeville mentions but does not emphasize: it encourages males to retain "normal" heterosexual desires and thus keeps them from practicing sodomy or homosexuality. On the homosexual subculture of Mandeville's time, see the bibliographical entries under Randolph Trumbach and Rictor Norton.

offered as an improvement over the unregulated prostitution that spread disease and crime wherever it was found. What he defends, in other words, is a plan for brothels that do not yet exist, a product of his imagination. Consequently, it is simply wrong to think loosely or uncritically that he defends prostitution *as it is*. He actually defends prostitution *as it might be*, and even then his defense of his plan seems to be intentionally flawed.

Such considerations support the view that we are really dealing above all with a work of literary art, a piece of imaginative writing in the form of an academic declamation constructed according to the received rules of that art. Like many other literary works, it is also polemical. It is perfectly clear that he used this work to attack the aims and reputation of the SRMs. He was also sniping at those members of the clergy who supported the SRMs. Another of his targets was the kind of individual who refused to acknowledge the social problems of prostitution and even refused to discuss the sexuality of human beings at all. But it cannot be doubted that one of the serious purposes of his ambiguous essay was to publicize the plight of London's harlots and to suggest that Britain's Parliament needed to address their sufferings and other evils associated with their trade.

Considered from a certain angle, this plan for state-run brothels does appear to have some merits, for who would disapprove of eliminating or at least reducing the incidence of venereal disease, controlling related thievery and disorderly conduct, and improving the lot of the women who are thus employed? (The answer, of course, would be all persons who disapprove of prostitution in principle.) Keith Thomas, indeed, wrote that Mandeville in *A Modest Defence* "made a strong case for state-regulated brothels."[32] (Did he examine the "proofs" Mandeville invented to support his project?) As J.M. Robertson argued half a century earlier, a social benefit that degrades any member of society is not a "benefit" that anyone should desire.[33] Much of Mandeville's argument hinges upon our concurring with the old opinion that prostitution must be tolerated so that virtuous women will remain unmolested and in order to avoid worse evils that would ensue if it were prohibited. That article of belief is now widely viewed as outmoded but it still appears as a serious tenet in some modern writings on sexuality and prostitution.

★   ★   ★

The few responses we have by Mandeville's contemporaries express disapproval on moral and religious grounds, but some who dislike the book

---

[32] Keith Thomas, "The Double Standard," *Journal of the History of Ideas*, 20.2 (April 1959), 197.

[33] See J.M. Robertson, "Mandeville," in his *Essays towards a Critical Method* (1889), 217–218; reprinted in his *Pioneer Humanists* (1907). But earlier in the same essay (214) Robertson remarked that Mandeville's opinion that "the existence of prostitutes secures the 'chastity of a number of young women who would otherwise become 'unchaste,' is a statement which no thinking man will very confidently dispute."

today may dislike it for different, that is, newer reasons.[34] Feminists in particular will find it hard to see anything witty or amusing in a document that seems to support the double standard by upholding the superiority of men over women and by accepting the subjugation of women as an established fact within a cruel social system. The speaker is much concerned with finding the best ways to satisfy the sexual urges of young men, mainly because those urges are potentially more dangerous to society than any expressions of female sexuality. As Mandeville's speaker puts it, without dismay or outrage, certain lower-class women, early in their lives, are forced to choose between poverty, starvation, and homelessness on the one hand, and on the other, a degraded life in prostitution.

How to satisfy female desire is not at all on this speaker's agenda, and it is necessary to ask why he privileges male lust over that of females. The answer, quite likely, is not that the speaker is a male defending male prerogatives, but rather that he finds the unruliness and power of the male sex drive to be potentially far more menacing to civil society than any sexual urges felt by women. The highest value for this author is not, as it might seem, the satisfaction of male sexual desire but the flourishing of his modern commercial state. Much of his essay is devoted to devising a method for taming the sexual energies of males because it is the men and not the women who are more prone to creating disturbance and disorder in their society.

That he shows no similar motivation to satisfy women's lust is not an indication that he thinks they have none. In his four types of women classified according to the coldness or warmth of their amorous proclivities, women in his fourth class are particularly desirous of enjoying sex with men. On the other hand, he describes the sexuality of the hardened prostitute in negative terms: "indeed there appears nothing in it so very alluring and bewitching, especially to People [i.e., prostitutes] who have had that Inclination to Lewdness intirely extinguish'd, which is the only thing [that] could possibly make it supportable [9]." As for the sexuality of adult women in general, the speaker seems to adopt the myth of female passivity, a belief that became more prominent later in his century.

Even when he professes a desire to improve the lot of the fallen woman, his representation of women here is on the whole unsympathetic. And even though he states briefly that marriage is far more desirable than loveless promiscuous sex, in most of this pamphlet he seems to favor the double standard. Promiscuous men who tire of purchasing sexual favors may well decide to marry, and that resolution will gain approval in upright, respectable middle-class circles. But for the prostitute in Mandeville's era, the possibility of social redemption or reintegration into "honest" or "virtuous" society simply does not exist. In that society she is an outcast

---

[34] See our survey of Mandeville's early critics in the Commentaries.

whom no "honest" persons would wish to hire. Her fall into prostitution is irreversible.[35]

There are many questions about her possible career in the proposed public brothels that the speaker does not choose to ask, yet they should be asked. What kind of life would she lead as a government employee in these new brothels? Would she, for instance, have to service a required number of customers in a given period—a daily quota? Would she have to be available for such work on each of the six business days of the week? Would the proposed new stews be open for business on Sundays, the day of rest for most adult males? What would happen to her income and her very position if customers for whatever reason decided to avoid her? Would the new system apply "Hobson's choice" as a working principle, which stipulates that the customer must accept the next available prostitute? (The plan to have four grades or levels of prostitutes depending on their desirability and other factors suggests that Hobson's choice would not be applied as a universal rule.) Moreover, will there be a dress code, or uniforms? Will she purchase her own meals, or will the food and drink be perquisites of her employment? How would she survive if she wanted to leave that mode of employment? Finally, How much regimentation will she have to endure?

Those engaged in what Mandeville calls private whoring were ostensibly in charge of their own hours; they could set their own prices and at least theoretically were at liberty to refuse a customer. In many cases their gnawing hunger and poverty would cause them to forego the luxury of refusal. The most drastic alteration that might be expected in the changeover from the old freelance entrepreneurial mode of private whoring to a state-regulated system of public brothels would probably entail some loss of freedom for the individual prostitute. Those who chose to continue their "private" unregulated whoring, finding their private customers as chance would dictate, could expect harsher measures and punishments from a government now seriously committed to quelling that private practice. The old image of the itinerant or "wandering" whore would disappear. In its place one would find presumably a more efficient and rationally organized system of regulated sex, at least in the urban centers.

As Mandeville or his speaker envisions it, the improvements in the lives of these sex workers would include greater safety and security, a steadier income, a healthier environment (including medical care when needed), suitable provision for retirement or superannuation, and suitable care and education for any children they may have as a result of their employment. Though such an existence is morally abhorrent to the prudent and industrious

---

[35] This was a commonplace in Mandeville's era. The most famous series of periodical essays in his time, the *Spectator* papers by Addison and Steele, includes a fictional letter by a prostitute who informs "Mr. Spectator" that "There are Crowds of us whose Manner of Livelihood has long ceased to be pleasing to us; and who would willingly lead a new Life, if the Rigour of the Virtuous did not for ever expel us from coming into the World again." From No. 190, Monday, October 8, 1711, in *The Spectator* ed. Donald F. Bond, II, 80.

middle classes, it does promise certain improvements in the lives of these sex workers. Whether the loss of their freedom to trade freely in the open sex market is too high a cost for these improvements is not easily determined for each individual.

The advantages of the proposed system of managed sex might suggest that it is quasi-utopian. It seems likelier, however, that that system would eventually prove to be dystopian. Mandeville seems incapable of imagining the brutality and criminality of at least a portion of our current global sex industry in which unsuspecting women are seduced or kidnapped, then raped and beaten into submission, and finally offered for sale many times a day until they are no longer serviceable as sex slaves.[36] The impetus behind his plan seems to be the elimination of the crimes, social disorder, and the diseases spread through uncontrolled and unlicensed whoring. By contrast, in the far more criminal and totalitarian variety of prostitution involving stables of sex slaves (as is documented in recent articles and news reports), disorderliness is forbidden and improved medical procedures may or may not be available, but the major consideration that Mandeville refused to entertain—the possibility of generating extraordinary profits—is now the driving force behind this controlled application of large-scale brutality and dehumanization.[37]

Whether such extreme degrees of sexual slavery existed in Mandeville's London may be doubted, but the existence of sexual slavery elsewhere would have been known through the writings of the voyagers and other travelers. The fact that he makes no mention of it suggests that it was not a local problem requiring the attention of social engineers. The worst picture that he paints for us is of the ways in which women fall into prostitution through hunger and poverty or seduction or rape.

Whether he thought that his proposal really deserved to be implemented will remain an open question. That the plan itself would ever be legally adopted by the members of Parliament during Mandeville's lifetime was simply unrealistic or unthinkable. Yet on the European continent in the earlier nineteenth century various governments including France and Germany did indeed institute medical inspections that eventually resulted in a de facto system of state-regulated prostitution.[38] Thus his early eighteenth-century pamphlet advocating the regulation of brothels turned out to be a prophecy of some things to come. But he did not foresee the patterns of organized international trafficking in women and children and their sexual enslavement that are reported in our media.

We now know enough about the literary characteristics of his pamphlet to challenge the simplistic view that he simply means what he says. If some

---

[36] See Kathleen Barry's *Female Sexual Slavery* (1979) and her later book *The Prostitution of Sexuality* (1995).

[37] No one, so far as I know, has ever tried to argue that the extreme degree of what Kathleen Barry and others call industrialized sexual slavery also existed in Mandeville's London.

[38] Barry, *The Prostitution of Sexuality*, 91ff.

of his arguments in behalf of the public stews employ false logic revealing non sequiturs and untenable syllogisms, how can we possibly believe that he himself seriously supported that proposal? The project is suspect, it has affinities with utopian planning, and Mandeville generally disapproved of utopian schemes. Yet learned writers and thinkers on the whole appear to believe that he wished to see his plan become a reality. Without reliable external evidence we cannot pretend to know what he thought of his proposal. On the other hand, his account of the sufferings of the whores and of the corruption and hypocrisy in the system that keeps them subjugated has never been challenged. No one has ever argued that his depiction of the evils of prostitution is false or exaggerated. For publicizing these evils and implying that they need to be mitigated or removed, he surely deserves some recognition.

The regulationism that he seems to recommend became widely operative not in his century but in the mid- and later nineteenth century in western European countries, with some very unfortunate results.[39] As the urban population continued to expand after Mandeville's death, so did the numbers of prostitutes. In Britain the Magdalen hospitals for repentant prostitutes that were first established in the 1750s did nothing to stem the increasing tide of commercial sex. Nor could anyone ever prove what Mandeville and others asserted, that prostitution had a positive effect in preserving women's honor, and, as he in particular argued, that it actually produced better marriages. In the 1790s the most moving indictment of a social system that still had to deal with the unchanging evils of prostitution was expressed in William Blake's "London":

> But most thro' midnight streets I hear
> How the youthful Harlot's curse
> Blasts the new born Infant's tear,
> And blights with plagues the Marriage hearse.

Blake's image of the night-walking harlot became well known to later English readers. Like Mandeville's brief incursions into the sufferings of fallen women, it points to a class of persons without reference to any individual or offsetting differences. Another picture of prostitution, that of Fanny in *Memoirs of a Woman of Pleasure*, reveals a much warmer image. The good-hearted prostitute was as much a fixture in the English imagination as the bitter, angry, and cursing variety.

Essentially, the conditions described by Mandeville in 1724 had not changed much, if at all, by the end of the century, but the numbers who practiced that trade had certainly increased. We see no sign today that the

---

[39] Though almost no commentators on Mandeville's pamphlet in his own time expressed any approval of it, it is interesting to find that in mid-century some writers were again arguing that the brothels or stews ought to be regulated. Two of these anonymous pieces, dated 1749 and 1756, are excerpted below.

selling of sex will ever taper off or disappear, and we still are challenged by the problem that Mandeville tried to solve: how to channel the sexual urges of men and women in ways that would benefit individuals and our society most efficiently. Sex workers and their supporters believe that the first step society needs to take to deal with this problem is to decriminalize prostitution. Their opponents claim that prostitution dehumanizes women by allowing them to be exploited as mere objects for sexual pleasure, and they see prostitution as one more example of the evils of patriarchalism or male domination. Of the two positions, Mandeville's *A Modest Defence* seems to favor the first.

We are confident that he was the author, but we do not know how serious he was in offering his plan because it is embedded within a pamphlet that is rich in sexual humor. Some readers may be disturbed to find that an author who deals seriously with prostitution can yet make light of it. It is true that he includes a stream of sexual jokes, puns, and erotic innuendos, but his humor is never aimed at any single prostitute or at that class as a whole. In other words, it may be less offensive than some of his critics thought it was. It seems unlikely that his argument for regulated prostitution (now almost three centuries old) will persuade most readers to change their minds about this important and vexing issue, but it will surely encourage them to rethink and extend the views they already have.

Notes on the Text

During Mandeville's lifetime his name was never printed on a title page or anywhere else between the covers of his *A Modest Defence*. This fact makes it different from the kind of publication in which a known author was responsible for the changes in successive editions of a given work. It has always been assumed, for example, that until 1733, the year in which he died, Mandeville supervised each of the successive editions of his *Fable of the Bees*, making whatever alterations he saw fit. But the only editions of *A Modest Defence* known to have been published in his lifetime are those of 1724 and 1725; the French translation of that work, *Venus la populaire*, published in 1727; and possibly the edition containing the Glasgow imprint, which may have appeared in 1730. Whether that edition was indeed published in Glasgow and in 1730 is unknown, but it is obvious that the booksellers "J. Moral" and "Jocolo Itinerant" are playful fabrications. We may suspect that Mandeville worked with the pseudonymous publisher "A. Moore" for the 1724 edition, but we lack any evidence to prove that he was involved in the production of that or of any other edition of this work.[40] Changes in the text that appear in editions published after he died in 1733 very likely did not proceed from his hand.

It is well known that *A Modest Defence* was first published in 1724, yet almost no one, apart from the compilers of the English Short Title Catalogue (the ESTC), has taken note of the differences between the two forms of that edition. In this electronic database two separate ESTC identification numbers are assigned for the 1724 edition, N4820 and T114402, which suggests that their cataloguers found two editions of this work, both dated 1724. If, as Philip Gaskell wrote (p. 313), "there is a new edition when more than half the type has been reset," then we are probably dealing with two editions of this work, both published in the same year. For greater convenience I shall call ESTC's no. N4820 the 1724A edition, and

---

[40] Michael Treadwell informs us that "By the end of the [second] decade [in eighteenth-century England] the name [Moore] had been used more than a hundred times [in false imprints], with A. Moore emerging the clear favourite and the total was to reach several hundred by the mid-century with a particular flowering in the 1720s and early 1730s." See "On False and Misleading Imprints in the London Book Trade, 1660–1750," in *Fakes and Frauds*, 43.

ESTC no. T114402 will be called 1724B.[41] Since both editions are octavos and both end on p. 78, the easiest way to tell them apart is to look for the word "Layman" on the title page. If it is misspelled "Laymam," then it will most likely be the 1724A edition. In 1724B this typographical error is corrected to "Layman" and many other changes in spelling, punctuation, capitalization, and typography (i.e., the accidentals) are introduced. Interestingly, in creating 1724B Mandeville or the unknown reviser of 1724A chose to delete ten words (or, substantives) from the 1724A edition, as follows

Removed from page [*i*]:   FOR *Reformation of* Manners.
Removed from page [*xv*]:   ★A Sermon lately Preach'd against
                                  Masquerades.

Thus, because the 1724A edition, with "Laymam" on the title page, appears to have preceded the "corrected" or normalized text of 1724B, it should be regarded as the true first edition.

In the process of revising 1724A the unknown editor changed various spellings, generally in accordance with the following pattern: (1724A, p. 8) "seperated" becomes (1724B, p. 8) "separated." Other examples are (p. 4) intirely > entirely; (p. 7) exterpate > extirpate; (p. 14) impower'd > empower'd; (p. 34) belov'd > beloved; (p. 35) marry'd > married; (p. 36) dazling > dazzling; (p. 48) Strugling > Struggling; (p. 49) Licurgus > Lycurgus; (p. 62) deflour'd > deflower'd; and so forth. The list of further changes in accidentals, specifically in punctuation and capitalization, is much longer, and in more than half of all of the pages of text one finds alterations in the catchwords.

While both editions have an octavo format and in both the text ends on page 78, one does not always find the half-title page preceding the title page. Thus those that lack the half-title page will have 48 leaves (or 96 pages) and those that do have the half-title page will have 49 leaves (or 98 pages). But the two editions differ markedly in their collations: 1724A has gatherings in fours while 1724B has them in eights.

We do not know how many copies of either of these editions were printed. I have found only five locations for copies of 1724A recorded in bibliographies or catalogues, which suggests that relatively few were printed in comparison with the print run of 1724B. This suggests that whatever errors or undesirable idiosyncrasies were visible in 1724A were promptly altered in a reset edition, 1724B, during the same year. The 1724B edition differs on almost every page from 1724A, but the changes one sees almost always involve punctuation, spelling, and capitalization—the accidentals. The nature of these changes suggests that the bookseller/publisher, whose

---

[41] Ursula Pia Jauch, who recently translated *A Modest Defence* into German, observed briefly in her critical essay that the photographic reprint published by the Augustan Reprint Society in 1973 should preferably have been made from UCLA's copy of what I now call the 1724A edition. The A.R.S. reprint—the edition of *A Modest Defence* most widely used in the last three decades—was made from a copy of 1724B owned by the British Library.

true identity is unknown, may have engaged in normalizing the text of 1724A, thus creating a second edition. Very few changes were made in the choice and placement of the actual words, the substantives, and those changes are recorded in footnotes to the relevant passages. In other notes I describe some textual changes made in later editions (1730? 1740 [at least two editions] and 1745), all of which are of lesser authority.

Collations of editions published during Mandeville's lifetime:
(1724A): 8°: $\pi^2 A^4 a^4 B$ - $K^4 L^4$(-L4);49 leaves;$2 signed; pp. [4], xii, [4], 78.
(1724B): 8°: $\pi^2 A$ - F^8(-F8); 49 leaves; $4 signed; pp. [4], xii, [4], 78.
(1725): 8°: A - E^8; 40 leaves; $4 signed (B4 mis-signed as D4); pp. x, [4], 65, [1].

The 1725 edition contains further alterations and is more problematic than either 1724A or 1724B because it is accompanied by an anonymous "Answer" (pp. 58–59; transcribed below) followed by: "The Thirtieth Account of the Progress made in the Cities of London and Westminster, And Places adjacent, By the Societies for Promoting a Reformation of Manners; By Furthering the Execution of the Laws against Prophaneness and Immorality, and other Christian Methods" (pp. 60–65).

In this "Answer" the anonymous writer says of *A Modest Defence* that "To confute such a Libel as this Paragraphically wou'd be raking in a Laystall, and making the Stink more unsufferable" (p. 58). But if he equates *A Modest Defence* with a laystall, a dump for refuse and dung, why reproduce the whole of this presumably stinking heap—more than fifty pages—in order to append a two-page "Answer" followed by a six-page annual report of the SRMs? In pondering this question I wondered whether Mandeville himself had written that answer, tongue-in-cheek, in order to increase the sales of his book. But I eventually came upon William Pittis's *The True Born Englishman: A Satyr, Answer'd, Paragraph by Paragraph* (London, 1701), in which Pittis reprinted all of Defoe's long poem in order to answer it "paragraphically." But this, says the unknown author of the "Answer" in 1725, he refused to do in order not to be soiled by the contents of this pamphlet on the stews. If the answerer (as seems likely) was not Mandeville but another hidden author, then his reprint of Mandeville's text was probably unauthorized. It appears, moreover, that "A. Bussy," the bookseller in the imprint of the 1725 edition, was just as fictitious as the "A. Moore" of the 1724 edition.[42]

The most convincing evidence that someone other than Mandeville was responsible for the publication of the 1725 edition is the fact that this reprint of the 1724 text is very faulty. The omission of the word "as" on page 1 of the main essay transforms a perfectly good complex sentence into a run-on sentence that is uncharacteristic of this author. In 1724B (p. vi) we find these words: "*Demetrius Phalereus*, who had 360 Statues in *Athens*, kept

---

[42] A. Bussy is not listed in H.R. Plomer's *Dictionary of the Printers and Booksellers who were at work in England, Scotland and Ireland from 1726 to 1775.*

Lamia for his Concubine. . . ." In the 1725 edition Phalereus becomes Phalerus, statues becomes statutes (which sounds nonsensical), and Lamia is erroneously converted to Lemia; the last two changes seem positively unjustifiable. "Peripateticks" in 1724B (p. viii) collapses into "Peripaticks" in 1725 (p. viii). The phrase "Modern Butcher" in 1724B (xi) becomes "Mordern Butcher" in 1725 (x). "Occasion" (xiv) becomes "occasien" (xii); "alienating" in 1724B (p. 5) is ridiculously twisted into "alineating" in 1725 (p. 5); "the neighbouring" (7) becomes "their neigbouring" (7); "such Rules" (13) becomes "the Rules" (10); "require" (14) becomes "requrie" (10); and "they," which in 1724B is the subject of "ought" (15), is entirely omitted, leaving "ought" in 1725 (12) without a subject.

The only conclusion to be drawn from this sampling is that the 1725 edition, far from revealing any improvements in Mandeville's text, is actually a debased copy, full of faults that suggest ignorance, carelessness, and haste in the typesetting. This edition is so full of errors and omissions that we must conclude that it was reprinted without the author's approval or permission. Of the three editions that unquestionably appeared in his life-time, the 1725 is the most degraded and the least reliable.

Since the 1724B edition makes a needed correction to the 1724A edition and normalizes some idiosyncratic spellings, and since 1724B is so clearly superior to the 1725 edition, it seems advisable, on the whole, to use the 1724B as the base text for this new edition because it is not only a corrected text but it is also closer to the earliest printing of this work than any later edition. Another reason for selecting 1724B—a reason that has nothing to do with the issue of textual authority—is that since 1973 scholars have almost always used the A.R.S. reprint of 1724B for their quotations and citations. Thus by common practice that facsimile reprint became in a sense "standard." In the absence of major substantive differences between 1724A and 1724B, it makes sense to continue with the established pattern, that is, by using 1724B as our base text. Those who insist upon following the Greg-Bowers guidelines will regard the text of 1724A as the most authoritative one precisely because it is the earliest, and they would insist upon retaining the accidentals of that edition. For such readers and for anyone else who wishes to see the first edition, a transcription of the text of 1724A is included here as a supplement.

In this new edition my main purpose is to present a reasonably faithful transcription of the substantives and the accidentals of one copy of 1724B. By "reasonably faithful" I mean that I am not including a list of all of the catchwords, nor am I listing all of the end-of-line hyphenations, as is recommended by the MLA's "Guidelines for Scholarly Editions." Readers who want such information can turn to the commonly available facsimile reprint published in 1973 and reprinted in 2000. To make my basic text more meaningful to the modern reader I have supplied an introduction, footnotes, other relevant texts from Mandeville's era, together with supplementary essays on specific topics. This new edition, reproducing a single copy of a text, is usually called a diplomatic edition. I have not attempted to produce a "critical edition" in which a copy-text is selected and then emended in order to produce an "eclectic edition" with superior readings. Nor have I tried to produce a "definitive edition," if that notion is still current. My inclusion of a transcription of 1724A may suggest to some readers that I am relying upon Donald H. Reiman's account of "versioning" as a useful alternative to the editorial procedures elaborated by W.W. Greg, Fredson Bowers, and Thomas Tanselle. Reiman's argument for versioning is persuasive, but I cannot claim that it shaped this current edition in any way.[43]

In preparing this edition I have relied primarily on the British Library's copy of 1724B, shelfmark 1080.i.45, and the copy of 1724B owned by the Beinecke Library at Yale (call number 1985/214). The Yale copy lacks the half-title leaf that precedes the title page but otherwise closely resembles the British Library copy.

The 1724A edition (ESTC no. N4820) is owned by the Biomedical Library at UCLA, the Howard-Tilton Memorial Library at Tulane University, the Lilly Library at Indiana University, the Folger Library, and the Firestone Library at Princeton University.

Among the libraries that own the 1724B edition (ESTC no. T114402) are the British Library (2 copies); Cambridge University Library, Trinity College, Cambridge; the Goldsmiths' collection at the University of London Library; the National Library of Scotland; the Bodleian Library at Oxford; the Lilly Library at Indiana University; the Newberry Library; the Houghton Library at Harvard University; and the Beinecke Library at Yale University. (Note: the Lilly Library's copy of this edition is reported to have a blank leaf F8 as its last leaf. The leaf seems to be absent from all other recorded copies).

Contents of the 1724B edition

π1r half-title; π1v blank; π2r title page [see our photographic reproduction]; π2v blank; A1 double horizontal rule, then dedication "TO THE | GENTLEMEN | OF THE | SOCIETIES" and the text begins with "Gentlemen,"; dedication ends on *A6v* and is signed "Phil-Porney"; *A7r* double horizontal rule followed by "THE PREFACE" on unnumbered pages through *A8v*; B1r double horizontal rule followed by "A MODEST DEFENCE, *&c.*" and then the text, through *F7v* with "*FINIS*" at the end.

Press Figures

No press figures occur in 1724B, but in 1724A a press figure (in this case, a dagger, †) appears twice, once below the last line of text on page 10 and again on page 23.

---

[43] See Reiman's essay " 'Versioning': The Presentation of Multiple Texts."

Catchwords and hyphenation in 1724B

Following common typographical practice at that time, the printer, at the bottom right corner of most pages, inserted catchwords consisting either of full words or of first syllables that would be completed by other syllables on the first line of the next page. Most of the catchwords in 1724B accurately anticipate the expected word or syllable that appears on the top of the next page. The shorter one-syllable catchwords such as "is," "of," "has," and the like were simply repeated at the top of the next page. In cases involving a multisyllabic word, the word was usually split into two parts and hyphenated, so that only the second half of the word would appear at the top of the next page. Thus the last word on page 46 is simply the first syllable of the word "maturity," which appears as "Ma-" and the catchword "turity" appears immediately below it. At the top of page 47 the text begins with "turity."

The following list includes the only irregularities that I have found among the catchwords in the 1724B edition:

1. On p. 31 (or C8r) the catchword is "proceed," but at the top of p. 32 (or C8v) the first syllable "pro" is dropped, leaving only "ceed."
2. The catchword at the bottom of p. 32 should be "is," but only the "i" is visible at that place.
3. Similarly, the catchword on p. 37 (or D3r) is "a" but it should be "an." This catchword in the Beinecke copy is indeed "an."

Page numbering in 1724B

F.B. Kaye in his edition of *The Fable of the Bees* indicated the original page numbers by placing them within brackets in the outer margin of each page. Thus in vol. I, p. 80 of his edition we see **[74]** in the outer margin and on the same line a typographical "pipe" (|)inside the word "Ho-|nour," which means that the catchword "nour" must have appeared at the bottom of **[73]** and that the last word of the main text on that page is "Ho-". I have adopted Kaye's method of indicating split or divided words by means of a vertical bar or slash. I also follow Kaye's practice of placing the original page numbers within brackets (with numbers and brackets in boldface), but instead of placing these page numbers in the margins I include them within the body of the text. The bracketed page number will now signify the start of a new page. If it precedes a hyphenated word, then the new page (in 1724B) began with the second part of that word. Thus "**[62]** Cha-|racter" signifies that in the 1724B edition, p. 62 begins with "racter" and "Cha-" is the hyphenated syllable that concludes the last line of the main text on p. 61; "racter" is also the catchword at the bottom of p. 61.

★ ★ ★

In the texts that follow, the editor's annotations deal with a wide range of subjects in literature, law, history, and philosophy. A few subjects, those needing more space than a footnote, are explored under the heading "Commentaries." There the reader will find paragraphs and essays on audience, authorship, marriage, economics, the law, language (including Mandeville's lexicon of sexual terms), and the modern debate on prostitution. Separate essays are devoted to the critical reception of this work from 1725 on, and to a sixteenth-century poem that anticipates some of Mandeville's thoughts on this subject.

What has the sexual act, so natural, so necessary, and so just, done to mankind, for us not to dare to talk about it without shame and for us to exclude it from serious and decent conversation?

—Montaigne, *Essays* III, 5 (Frame, tr. p. 644)

. . . for the ingenious Author [i.e., Mandeville] has such a way with him, that it is very hard to know, when he is in earnest and when not. . . .

—George Bluet, *An Enquiry . . . With some Thoughts concerning a Toleration of Publick Stews* (1725), p. 160; in Stafford's edition, p. 345

[Mandeville's] writing is so largely ironic that it is hard to be sure when he is serious. . . .

—Arthur O. Lovejoy, Letter to F.B. Kaye (March, 1922), in Kaye's edition of *The Fable*, II, 432.

With several of Bernard Mandeville's works, it is an open question how far they were serious or designed to titillate; see, for example, his anonymous *A Modest Defence . . .*

—Roy Porter, "A touch of danger . . . ," p. 226, n. 19

From The Fable of the Bees, *Remark (H.)*

[The "Remarks" in the first edition of Mandeville's *Fable of the Bees* (1714) were prose notes to different passages in his core poem, "The Grumbling Hive: or, Knaves Turn'd Honest." Remark (H.) appeared with nineteen other "Remarks" in the first edition. The following reprint of this Remark is transcribed from pp. 62–67 of the sixth edition of Part One of the *Fable* (1729), the last in the author's lifetime.]

(H.)   *Parties directly opposite,*
   Assist each other, as 'twere for spight.

Nothing was more instrumental in forwarding the Reformation, than the Sloth and Stupidity of the *Roman* Clergy; yet the same Reformation has rouz'd 'em from the Laziness and Ignorance they then labour'd under; and the followers of *Luther*, *Calvin*, and others, may be said to have reform'd not only those whom they drew into their Sentiment, but likewise those who remain'd their greatest Opposers. The Clergy of *England* by being severe upon the Schismaticks, and upbraiding them with want of Learning, have raised themselves such formidable Enemies as are not easily answer'd; and again, the Dissenters by prying into the Lives, and diligently watching all the Actions of their powerful Antagonists, render those of the Establish'd Church more cautious of giving Offence, than in all probability they would, if they had no malicious Over-lookers to fear. It is very much owing to the great number of *Hugonots* [*sic*] that have always been in *France*, since the late utter Extirpation of them, that that Kingdom has a less dissolute and more learn'd Clergy to boast of than any other *Roman Catholick* Country.[44] The Clergy of that Church are no where more Sovereign than in *Italy*, and therefore no where more debauch'd; nor any where more Ignorant than they are in *Spain*, because their Doctrine is no where less oppos'd.

   Who would imagine, that Virtuous Women, unknowingly, should be instrumental in promoting the Advantage of Prostitutes? Or (what still

---

[44] The Huguenots or French Protestants were persecuted on numerous occasions from their beginnings in the sixteenth century. In 1685, with the Revocation of the Edict of Nantes, they were no longer freely tolerated and large numbers of them went into exile in Holland, England, and the New World.

seems the greater Paradox) that Incontinence should be made serviceable to the Preservation of Chastity? and yet nothing is more true. A vicious young Fellow, after having been an Hour or two at Church, a Ball, or any other Assembly, where there is a great parcel of handsome Women dress'd to the best Advantage, will have his Imagination more fired than if he had the same time been Poling[45] at *Guildhall*, or walking in the Country among a Flock of Sheep. The consequence of this is, that he'll strive to satisfy the Appetite that is raised in him; and when he finds honest Women obstinate and uncomatable,[46] 'tis very natural to think, that he'll hasten to others that are more compliable. Who wou'd so much as surmise, that this is the Fault of the Virtuous Women? They have no Thoughts of Men in dressing themselves, Poor Souls, and endeavour only to appear clean and decent, every one according to her Quality.[47]

I am far from encouraging Vice, and think it would be an unspeakable Felicity to a State, if the Sin of Uncleanness could be utterly Banish'd from it; but I am afraid it is impossible: The Passions of some People are too violent to be curb'd by any Law or Precept; and it is Wisdom in all Governments to bear with lesser Inconveniences to prevent greater.[48] If Courtezans and Strumpets were to be prosecuted with as much Rigour as some silly People would have it, what Locks or Bars would be sufficient to preserve the Honour of our Wives and Daughters?[49] For 'tis not only that the Women in general would meet with far greater Temptations, and the Attempts to ensnare the Innocence of Virgins would seem more excusable even to the sober part of Mankind than they do now: But some Men would grow outrageous, and Ravishing would become a common Crime. Where six or seven Thousand Sailors arrive at once, as it often happens at *Amsterdam*, that have seen none but their own Sex for many months together, how is it to be suppos'd that honest Women should walk the Streets unmolested, if there were no Harlots to be had at reasonable Prices? For which Reason the Wise Rulers of that well-ordered City always

---

[45] Voting—either for the Lord Mayor of London or for the City of London's parliamentary representatives. The Corporation of the City of London still meets at the Guildhall, which was first built in the fifteenth century.

[46] A recently coined word (1694) used by the dramatist Congreve, meaning "un-come-at-able," as when a woman resists the blandishments of all suitors. Mandeville had previously used this term in his earliest pamphlet of fables, *Some Fables after the Easie and Familiar Method of Monsieur de la Fontaine* (1703), p. 69. This passage can be more easily seen in the expanded edition of this work published in 1704 as *Æsop Dress'd; or a Collection of Fables Writ in Familiar Verse*, p. 57.

[47] Mandeville's sarcasm should be obvious to all readers. This is merely one of his passages illustrating female hypocrisy.

[48] In *A Modest Defence* Mandeville later expanded this argument that it is wise and prudent to choose the lesser of two evils.

[49] This sentence reappears in various collections of maxims or aphorisms on sexuality, prostitution, and related concepts. It is Mandeville's most memorable and best-known utterance about prostitution.

tolerate an uncertain number of Houses, in which Women are hired as publickly as Horses at a Livery-Stable; and there being in this Toleration a great deal of Prudence and Oeconomy to be seen, a short Account of it will be no tiresome digression.

In the first place the Houses I speak of are allowed to be no where but in the most slovenly and unpolish'd part of the Town, where Seamen and Strangers of no Repute chiefly Lodge and Resort. The Street in which most of them stand is counted scandalous, and the Infamy is extended to all the Neighbourhood round it. In the second, they are only Places to meet and bargain in, to make Appointments, in order to promote Interviews of greater Secrecy, and no manner of Lewdness is ever suffer'd to be transacted in them; which Order is so strictly observ'd, that bar the ill Manners and Noise of the Company that frequent them, you'll meet with no more Indecency, and generally less Lasciviousness there, than with us are to be seen at a Playhouse. Thirdly, the Female Traders that come to these Evening Exchanges are always the Scum of the People, and generally such as in the Day time carry Fruit and other Eatables about in Wheel-Barrows. The Habits indeed they appear in at Night are very different from their ordinary ones; yet they are commonly so ridiculously Gay, that they look more like the *Roman* Dresses of stroling Actresses than Gentlewomen's Clothes: If to this you add the aukwardness, the hard Hands, and course breeding of the Damsels that wear them, there is no great Reason to fear, that many of the better sort of People will be tempted by them.

The Musick in these Temples of *Venus* is performed by Organs, not out of respect to the Deity that is worship'd in them, but the frugality of the Owners, whose Business it is to procure as much Sound for as little Money as they can, and the Policy of the Government, who endeavour as little as is possible to encourage the Breed of Pipers and Scrapers. All Sea-faring Men, especially the *Dutch*, are like the Element they belong to, much given to loudness and roaring, and the Noise of half a dozen of them, when they call themselves Merry, is sufficient to drown twice the number of Flutes and Violins; whereas with one pair of Organs they can make the whole House ring, and are at no other Charge than the keeping of one scurvy Musician, which can cost them but little: yet notwithstanding the good Rules and strict Discipline that are observ'd in these Markets of Love, the *Schout*[50] and his Officers are always vexing, mulcting, and upon the least Complaint removing the miserable Keepers of them: Which Policy is of two great uses; first it gives an opportunity to a large parcel of Officers, the Magistrates make use of on many Occasions, and which they could not be without, to squeeze a Living out of the immoderate Gains accruing from the worst of Employments, and at the same time punish those necessary

---

[50] A police official—a bailiff or sheriff.

Profligates the Bawds and Panders, which, tho' they abominate, they desire yet not wholly to destroy. Secondly, as on several accounts it might be dangerous to let the Multitude into the Secret, that those Houses and the Trade that is drove in them are conniv'd at, so by this means appearing unblameable, the wary Magistrates preserve themselves in the good Opinion of the weaker sort of People, who imagine that the Government is always endeavouring, tho' unable, to suppress what it actually tolerates: Whereas if they had a mind to rout them out, their Power in the Administration of Justice is so sovereign and extensive, and they know so well how to have it executed, that one Week, nay one Night, might send them all a packing.

In *Italy* the toleration of Strumpets is yet more barefac'd, as is evident from their publick Stews. At *Venice* and *Naples* Impurity is a kind of Merchandize and Traffick; the *Courtezans* at *Rome*, and the *Cantoneras* in *Spain*, compose a Body in the State, and are under a Legal Tax and Impost. Tis well known, that the Reason why so many good Politicians as these tolerate Lewd Houses, is not their Irreligion, but to prevent a worse Evil, an Impurity of a more execrable kind, and to provide for the Safety of Women of Honour.[51] *About Two Hundred and Fifty Years ago*, says Monsieur *de St. Didier*, Venice *being in want of Courtezans, the Republick was obliged to procure a great number from Foreign Parts. Doglioni*, who has written the memorable Affairs of *Venice*, highly extols the Wisdom of the Republick in this Point, which secured the Chastity of Women of Honour daily exposed to publick Violences, the Churches and Consecrated Places not being a sufficient Azylum for their Chastity.[52]

Our Universities in *England* are much bely'd, if in some Colleges there was not a Monthly Allowance *ad expurgandos Renes:* and time was when the Monks and Priests in *Germany* were allow'd Concubines on paying a certain Yearly Duty to their Prelate. *'Tis generally believ'd*, says Monsieur *Bayle*, (to whom I owe the last Paragraph) that *Avarice was the Cause of this shamefull Indulgence; but it is more probable their design was to prevent their tempting modest Women, and to quiet the uneasiness of Husbands, whose Resentments the Clergy do well to avoid.* From what has been said it is manifest, that there is a Necessity of sacrificing one part of Womankind to preserve the other, and prevent a Filthiness of a more heinous Nature. From whence I think I may justly conclude (what was the seeming Paradox I went about to prove) that

---

[51] Mandeville continued to employ this lesser-of-two-evils argument ten years later in his *A Modest Defence*. By his time this argument was already centuries old.

[52] As F.B. Kaye informs us (*Fable* (I, 99), Mandeville acquired this paragraph and some later words from Pierre Bayle's *Pensées diverses* or *Miscellaneous Reflections, Occasion'd by the Comet Which appear'd in December 1680* (English translation, 1708). In that work Bayle quotes from a book on Venice by Alexandre Toussaint de Limojon de Saint-Didier (d. 1689), who in turn quoted from a work by Giovanni Nicolo Doglioni on the city and republic of Venice.

Chastity may be supported by Incontinence, and the best of Virtues want the Assistance of the worst of Vices.

★   ★   ★

From The Fable of the Bees, *Remark (N.)*

[First published in 1723, one year before *A Modest Defence* appeared, this Remark opens with an analysis of the passion of envy and then focuses upon the distinctions between love and lust. Before concluding it Mandeville also examines the nature of jealousy and how that passion relates to love, marriage, and illicit or extramarital affairs of the heart. He continues to discourse upon love, lust, matrimony, and illicit sex in *A Modest Defence*. The text that follows is transcribed from the sixth edition of his *Fable* (1729), pp. 103–108; it begins with the fourteenth paragraph of this Remark.]

Love in the first Place signifies Affection, such as Parents and Nurses bear to Children, and Friends to one another; it consists in a Liking and Well-wishing to the Person beloved. We give an easy Construction to his Words and Actions, and feel a Proneness to excuse and forgive his Faults, if we see any; his Interest we make on all Accounts our own, even to our Prejudice, and receive an inward Satisfaction for sympathizing with him in his Sorrows, as well as Joys. What I said last is not impossible, whatever it may seem to be; for when we are sincere in sharing with another in his Misfortunes, Self-Love makes us believe, that the sufferings we feel must alleviate and lessen those of our Friend, and while this fond Reflexion is soothing our pain, a secret Pleasure arises from our grieving for the Person we love.[53]

Secondly, by Love we understand a strong Inclination, in its Nature distinct from all other Affections of Friendship, Gratitude, and Consanguinity, that Persons of different Sexes, after liking, bear to one another: It is in this Signification that Love enters into the Compound of *Jealousy*, and is the Effect as well as happy Disguise of that Passion that prompts us to labour for

---

[53] Mandeville in this sentence may be alluding to the following maxim (in *Maximes*, 1665 edition, no. 99) by La Rochefoucauld: "Dans l'adversité de nos meilleurs amis, nous trouvons toujours quelque chose qui ne nous déplaît pas." Though at least five English translations of this maxim had appeared between 1670 and 1706, the first published English translation was probably that of Jonathan Swift in 1731: "In the adversity of our best friends, we find something that doth not displease us." Swift used this maxim as the epigraph to his poem "Verses on the Death of Dr. Swift, D.S.P.D."

the Preservation of our Species. This latter Appetite is innate both in Men and Women, who are not defective in their Formation, as much as Hunger or Thirst, tho' they are seldom affected with it before the Years of Puberty. Could we undress Nature, and pry into her deepest Recesses, we should discover the Seeds of this Passion before it exerts it self, as plainly as we see the Teeth in an Embrio, before the Gums are form'd. There are few healthy People of Either Sex, whom it has made no Impression upon before Twenty: Yet, as the Peace and Happiness of the Civil Society require that this should be kept a Secret, never to be talk'd of in Publick; so among well-bred People it is counted highly Criminal to mention before Company any thing in plain Words, that is relating to this Mystery of Succession: By which Means the very Name of the Appetite, tho' the most necessary for the Continuance of Mankind, is become odious, and the proper Epithets commonly join'd to Lust are *Filthy* and *Abominable.*

This Impulse of Nature in People of strict Morals, and rigid Modesty, often disturbs the Body for a considerable Time before it is understood or known to be what it is, and it is remarkable that the most polish'd and best instructed are generally the most ignorant as to this Affair; and here I can but observe the Difference between Man in the wild State of Nature, and the same Creature in the Civil Society. In the first, Men and Women, if left rude and untaught in the Sciences of Modes and Manners, would quickly find out the Cause of that Disturbance, and be at a Loss no more than other Animals for a present Remedy: Besides, that it is not probable they should want either Precept or Example from the more experienc'd. But in the second, where the Rules of Religion, Law and Decency, are to be follow'd, and obey'd before any Dictates of Nature, the Youth of both Sexes are to be arm'd and fortify'd against this Impulse, and from their Infancy artfully frighten'd from the most remote Approaches of it. The Appetite it self, and all the Symptoms of it, tho' they are plainly felt and understood, are to be stifled with Care and Severity, and in Women flatly disown'd, and if there be Occasion, with Obstinacy deny'd, even when themselves are visibly affected by them. If it throws them into Distempers, they must be cured by Physick, or else patiently bear them in Silence; and it is the Interest of the Society to preserve Decency and Politeness; that Women should linger, waste, and die, rather than relieve themselves in an unlawful manner; and among the fashionable Part of Mankind, the People of Birth and Fortune, it is expected that Matrimony should never be enter'd upon without a curious Regard of Family, Estate, and Reputation, and in the making of Matches the Call of Nature be the very last Consideration.

Those then who would make Love and Lust Synonimous confound the Effect with the Cause of it; Yet such is the force of Education, and a Habit of thinking as we are taught, that sometimes Persons of either Sex are actually in Love without feeling any Carnal Desires, or penetrating into the Intentions of Nature, the end proposed by her without which they could never have been affected with that sort of Passion. That there are such is certain, but many more whose Pretences to those refin'd Notions are only upheld by Art and Dissimulation. Those, who are really such Platonick Lovers are commonly the pale-faced weakly People of cold and phlegmatick Constitutions in either Sex; the hale and robust of bilious Temperament and a sanguine Complexion never entertain any Love so Spiritual as to exclude all Thoughts and Wishes that relate to the Body.[54] But if the most Seraphick Lovers would know the Original of their Inclination, let them but suppose that another should have the Corporal Enjoyment of the Person beloved, and by the Tortures they'll suffer from that Reflexion they will soon discover the Nature of their Passions: Whereas on the contrary, Parents and Friends receive a Satisfaction in reflecting on the Joys and Comforts of a happy Marriage, to be tasted by those they wish well to.

The curious, that are skill'd in anatomizing the invisible Part of Man, will observe that the more sublime and exempt this Love is from all Thoughts of Sensuality, the more spurious it is, and the more it degenerates from its honest Original and primitive Simplicity. The Power and Sagacity as well as Labour and Care of the Politician in civilizing the Society, has been no where more conspicuous, than in the happy Contrivance of playing our Passions against one another. By flattering our Pride and still encreasing the good Opinion we have of ourselves on the one hand, and inspiring us on the other with a superlative Dread and mortal Aversion against Shame, the Artful Moralists have taught us chearfully to encounter our selves, and if not subdue, at least so to conceal and disguise our darling Passion, Lust, that we scarce know it when we meet with it in our own Breasts; Oh! The mighty Prize we have in view for all our Self-Denial! can any Man be so serious as to abstain from Laughter, when he considers that for so much deceit and insincerity practis'd upon our selves as well as others, we have no other Recompense than the vain Satisfaction of making our Species appear more exalted and remote from that of other Animals, than it really is; and we in our Consciences know it to be? Yet this is fact, and in it we plainly perceive the reason why it was necessary to render odious every Word or Action by which we might discover the innate Desire we feel to perpetuate our Kind; and why tamely to submit to the violence of a Furious Appetite (which it is painful to resist) and innocently to obey the most pressing demand of Nature without Guile or Hypocrisy, like other Creatures, should be branded with the Ignominious Name of Brutality.

What we call Love then is not a Genuine, but an Adulterated Appetite, or rather a Compound, a heap of several contradictory Passions blended in one. As it is a product of Nature warp'd by Custom and Education, so the true Origin and first Motive of it, as I have hinted already, is stifled in

---

[54] The phrases "phlegmatic Constitutions" and "sanguine Complexion" refer to the centuries-old system that treated human personalities or characters as governed by the balance of the four humors (liquids) within each person: blood, phlegm or white bile, choler, and melancholy or black bile. The predominance of any one of these humors was thought to produce the sanguine, phlegmatic, choleric, or melancholic personality.

well-bred People, and almost concealed from themselves: all which is the reason that as those affected with it vary in Age, Strength, Resolution, Temper, Circumstance, and Manners, the effects of it are so different, whimsical, surprizing and unaccountable.

It is this Passion that makes Jealousy so troublesome, and the Envy of it often so fatal; those who imagine that there may be Jealousy without Love, do not understand that Passion. Men may not have the least Affection for their Wives, and yet be angry with them for their Conduct, and suspicious of them either with or without a Cause: But what in such Cases affects them is their Pride, the Concern for their Reputation. They feel a Hatred against them without Remorse; when they are Outrageous, they can beat them and go to sleep contentedly: such Husbands may watch their Dames themselves, and have them observed by others; but their Vigilance is not so intense; they are not so inquisitive or industrious in their Searches, neither do they feel that Anxiety of Heart at the Fear of a Discovery, as when Love is mix'd with the Passions.

What confirms me in this Opinion is, that we never observe this Behaviour between a Man and his Mistress; for when his Love is gone and he suspects her to be false, he leaves her, and troubles his Head no more about her: Whereas it is the greatest Difficulty imaginable, even to a Man of Sense, to part with a Mistress as long as he loves her, what ever Faults she may be guilty of. If in his Anger he strikes her he is uneasy about it; his Love makes him reflect on the Hurt he has done her, and he wants to be reconcil'd to her again. He may talk of hating her, and many times from his Heart wish her hang'd, but if he cannot get entirely rid of his Frailty, he can never disentangle himself from her: tho' she is represented in the most monstrous Guilt to his Imagination, and he has resolved and swore a thousand Times never to come near her again, there is no trusting him; even when he is fully convinc'd of her Infidelity, if his Love continues, his Despair is never so lasting, but between the blackest Fits of it he relents, and finds lucid Intervals of Hope; he forms Excuses for her, thinks of pardoning, and in order to it racks his Invention for Possibilities that may make her appear less criminal.

★   ★   ★

A

Modest D E F E N C E

OF

Publick STEWS :

OR, AN

E S S A Y

UPON

W H O R I N G,

As it is now practis'd in these Kingdoms.

Nimirum propter Continentiam Incontinentia necessaria
est, incendium ut ignibus extinguitur.   Seneca.[A]

Omne adeo genus in terris, hominumq; ferarumq;
Et genus æquoreum, pecudes, pictæq; volucres,
In furia, ignemq; ruunt.   Virg. Georg. 3.[B]

Written by a L A Y M A N.

L O N D O N;
Printed by A. MOORE near St. PAUL'S.

M.DCC.XXIV.

Notes to the Title Page

(A). Tertullian, *Liber de Pudicitia*, no. 16. Mandeville probably found this Latin excerpt in a French edition of Montaigne's *Essais*, where it is quoted in III, 5 "On Some Verses of Virgil." This identification and the broad indebtedness of Mandeville to Montaigne were first pointed out by Dario Castiglione in an essay accompanying his translation of this work, *Modesta Difesa delle Pubbliche Case di Piacere*. On the title page of a 1740 edition of *A Modest Defence* ("By the late Colonel Harry Mordaunt"and "Printed for T. Read"), the two Latin quotations are absent and in their places are English translations of those passages. The first quotation, still attributed to Seneca, reads: "*Certainly some Kind of Incontinency may be necessary to preserve Chastity, as one Fire is extinguished by another.*" In the earlier Florio translation (1603) it is rendered as: "Belike we must be incontinent that we may be continent, burning is quenched by fire." (Modern Library edition, p. 773). As rendered in Donald Frame's translation of Montaigne: "Doubtless incontinence is necessary for the sake of continence; a conflagration is extinguished by fire." (Stanford University Press, 1958, 1965, p. 652). We supply these quotations from Montaigne because this epigraph and the one that follows appear one page apart in Montaigne's *Essais* III, 5: "On Some Verses of Virgil." Other Latin passages, and a few passages from Montaigne's own prose (in translation) appear throughout Mandeville's essay. He may have seen this passage attributed somewhere to Seneca, but in the Pléiade edition of Montaigne (p. 960) the note to this passage indicates that its author is unknown. In selecting this quotation Mandeville was characteristically indulging his taste for paradox. Only ten years earlier he had published what became the eighteenth-century's most famous paradox, "private vices, publick benefits."

(B). Virgil, *Georgics* III, 244–246. On the title page of the 1740 edition mentioned in the preceding note, the Latin lines are replaced by Dryden's verse translation of this passage:

> *Not only Man's Imperial Race, but they*
> *That wing the liquid Air, or swim the Sea,*
> *Or haunt the Desart, rush into the Flame,*
> *For Love is Lord of All, and is in All the same.*

In Donald Frame's translation (p. 653), "Yes, everything on earth, the race of man and beast, / Fish of the sea, and flocks, and gaily painted birds, / Rush into passionate flame." For Florio's translation, see the Modern Library edition, p. 774.

[Each of the two earliest editions of Mandeville's *A Modest Defence* (1724A and 1724B) consists of two introductory parts, the Dedication (12 pages) and the Preface (4 pages), followed by the main body of the essay (78 pages). In both editions the pages of the Dedication are numbered in lower-case roman font, the pages of the Preface are unnumbered, and those of the main text have arabic numbers. Page numbers for all pages of both editions now appear within brackets at the beginning of each new page in those editions. Italicized numbers within brackets indicate pages that were unnumbered in these two editions. The text that follows is transcribed from the 1724B edition.]

[Mandeville's Dedication]

[i]   TO THE

GENTLEMEN

OF THE

SOCIETIES.[55]

Gentlemen,

THE great Pains and Diligence You have employ'd in the Defence of Modesty and Virtue, give You an undisputed Title, to the Address of this Treatise; tho' it is with the utmost Concern that I find myself under a Necessity of writing it, and that after so much Reforming, there should be any Thing left to say upon the Subject, besides congratulating You upon Your happy Success. It is no small Addition **[ii]** to my Grief to observe, that Your Endeavours to suppress Lewdness, have only serv'd to promote it; and that this *Branch* of Immorality has grown under Your Hands, as if it was *prun'd* instead of being *lopp'd*.[56] But however Your ill Success may grieve, it cannot astonish me: What else could we hope for, from Your persecuting of poor strolling Damsels? From Your stopping up those *Drains* and *Sluices* we had to let out Lewdness?[57] From Your demolishing those

---

[55] In the first edition, 1724A, this title continues with the following words: "FOR *Reformation of* MANNERS." Whoever removed these words could have been acting prudentially by avoiding the common name for these societies. Making the title less specific and therefore more ambiguous also fits in with Mandeville's playful humor in this work.

[56] In his doggerel poem, *The Grumbling Hive: Or, Knaves turn'd Honest* (1705), the basis for Mandeville's *Fable of the Bees* (1714 and later editions), Mandeville included this couplet:

So Vice is beneficial found,
When it's by Justice lopt and bound. (Kaye's edition, I, 37)

Lopping for Mandeville implied major surgical amputation, something that would halt further growth. Pruning, on the other hand, involves removal of smaller portions of vegetation in order to encourage and stimulate new growth.

[57] This is Mandeville's first reference to the function of prostitutes as sewers or drains that remove "peccant humours" or troublesome liquids from society. We do not know whether he

Horn-works and *Breast-works* of Modesty? Those *Ramparts* and *Ditches* within which the Virtue of our Wives and Daughters lay so conveniently *intrench'd?*[58] An Intrenchment so much the safer, by how much the Ditches were harder to be fill'd up. Or what better could we expect from Your Carting of Bawds, than that the Great Leviathan of Leachery, for Want of these Tubs to play with, should, with one Whisk of his Tail, **[iii]** overset the *Vessel* of Modesty?[59] Which, in her best Trim, we know to be somewhat *leaky*, and to have a very unsteady *Helm*.

An antient Philosopher compares Lewdness to a wild, fiery, and headstrong young Colt, which can never be broke till he is rid into a Bog: And *Plato*, on the same Subject, has these words; *The Gods*, says he, *have given us one disobedient and unruly Member, which, like a greedy and ravenous Animal that wants Food, grows wild and furious, till having imbib'd the Fruit of the common Thirst, he has plentifully besprinkled and bedewed the Bottom of the Womb.*[60]

was aware that this explanation of the utility of the prostitute goes back to passages in the writings of St. Augustine and St. Thomas Aquinas. St. Augustine remarked that if prostitutes are removed then society will be disturbed by all kinds of lusts: "Aufer meretrices de rebus humanis, turbaveris omnia libidinibus."—from *De Ordine*, Book II, ch. iv. Aquinas said essentially the same thing: "Prostitution in towns is like the sewer in a palace; take away the sewers and the palace becomes an impure and stinking place."—from Aquinas's *De Regimine Principum* (*Opuscula* XX), Book IV, ch. xiv. These Latin references and the translation can be found in Havelock Ellis's *Studies in the Psychology of Sex* (New York: Random House, 1936), vol. 2, part 3, pp. 282–283. As Michael Rocke reports (p. 159), this idea reappeared in the fourteenth century in a passage by Giordano da Pisa, who wrote that the removal of prostitution from society would result in an increase of worse evils including adultery and sodomy.

[58] Mandeville's reliance upon military metaphors to express courtship, sexual pursuit, and the "wars" of love was already centuries old and continued to appear in literary works well into the eighteenth century. "Horn-works" and "breast-works" were technical terms relating to military strategy and fortifications, but they could easily be made to convey sexual meanings as well. The military metaphor for female chastity as a town, castle, or fortress that needs to be protected from direct external assaults and from frauds working secretly from within reappears a few times in this work; see Mandeville's pages 42–43, for example. A typical earlier example occurs in Richard Head's picaresque novel, *The English Rogue* (1665), where a young lady complains that other women "will surrender their maiden forts upon first summons" (Boston 1961 reprint, p. 81). The term "ditch" as used here with obvious reference to the female pudendum also has a biblical source: "For a whore is a deep ditch; and a strange woman is a narrow pit" Proverbs 23: 27. Anthony E. Simpson reports (p. 52) that Josiah Woodward, a major supporter of the Societies for the Reformation of Manners, used this passage from Proverbs in his often reprinted *Soldier's Monitor*, and it would have been an obvious favorite with all those preaching against prostitution. Hence, when Mandeville uses the term "ditch" it is loaded with sexual meaning. His sexual puns and double entendres all contribute, as a strategy of ridicule, to his polemic against the repressive activities of the "gentlemen" of the Societies. As discrete bursts of humor, to be sure, they are also ends in themselves.

[59] Leviathan, a mythical sea monster, is mentioned in the biblical books of Psalms, Job, and Amos. In this sentence Mandeville also alludes to two major works that were controversial in his time, Hobbes's *Leviathan* (1651) and Swift's *A Tale of a Tub* (1704); see p. 40 in Swift's *Tale*, ed. A.C. Guthkelch and D. Nichol Smith (second edition, 1958). Later in this work Mandeville names Hobbes as the author of *Leviathan*.

[60] This is thus far the strongest piece of evidence that Mandeville was borrowing with some frequency from Montaigne's essay III, 5, "Upon Some Verses of Virgil." In that essay Montaigne mentions Plato's comment on the "unruly member," the penis, immediately after he quotes from

And now I have mention'd the Philosophers, I must beg Your Patience for a Moment, to hear a short Account of their Amours: For nothing will convince us of the irresistible Force of Love, and the Folly of hoping to suppress it, sooner than reflecting, that those venerable *Sages*, **[iv]** those Standards of Morality, those great *Reformers* of the World, were so sensibly touch'd with this tender Passion.

Socrates confess'd, that, in his old Age, he felt a strange tickling all over him for five Days, only by a Girl's touching his Shoulder.[61]

Xenophon made open Profession of his passionate Love to *Clineas*.[62]

Aristippus, of *Cyrene*, writ a lewd Book of antient Delights; he compar'd a Woman to a House or a Ship, that was the better for being used: He asserted, that there was no Crime in Pleasure, but only in being a Slave to it: And often used to say, *I enjoy* Lais, *but* Lais *does not enjoy me.*[63]

Theodorus openly maintain'd, that a wise Man might, without Shame or Scandal, keep Company with common Harlots.[64]

Plato, our great Pattern for chaste Love, proposes, as the greatest Reward for publick Service, that he who **[v]** has perform'd a signal Exploit, should not be deny'd any amorous Favour.[65] He writ a Description of the Loves of his Time, and several amorous Sonnets upon his own Minions: His chief

---

Virgil's *Georgics* III, the same passage that Mandeville uses as the second epigraph on his title page. Mandeville extracted this paragraph from the following more involved statement in Montaigne: "The Gods, says Plato, have furnished us with a disobedient and tyrannical member, which, like a furious animal, undertakes by the violence of its appetite to subject everything to itself. To women likewise they have given a gluttonous and voracious animal which, if denied its food in due season, goes mad, impatient of delay, and, breathing its rage into their bodies, stops up the passages, arrests the breathing, causing a thousand kinds of ills, until it has sucked in the fruit of the common thirst and therewith plentifully irrigated and fertilized the depth of the womb." Translated by Donald Frame (Stanford University Press, 1958, p. 654). For Florio's translation, see the Modern Library edition, p. 774; for the French, see the Pléiade edition (1953), p. 961. The original source is Plato's *Timaeus*, Sec. 91, toward the conclusion of that work.

[61] The amours of the ancient philosophers mentioned in this and the following paragraphs derive mainly from Mandeville's readings in Montaigne. The arousal of Socrates in advanced age appears in Montaigne's essay "On Some Verses of Virgil," but in transcribing this passage Mandeville arbitrarily substituted "girl" in place of the male who caused Socrates' erotic reaction. See Frame's translation, p. 680; Florio (Modern Library), p. 805; the Pléiade edition, p. 999.

[62] A description of how much Xenophon, a student of Socrates, admired Clinias can be found in *Lives of the Philosophers* (II, 48–49) by Diogenes Laertius, who reports that he found this information in the fourth book of *On the Luxury of the Ancients* by Aristippus. See vol. I, p. 179 of the Loeb Classical Library edition of Diogenes Laertius.

[63] For Aristippus and Lais, see Athenaeus, *The Deipnosophists* (Loeb Library edition, VI, 173–175). Aristippus's book "Of Ancient Delights" is mentioned in Montaigne, III, 5; see Frame's translation, p. 652; Pléiade edition, p. 959. Mandeville may also have used the article "Lais," Remark [G], in Bayle's *Dictionnaire historique et critique*. See the English translation of Bayle in Thomas Birch et al., *A General Dictionary*, vol. VI, p. 598, col. a (London, 1738). Lais as a love partner of Aristippus also appears in Diogenes Laertius's *Lives of the Philosophers*, II, 74 and 84 (Loeb Library, I, pp. 203 and 213).

[64] For Theodorus see Diogenes Laertius, II, 97ff. (Loeb Library, I, 225–233).

[65] Montaigne, *Essais*, III, 5; Frame's translation, p. 684; the Pléiade edition, p. 1004; Florio's translation (Modern Library), p. 809.

Favourites were *Asterus, Dio, Phaedrus*, and *Agatho*; but he had, for Variety, his Female Darling *Archeanassa*; and was so noted for Wantonness, that *Antisthenes* gave him the Nick-name of *Satho*, i.e. *Well-furnish'd*.[66]

Polemo was prosecuted by his Wife for Male Venery.[67]

Crantor made no Secret of his Love to his Pupil *Arcesilaus*.[68]

Arcesilaus made Love to *Demetrius* and *Leocharus*; the last, he said, he would fain have open'd: Besides, he openly frequented the two *Elean* Courtezans, *Theodota* and *Philæta*, and was himself enjoy'd by *Demochares* and *Pythocles*: He suffer'd the last, he said, for Patience-sake.[69]

Bion was noted for debauching his own Scholars.[70]

[vi]   *Aristotle*, the first *Peripatetick*, had a Son call'd *Nichomacus*, by his Concubine *Herpilis*: He lov'd her so well, that he left her in his Will a Talent of Silver, and the Choice of his Country-Houses; that, as he says, the Damsel might have no Reason to complain: He enjoy'd, beside the Eunuch *Hermias*, others say only his Concubine *Pythais*, upon whom he writ a Hymn, call'd, *The Inside*.[71]

Demetrius Phalereus, who had 360 Statues in *Athens*, kept *Lamia* for his Concubine, and at the same time was himself enjoy'd by *Cleo*: He writ a Treatise, call'd, *The Lover*, and was nick-nam'd by the Courtezans, *Charito Blespharus*, i.e. *A Charmer of Ladies*; and *Lampetes*, i.e. *A great Boaster of his Abilities*.[72]

Diogenes, the *Cynick*, us'd to say, that Women ought to be in common, and that Marriage was nothing but a Man's getting a Woman in the Mind to be lain with: He often us'd Manual **[vii]** Venery in the Publick Market-place, with this Saying. *Oh! that I could assuage my Hunger thus with rubbing of my Stomach!*[73]

---

[66] For Aster, Dion, Phaedrus, and Archeanassa, as well as for Antisthenes calling Plato "Sathon," see the life of Plato in Diogenes Laertius's *Lives of the Philosophers* III, 29ff. (Loeb Library, I, 303–309). Plato and Archeanassa are mentioned in Athenaeus's *Deipnosophists* (Loeb Library edition, VI, 179.

[67] Montaigne, *Essais*, III, 5. Frame, p. 651; Pléiade edition, p. 957; Florio, p. 770. Recorded in Diogenes Laertius, IV, 17; in the Loeb Library edition, I, p. 395.

[68] Diogenes Laertius, IV, 29; Loeb Library edition, I, p. 407.

[69] Diogenes Laertius, IV, 40–41; Loeb edition, I, pp. 417–419. In the Loeb translation (by R.D. Hicks), the names are rendered as Theodete, Phila, and Cleochares.

[70] Diogenes Laertius, IV, 53; Loeb edition, I, p. 431.

[71] Diogenes Laertius, V, 1–3 (Loeb edition, I, pp 445–447); see also Athenaeus, *The Deipnosophists*, Bk. XIII, 589 (Loeb edition, VI, p. 179).

[72] Diogenes Laertius, V, 75–76; Loeb edition, I, pp. 527–529. In par. 76 on p. 529 this passage appears: "a certain courtesan nicknamed him Charito-Blepharos ('having the eyelids of the Graces'), and Lampito ('of shining eyes')."

[73] Diogenes Laertius, VI, 46 and 69 (re: masturbation and stomach rubbing); Loeb edition, II, pp. 47 and 71. For his remark on community of wives or female sexual partners, see VI, 72; Loeb edition, II, p. 75. Diogenes the Cynic's remark about masturbation and hunger also appears twice in Bayle's *Dictionnaire*, first in his article "Diogenes," Remark [L] and later in his article "Hipparchia," Remark [D]. For an English translation see *A General Dictionary*, IV, 604, col. b, and VI, 176–177.

But what Wonder if the old *Academicks*, the *Cyrenaicks*, and *Peripateticks*, were so lewdly Wanton, when the very *Stoicks*, who prided themselves in the Conquest of all their other Passions, were forc'd to submit to this?

Zeno, indeed, the Founder of that Sect, was remarkable for his Modesty, because he rarely made Use of Boys, and took but once an ordinary Maid-Servant to Bed, that he might not be thought to hate the Sex; yet, in his *Commonwealth*, he was for a Community of Women; and writ a Treatise, wherein he regulated the Motions of getting a Maidenhead, and philosophically prov'd Action and Reaction to be equal.[74]

Chrysippus and *Apollodorus* agree with *Zeno* in a Community of Women, **[viii]** and say, that a wise man may be in Love with handsome Boys.

Erillus, a Scholar of Zeno's, was a notorious Debauchee.

I need not mention the *Epicureans* that were remarkable for their Obscenity.

Epicurus used to make a Pander of his own Brother; and his Scholar, the Great *Metrodorus*, visited all the noted Courtezans in *Athens*, and publickly kept the famous *Leontium*, his Master's *Quondam* Mistress. Yet, if you will believe *Laertius*, he was every Way a good Man.[75]

But what shall we say of our Favourite *Seneca*, who, with all his Morals, could never acquire the Reputation of Chastity? He was indeed somewhat Nice in his Amours, like the Famous *Flora*, who was never enjoy'd by any Thing less than a Dictator or a Consul; for he scorn'd to intrigue with any Thing less than the Empress.[76]

[ix] Now, if those Reverend School-Masters of Antiquity, were so Loose in their Seminals; shall we, of this Age, set up for Chastity? Have our

---

[74] For Zeno's rules on deflowering a virgin, see Montaigne, *Essais*, III, 5: Frame's translation, p. 652; the Pléiade edition, p. 959; Florio's translation (Modern Library), p. 772. For Zeno and the maid-servant, see Montaigne, *Essais*, III, 5: in Frame's translation, p. 669; in the Pléiade edition, p. 983; in Florio's translation (Modern Library), p. 792. "Community of Women" here and in the next paragraph again signifies the sharing of women as sexual partners, or free love. See Diogenes Laertius's *The Lives and Opinions of Eminent Philosophers*: Book VII: The Stoics, "Life of Zeno," sec. xxviii.

"philosophically prov'd Action and Reaction to be equal": Ursula Pia Jauch in a note to her German translation of *A Modest Defence* reminds us (p. 91) that this phrase alludes to Newton's Third Law of Motion (every action has an equal and opposite reaction), as stated in his *Mathematical Principles of Natural Philosophy* (first edition, in Latin, 1687).

[75] For Epicurus and Leontion, see Athenaeus, *The Deipnosophists* (Loeb Library edition, VI, 171). In the above paragraph Mandeville mischievously reports as fact some charges against Epicurus that were warmly debated by various scholars in the seventeenth century, to the effect that he and his students enjoyed the favors of the Athenian courtesan Leontium. In his article on Epicurus, Remark [I], and again in his article on Leontium, Pierre Bayle reviews these charges and concludes by sending the reader to Book 7 of Pierre Gassendi's *De Vita & Moribus Epicuri* (*Of the Life and Death of Epicurus*), where Gassendi defends the reputation of Epicurus against such calumnies (as Bayle puts it). See *A General Dictionary*, V, 51–52, and VI, 715. In naming "Laertius," i.e., Diogenes Laertius, Mandeville tells his readers where they might find sources for his remarks not only about Epicurus but about the other named philosophers as well.

[76] The translation of Seneca's *Morals* by Sir Roger L'Estrange (1616–1704) was often reprinted. The author uses "nice" in its older sense of particular or discriminating. The empress is Agrippina the younger, mother of Nero, who ordered her death.

Oxford Students more Command of their Passions than the *Stoicks*? Are our Young *Templars*[77] less Amorous than *Plato*? Or, is an *Officer* of the Army less *Ticklish* in the Shoulder than *Socrates*?

But I need not waste any Rhetorick upon so evident a Truth; for plain and clear Propositions, like Windows painted, are only the more Obscure the more they are adorn'd.

I will now suppose, that you have given up the Men as Incorrigible; since You are convinc'd, by Experience, that even Matrimony is not able to reclaim them. Marriage, indeed, is Just such a Cure for Lewdness, as a Surfeit is for Gluttony; it gives a Man's Fancy a Distaste to the particular Dish, but leaves his Palate as Luxurious as ever: for this Reason **[x]** we find so many marry'd Men, that, like *Sampson*'s Foxes,[78] only do more Mischief for having their Tails ty'd. But the Women, You say, are weaker Vessels, and You are resolv'd to make them submit; rightly judging, if You cou'd make all the Females Modest, it would put a considerable Stop to Fornication. It is great Pity, no doubt, so Fine a Project should Miscarry: And I would willingly entertain Hopes of seeing one of these *Bridewell*[79] Converts. In the mean Time it would not be amiss, if You chang'd somewhat your present Method of Conversion, especially in the Article of Whipping. It is very possible, indeed, that leaving a Poor Girl Penny-less, may put her in a Way of living Honestly, tho' the want of Money was the only Reason of her living otherwise; and the Stripping of her Naked, may, for aught I know, contribute to Her Modesty, and put Her in a State of **[xi]** Innocence; but surely, *Gentlemen*, You must all know that Flogging has a quite contrary Effect.[80] This Project of pulling down Bawdy-houses to prevent Uncleanness, puts me in Mind of a certain Over-nice Gentleman, who cou'd never Fancy his Garden look'd Sweet, till he had demolish'd a Bog-house that offended his Eye in one Corner of it; but it was not long before every Nose in the Family was convinc'd of His Mistake.[81] If Reason

---

[77] By "Templars" Mandeville means not the "Knights Templars" who participated in the Crusades, but rather the law students or barristers associated with the Inner Temple or Middle Temple, old law schools, and centers of law practice in the heart of London.

[78] Judges 15: 4–5. Mandeville does not customarily take libertine freedoms with a biblical text, as he does here by applying a sexual meaning to the word "tails." But his imputation of sexual significance to the ignited tails of Sampson's foxes was not original. He could have seen it in *The London-Bawd* (1711, p. 3), whose main character "was once 'one of *Sampson's Foxes*, and has carried so much Fire in her Tail, as has burnt all those that have had to do with her.'" The fire in the tail, of course, is syphilis or gonorrhea. Quoted from April London, "Avoiding the Subject: The Presence and Absence of Venereal Disease in the Eighteenth-Century English Novel," in *The Secret Malady* (ed. Merians), 216.

[79] Bridewell, first built near the Thames River in London during the reign of Henry VIII, eventually became a prison which, in Mandeville's time, was a place of punishment and incarceration for harlots.

[80] Here flogging suggests not only punishment but also deviant sexual behavior which would be far from modest or innocent. The bookseller Edmund Curll, Mandeville's notorious contemporary, published *A Treatise of the Use of Flogging in Venereal Affairs* in 1718.

[81] Bog-house, a term used in the seventeenth and eighteenth centuries, is the equivalent of the later outhouse, a separate structure containing a toilet or latrine.

fails to Convince let us profit by Example: Observe the Policy of a Modern Butcher, persecuted with a Swarm of Carnivorous Flies; when all his Engines and Fly-Flaps have prov'd ineffectual to defend his Stall against the Greedy Assiduity of those Carnal Insects, he very Judiciously cuts off a Fragment, already blown, which serves to hang up for a Cure; and thus, by Sacrificing a Small Part, already Tainted, and not worth Keeping, he wisely **[xii]** secures the Safety of the Rest.[82] Or, let us go higher for instruction, and take Example by the Grazier, who far from denying his Herd the Accustom'd Privilege of Rubbing, when their Sides are Stimulated with Sharp Humours, very industriously fixes a Stake in the Center of the Field, not so much, you may imagine, to Regale the Salacious Hides of his Cattle, as to preserve his Young Trees from Suffering by the Violence of their Friction.

I could give You more Examples of this Kind, equally full of Instruction, but that I'm loth to detain You from the Perusal of the following Treatise; and at the same Time Impatient to have the Honour of Subscribing Myself

Your Fellow-Reformer,

and Devoted Servant,

PHIL-PORNEY.[83]

[82] In a lengthy book about Hogarth's series "The Harlot's Progress," Ronald Paulson italicizes "sacrificing" in this sentence and then tells us that he has "emphasized the word [sacrificing] that connects Mandeville's analogy with vicarious Atonement." See his *Hogarth's Harlot*, 97. In Paulson's comparison (98) between Mandeville and Hogarth on prostitution, Mandeville's words are used to emphasize the superiority of Hogarth's treatment of Moll Hackabout: "By introducing the analogies to the scriptural story, Hogarth replaces Mandeville's ironic 'already tainted, and not worth Keeping' with a deeper, more resonant and shocking irony." No one else, I think, has ever tried to elevate the reputation of Hogarth by depressing that of Mandeville.

[83] This pseudonym means "lover of harlots." On the issue of authorship see the Commentaries that follow the eighteenth-century texts.

[*xiii*]   THE PREFACE.

Lest any inquisitive Reader should puzzle his Brains to find out why this Foundling *is thus clandestinely dropt at his Door, let it suffice him, that the* Midwife *of a Printer was unwilling to help bring it into the World, but upon that Condition, or a much harder, that of my openly* Fathering *it. I could make many other reasonable Apologies, if requisite: For, besides my having follow'd the modest Example of several other pious* Authors, *such as that of* Ἐικὼν Βασιλική, the Whole Duty of Man,*[84] &c. who have studied rather their Country's Publick Good, than their own Private Fame; I think, I have also play'd the Politick Part: for should my* Off-spring *be defective, why let it fall upon the Parish.[85] On the other hand, if* [*xiv*] *acci-|dentally it prove hopeful, 'tis certain I need be at no further Trouble: There will then be* Parents *enough ready to own the* Babe, *and take it upon themselves. Adoption amongst the* Machiavellian *Laws of the Muses,[86] is strictly kept up, and every day put in Practice: How few of our now bright* Noblemen *would otherwise have* Wit?

[84] The Greek transliterated reads "Eikon Basilike"; it means "portrait [icon] of the king" or "royal image." The full title of this controversial book—published shortly before the beheading of King Charles I of England on January 30, 1649—is *ΕΙΚΩΝ ΒΑΣΙΛΙΚΗ, The Portraiture of His Sacred Majesty in His Solitudes and Sufferings.* Philip A. Knachel in his modern edition of this work (Ithaca: Cornell University Press, 1966) examines the controversy that it generated in the decades following its appearance. It was ostensibly written by Charles I, who may have composed parts of it, but it is usually assigned to a clergyman, Dr. John Gauden, who became Bishop of Exeter in 1660 and Bishop of Worcester in 1662.

The next piece, one of the most popular books of devotional literature in Restoration and eighteenth-century England, was generally attributed to Richard Allestree (1619–1681). The full title reads, *The Whole Duty of Man, Laid down in a Plain and Familiar Way for the Use of All, but especially the Meanest Reader.* The earliest edition recorded in the *New Cambridge Bibliography of English Literature*, II, is that of 1658. For the biblical source of this title, see Ecclesiastes 12: 13. With a wicked smile, pretending to adopt them as models, Mandeville makes ironic use of the fact that these two famous works were, like the present work, also anonymous. These seventeenth-century works exude a piety that is quite alien to Mandeville's outlook in both religion and politics.

[85] The ironic speaker here not only compares this work (author unknown) to an infant bastard (father unknown), but also glances at the male progenitors who refuse to claim their offspring and abandon them to whatever care will be provided by the local parish.

[86] Mandeville was probably thinking of the following passage in chapter 10 of Machiavelli's *Discourses on the First Ten Books of Titus Livius*: "for all the Emperors that succeeded to the throne by inheritance, except Titus, were bad, and those who became Emperors by adoption were all good, such as the five from Nero to Marcus Aurelius; and when the Empire became hereditary, it came to ruin." (Translated by Christian E. Detmold, in *The Prince and the Discourses* by Niccolo Machiavelli, New York: The Modern Library, 1940; pp. 143–144).

Mandeville obviously enjoyed presenting his anonymous book on the stews as a foundling with a strong hint of bastardy. If any author (among his contemporaries) believes that this work will be successful, he will "adopt" it by claiming it as his own! A deeper implication of Mandeville's analogy between his book and a foundling is that his intellectual activity itself is libidinous, flouting the official code of morality by producing illegitimate literary progeny. His metaphor for this pamphlet as an illegitimate, fatherless offspring that may become a public ward anticipates and ties

How many of our present thriving Poets *would else want a* Dinner? *'Tis a vulgar Error to imagine Men live upon their own Wits, when generally it is upon others Follies; a Fund that carries by much the best Interest, and is by far upon the most certain Security of any*: The Exchequer *has been shut up, the* Bank *has stopt Payment,* South-Sea *has been demolish'd,*[87] *but* White's *was never known to fail; and indeed how should it, when almost every Wind blows to* Dover, *or* Holyhead, *some fresh* Proprietor *amply qualified with Sufficient* Stock.[88]

I am in some pain for the Event[89] *of this* Scheme, *hoping the* Wicked *will find it too Grave, and fearing the* Godly *will scarce venture beyond the Title-Page: And should they even, I know they'll object, 'tis here and there interwoven with too ludicrous Expressions, not considering that a dry Argument has occasion for the larding of Gaiety to make it the better relish and go down. Besides, finding by the exact Account tack'd to* [xv] *that most edifying* Anti-Heidegger[90] *Discourse, that eighty six Thousand Offenders have been lately punish'd, and that four hundred Thousand religious Books have been distributed about* Gratis (*not to mention the numberless Three-penny jobs daily publish'd to no Ends, or Purpose, but the Author's;) I say, finding all these Measures have been taken, and that Lewdness still so much prevails; I thought it highly proper to try this Experiment, being fully convinc'd that opposite Methods often take place. Own,* Preferment-Hunter! *when sailing on with the Tide avails nothing, does not tacking about steer you sometimes*

in with the same subject matter that he will discuss later on in this discourse. For a penetrating discussion of this topos, see chapter 3 in *The Yard of Wit* by Raymond Stephanson.

[87] The effects of the recent South Sea Bubble (1720), the earliest of the stock market crashes in the history of modern capitalism, were still strongly felt when Mandeville's *A Modest Defence* was published. The poet and dramatist John Gay, like many others including statesman and poet Matthew Prior, suffered a huge loss in the bubble. Gay later exposed the fraud and corruption of modern society in *The Beggar's Opera* (1728). Gay's hero, Macheath, appears in various scenes surrounded by harlots.

[88] White's, a famous chocolate house on St. James' Street dating from 1693, later became a gentleman's club and had a reputation as a center for gambling. Mandeville says that it owes its survival and success not to any special wisdom of its owners or managers, but to the folly of the wealthy who are attracted to that fashionable establishment. It is mentioned with other London coffee houses in the first issue of Sir Richard Steele's periodical, *The Tatler* (April 12, 1709). In the thirty-two papers that Mandeville contributed to the offshoot journal, *The Female Tatler*, he responded to a number of subjects raised in Steele's Tatler.

[89] By "event" Mandeville here means not an occasion or happening, but, as in the Latin *eventus*, outcome or result.

[90] At this point the first "uncorrected" edition, 1724A, inserts the following footnote, which is absent from 1724B: "*A Sermon lately Preach'd against Masquerades."

John James Heidegger (1659?–1749), son of a Swiss clergyman, moved from Zurich to London in 1708. Within a few years he became the major entrepreneur behind the rise of masquerades in England. In the 1720s he and George Frederick Handel were producing operas performed at the Royal Academy of Music. The courts of King George I and George II relied on his expertise in mounting their lavish masquerades. On January 6, 1724, in a sermon delivered to the members of the Societies for the Reformation of Manners, Edmund Gibson, the Bishop of London, praised his audience for their good work and also attacked the masquerades as sinful and immoral—hence Mandeville's modifier "anti-Heidegger." The statistics Mandeville uses here derive from this sermon's appendix or postscript which was essentially an annual report of the Societies.

into that snug Harbour, an Employment?[91] *Speak* Hibernian Stallion! *when a meek fawning Adoration turns to no Account, does not a pert assuming Arrogance frequently forward, nay, gain the critical Minute? And say,★* Mesobin!*[92] where a Purge fails, is not a Vomit an infallible* Recipe *for a Looseness?*

   To conclude; when my Arguments are impartially examin'd, I doubt not but my Readers will join with me, that as long as it is the Nature of Man (and Naturam expellas furcâ licet usque recurret[93]*) to have a Salt* Itch *in the Breeches, the* Brimstone *under* [**xvi**] *the Petticoat will be a necessary Remedy to* lay *it; and let him be ever so sly in the Application, it will still be found out: What avails it then to affect to conceal that which cannot be concealed, and that which if carried on openly*

---

[91] This sentence is the first of three consecutive "apostrophes," a rhetorical figure in which the speaker interrupts his discourse to address directly a person assumed to be present, as audience or reader.

[92] "An able Member of the College of Physicians" [Mandeville's footnote.] This characterization would have brought smiles to his sophisticated readers. Hogarth satirized the French doctor John (or Jean) Misaubin (d. 1734) in plate V of his series of engravings called "A Harlot's Progress," and Henry Fielding makes fun of "the great Doctor *Misaubin*" by ridiculing his poor pronunciation of English; see *Tom Jones*, Book V, chapter vii. Fielding had previously dedicated his play *The Mock Doctor* (1732) to Misaubin, in an ironic manner. Recently this negative view has been modified by Barry Hoffbrand in "John Misaubin, Hogarth's quack. . . ." It is useful to recall that Mandeville, who received his M.D. from the University of Leiden, never became a "Member of the College of Physicians."

   The author in this paragraph is again demonstrating his rhetorical virtuosity by elaborating satirically upon the simple notion that if one method does not work (that of the SRMs, using punishment and distributing religious literature), then one might succeed by trying the opposite method (tolerating prostitution but controlling it to prevent the spread of venereal diseases). The elaboration in the form of two character types (the preferment-hunter and the Irish "stallion") and one contemporary practitioner of medicine (Misaubin) shows each individual veering about and pursuing an "opposite" method to achieve his goal. In Misaubin's case, if the purge fails to empty out the patient's bowels, then a "vomit," a substance or mixture used to induce a vomit, is recommended in order to achieve that purpose in the upper half of a human body—"a vomit is an infallible recipe for a looseness"! Mandeville is enjoying himself at the expense of his satiric victim Misaubin. There is, finally, one more way in which Dr. Misaubin has a thematic connection with the content of *A Modest Defence*: Misaubin also sold pills which were supposed to cure venereal disease.

[93] "You may drive out Nature with a pitchfork, but still she will return." The most common source for this line is Horace's *Epistles* Book I, epistle 10, line 24, where it occurs as "Naturam expellas furca, tamen usque recurret." But in Mandeville's citation the word "licet" (an adverbial conjunction here meaning "granted that" or "although" and derived from the infinitive "licere") replaces "tamen." Was Mandeville simply misquoting this line? Or did he deliberately alter it? To each question the answer is "no." The line containing "licet" actually appears in the Latin comedy *Laelia* (author unknown) which was first performed at Queens' College, Cambridge in 1595, at a special occasion at which the Earl of Essex was present. Well known to Shakespearean scholars as a probable source for *Twelfth Night*, this comedy was an adaptation of a French play, which itself was based on the Italian comedy *Gl'Ingannati* ("The Deceived"), first published in 1532. Thus the line was invented by Horace and was later quoted, with an alteration, in *Laelia*. Mandeville could have taken his Latin quotation from *Laelia*, or perhaps he found it in a collection of *sententiae* containing this line in its later, altered form. See Dana F. Sutton's excellent hypertext edition of *Laelia* (*1595*), first published on the Internet July 9, 2000, at this website: http://eee.uci.edu/~papyri/laelia/intro.html.

and above-board, would become only less detrimental, and of consequence more justifiable?

Be the Success of this Treatise as it happens, the Good of Mankind is my only Aim; nor am I less hearty or zealous in the Publick Welfare of my Country, than that Noble Pattern of Sincerity,[94] who finishes his Preface with the following Paragraph. And now, O my G-, the G- of my Life, and of all my Mercies, I offer this Work to Thee, to whose Honour it is chiefly intended; that thereby I may awaken the World to Just Reflections on their own Errors and Follies, and call on them to acknowledge thy Providence, to adore it, and ever to depend on it.[95]

[94] "B———p B———t." Mandeville's footnote. He means Bishop Gilbert Burnet (1643–1715).

[95] See "The Preface" in *Bishop Burnet's History of his own Time* (Vol. I, 1723, 1724). Though Burnet died eight years before this posthumous work was published, Mandeville had no compunction in appropriating and satirizing Burnet's ejaculation of piety. Mandeville apparently made this prayer a bit more unctuous by adding these words which are not in the original: "the G- of my Life, and of all my Mercies." In Burnet's posthumous text the word "God" is spelled out. Was Mandeville's abbreviation of that term intended to elicit a smile? In some groups it is forbidden to write out the full name of God. Since Mandeville's writings occasionally reveal signs of anticlericalism, one might be tempted to think that his satire here falls under that general heading. But in this case there is something more specific to add: Bishop Burnet had earlier delivered a sermon at an annual meeting of the SRMs. It was soon published as *A Sermon Preached at The Church of St. Mary-le-Bow, to the Societies for Reformation of Manners, The 25th of March 1700. By the Right Reverend Father in God, Gilbert Lord Bishop of Sarum* [i.e., Salisbury]. London: . . . 1700. Gilbert Burnet was thus an early supporter of the SRMs and Mandeville could well have had that fact in mind when he parodied Burnet's pious passage.

A Modest Defence, &c.

There is nothing more idle, or shows a greater Affectation of Wit, than the modern Custom of treating the most grave Subjects with Burlesque and Ridicule. The present Subject of *Whoring*, was I dispos'd, would furnish me sufficiently in this kind, and might possibly, if so handled, excite Mirth in those who are only capable of such low Impressions. But, as the chief Design of this Treatise is to promote the general Welfare and Happiness of Mankind, I hope to be excus'd, if I make no farther Attempts to please, than are consistent with that Design. The Practice of *Whoring* has, of late Years, become so universal, and its Effects so prejudicial to Mankind, that several Attempts have been made to put a Stop to it; and a certain *Society* of Worthy *Gentlemen* have undertaken that Affair with a Zeal truly commendable, tho' the Success does but too plainly make it appear, that they were mistaken in their **[2]** Mea-|sures, and had not rightly consider'd the Nature of this Evil, which we are all equally sollicitous to prevent, however we may differ in our Opinions as to the Manner. And tho' the Method I intend to propose, of erecting *Publick Stews* for that purpose, may seem at first sight somewhat ludicrous, I shall, nevertheless, make it appear to be the only Means we have now left for redressing this Grievance. As this Redress is the whole Scope and Design of this Treatise, I hope to be acquitted of my Design, when I have prov'd the following Proposition; That publick Whoring is neither so criminal in itself, nor so detrimental to the *Society*, as private Whoring; and that the encouraging of publick Whoring, by erecting *Stews*, will not only prevent most of the ill Consequences of this Vice, but even lessen the Quantity of Whoring in general, and reduce it to the narrowest Bounds which it can possibly be contain'd in. But before we proceed, it is requisite that we examine what those mischievous Effects are which Whoring naturally produces, that we may the better judge whether or no they will be prevented by this Scheme.

The greatest Evil that attends this Vice, or could well befall Mankind, is the Propagation of that infectious Disease, called the *French Pox*,[96] which, in two Centuries, has made such incredible Havock all over *Europe*. **[3]** In these Kingdoms it so seldom fails to attend Whoring, now-a-days mistaken for Gallantry and Politeness, that a hale, robust Constitution is esteem'd a Mark of Ungentility; and a healthy young Fellow is look'd upon with the same View, as if he had spent his Life in a Cottage. Our Gentlemen of the Army, whose unsettled way of Life makes it inconvenient for them to marry, are hereby very much weaken'd and enervated, and render'd unfit to

---

[96] Syphilis, also called "the French disease."

undergo such Hardships as are necessary for defending and supporting the Honour of their Country: And our Gentry in general seem to distinguish themselves by an ill State of Health, in all probability the Effect of this pernicious Distemper: for the Secrecy which most People are obliged to in this Disease, makes the Cure of it often ineffectual; and tho' the Infection itself may possibly be remov'd, yet for want of taking proper Methods, it generally leaves such an ill Habit of Body as is not easily recover'd. 'Tis to this we seem to owe the Rise of that Distemper, the *King's-Evil*,[97] never known till the *French Disease* began to prevail here. But what makes this Mischief the more intolerable, is that the Innocent must suffer by it as well as the Guilty: Men give it to their Wives, Women to their Husbands, or perhaps their Children; they to their Nurses, and the Nurses again to other Children; so that no Age, [4] Sex, or Condition can be intirely safe from the Infection.

Another ill Effect of this Vice, is, its making People profuse, and tempting them to live beyond what their Circumstances will admit of; for if once Men suffer their Minds to be led astray by this unruly Passion, no worldly Consideration whatever will be able to stop it; and Wenching as it is very expensive in itself, without the ordinary Charges of Physick or Children, often leads Men into a thousand other Vices to support its Extravagance: Besides, after the Mind has once got this extravagant Turn, there naturally follows a Neglect and Contempt of Business; and Whoring of itself disposes the Mind to such a sort of Indolence, as is quite inconsistent with Industry, the main Support of any, especially a trading, Nation.

The murdering of Bastard Infants is another Consequence of this Vice, by much worse than the Vice itself: and tho' the Law is justly severe in this Particular, as rightly judging that a Mind capable of divesting itself so intirely of Humanity, is not fit to live in a civiliz'd Nation; yet there are so many ways of evading it, either by destroying the Infants before their Birth, or suffering them afterwards to die by wilful Neglect, that there appears but little Hope of putting any Stop to this Practice, which, besides the Barbarity of it, tends very much to dispeople the [5] Country.[98] And since the

---

[97] The King's Evil was scrofula, which, from the reign of Edward the Confessor (1043–1066) well into the eighteenth century, was thought to be curable by the King's touch. Queen Anne was the last English monarch to participate in this practice.

[98] Earlier however, in "Remark (C.)" of his *Fable* (1714), Mandeville gave a psychological explanation of infanticide by mothers that emphasized the force of the passions rather than the severity of the law in such cases:

> It is commonly imagined, that she who can destroy her Child . . . must have a vast stock of Barbarity, and be a Savage Monster . . . but this is likewise a mistake, which we commit for want of understanding . . . the force of Passions. The same Woman that Murders her Bastard . . . if she is Married afterwards, may . . . feel all the tenderness for her Infant that the fondest Mother can be capable of. (Kaye, ed., I, 75)

Following this, Mandeville asserts that "Common Whores . . . hardly ever destroy their Children . . . because they have lost their Modesty to a greater degree and the fear of Shame makes hardly any Impression on them" (I, 75–76). He may have thought that his earlier discussion of whores and infanticide would not serve his purposes in *A Modest Defence*.

Prosperity of any Country is allow'd to depend, in a great measure, on the Number of its Inhabitants,[99] the *Government* ought, if it were possible, to prevent any Whoring at all, as it evidently hinders the Propagation of the Species: How many thousand young Men in this Nation would turn their Thoughts towards Matrimony, if they were not constantly destroying that Passion, which is the only Foundation of it? And tho' most of them, sooner or later, find the Inconvenience of this irregular Life, and think fit to confine themselves to One, yet their Bodies are so much enervated, by the untimely or immoderate Increase of this Passion, together with the Relicks of Venereal Cures, that they beget a most wretched, feeble, and sickly Offspring: We can attribute it to nothing else but this, that so many of our antient Families of Nobles are of late extinct.

There is one thing more we ought to consider in this Vice, and that is the Injury it does to particular Persons and Families either by alienating the Affections of Wives from their Husbands, which often proves prejudicial to both, and sometimes fatal to whole Families; or else by debauching the Minds of young Women, to their utter Ruin and Destruction: for the Reproach they must undergo, when a Slip of this nature is discover'd, prevents their marrying in any Degree **[6]** suitable to their Fortune, and by degrees hardens them to all Sense of Shame; and when they have once overcome that, the present View of Interest as well as Pleasure, sways them to continue in the same Course, till at length they become common Prostitutes.[100]

These are the several bad Effects of Whoring; and it is an unhappy Thing, that a Practice so universal as this is, and always will be, should be attended with such mischievous Consequences: But since few or none of them are the necessary Effects of Whoring, consider'd in itself, but only proceed from the Abuse and ill Management of it; our Business is certainly to regulate this Affair in such sort as may best prevent these Mischiefs. And I must here beg pardon of those worthy *Gentlemen* of the *Society*, if I can't conceive how the Discouragement they have given, or rather attempted to give, to publick Whoring, could possibly have the desired Effect. If this was

Three years before the appearance of *A Modest Defence* Defoe pointed to the same evil in his novel *Moll Flanders*, in which almost all of Moll's progeny are given away and never followed up with any kind of maternal interest or devotion. See works in the Bibliography by P.C. Hoffer, Jennifer Thorn, Robert W. Malcolmson and Mark Jackson.

[99] Mandeville had previously stated this view in his "Essay on Charity and Charity-Schools" which he added to his *Fable of the Bees* in 1723:

in a free Nation where Slaves are not allow'd of, the surest Wealth consists in a Multitude of laborious Poor; for besides that they are the never-failing Nursery of Fleets and Armies, without them there could be no Enjoyment, and no Product of any Country could be valuable. (Kaye I, 287)

[100] The fall of women into degradation and prostitution following the loss of their chastity was a common theme in Mandeville's age. His is only one of many accounts of the "Harlot's progress." Eight years later, in 1732, Hogarth told essentially the same story, though with different details, in his famous series of engravings on that subject.

a Vice acquired by Habit or Custom, or depended upon Education, as most other Vices, there might be some Hopes of suppressing it; and then it would, no doubt, be commendable to attack it, without Distinction, in whatever Form or Disguise it should appear: But alas! this violent Love for Women is born and bred with us; nay, it is absolutely necessary to our being born at all: And however **[7]** some People may pretend, that unlawful Enjoyment is contrary to the Law of *Nature*; this is certain, that Nature never fails to furnish us largely with this Passion, tho' she is often sparing to bestow upon us such a Portion of Reason and Reflection as is necessary to curb it.

That long Course of Experience which most of these *Gentlemen* have had in the World, and which is of so great Use in other Cases, may probably occasion their Mistake in this; for Age is very liable to forget the violence of youthful Passions, and, consequently, apt to think them easier curb'd: whereas if we consider the true Source of Whoring, and the strong Impulse of Nature that way, we shall find, it is a Thing not to be too violently restrain'd; lest, like a Stream diverted out of its proper Channel, it should break in and overflow the neighbouring *Enclosures*.[101]

History affords us several Instances of this Truth; I shall mention but one, and that is of Pope *Sixtus* the Fifth, who was so strictly severe in the Execution of Justice, if such Severity may be call'd Justice, and particularly, against Offenders of this kind, that he condemned a young Man to the Galleys, only for snatching a Kiss of a Damsel in the Street: yet notwithstanding this his *Holiness's* Zeal, he never attempted once to extirpate Whoring intirely: But like a true *Pastor* separated the **[8]** clean Sheep from the unclean, and confin'd all the Courtezans to one Quarter of the City. It is true, he did attempt to moderate this Vice, and banish'd as many Courtezans as he thought exceeded the necessary Number; but he was soon convinc'd of the Error of his Computation, for *Sodomy* and a thousand other unnatural Vices sprung up, which forc'd him soon to recall them, and has left us a remarkable Instance of the Vanity of such Attempts.[102]

---

[101] The stream image mirrors the earlier sewer metaphor for prostitution and illicit sex. If the stream is diverted and prostitutes ("its proper channel") are no longer available, the honor of all virtuous women could be endangered. The term "enclosures" refers to the practice of removing arable or grazing lands held in common by enclosing and privatizing them. Roy Porter (*English Society in the Eighteenth Century*, p. 209) reports that half of such land in England had been enclosed by 1700, forcing peasants and cottagers into wage labor or beggary. "Enclosures" here also suggests the idea of wives as private property, and virtuous women endangered by rampant males seeking sexual outlets.

[102] Pope Sixtus the Fifth: Felice Peretti, 1520–1590; Pope from 1585–1590. Actively concerned to control abuses of sexuality, he issued in 1588 the Apostolic Constitution or bull *Effraenatam* ("without restraint") condemning abortion and contraception, on pain of excommunication. I have not traced the account of his having condemned a young man to the galleys for snatching a kiss. As for Sixtus V's role in ridding Rome of unneeded prostitutes, another account closely matching Mandeville's is connected with the Pontificate of Pope Pius V, Ghislieri (1566–1572), reputedly the first pope in sixteenth-century Italy who tried to expel prostitutes from Rome. See Kurzel-Runtscheiner, *Töchter der Venus*, 22–24. Mandeville may have meant Pius V rather than Sixtus V.

Let us now proceed to the Proof of our Proposition, in the first Part of which, it was asserted, That publick Whoring is neither so Criminal in itself, nor so Detrimental to the *Society*, as private Whoring.

Publick Whoring consists in lying with a certain Set of Women, who have shook off all Pretence to Modesty; and for such a Sum of Money, more or less, profess themselves always in a Readiness to be enjoy'd. The Mischief a Man does in this Case is entirely to himself, for with respect to the Woman, he does a laudable Action, in furnishing her with the Means of Subsistence, in the only, or at least most innocent way that she is capable of procuring of it. The Damage he does to himself, is either with regard to his Health, or the Expence of Money, and may be consider'd under the same View as Drinking, with this considerable Advantage, that it restores us to that cool Exercise of our Reason, **[9]** which Drinking tends to deprive us of. Indeed was there a Probability of a Woman's Amendment, and of her gaining a Livelihood by some honester Method, there might be some Crime in encouraging her to follow such a Profession: But the Minds of Women are observ'd to be so much corrupted by the Loss of Chastity, or rather by the Reproach they suffer upon that Loss, that they seldom or never change that Course of Life for the better; and if they should, they can never recover that good Name, which is so absolutely necessary to their getting a Maintenance in any honest Way whatever; and that nothing but meer Necessity obliges them to continue in that Course, is plain from this, That they themselves in Reality utterly abhor it: And indeed there appears nothing in it so very alluring and bewitching, especially to People who have that Inclination to Lewdness intirely extinguish'd, which is the only thing could possibly make it supportable.[103]

The other Branch of Whoring, viz. *Private*, is of much worse Consequence; and a Man's Crime in this Case, increases in proportion to the different Degree of Mischief done, if you consider his Crime with regard to the *Society*; for as to personal Guilt, Allowance ought to be made for the Increase of Temptation, which is very considerable in the Case of debauching *Married Women*; **[10]** upon account of the Safety to the Aggressor, either with Respect to his Health, or the Charge, and, if that affects him, the Scandal of having a Bastard. On the other hand, the injury done, is very considerable, as such an Action tends to corrupt a Woman's Mind, and destroys that mutual Love and Affection between Man and Wife, which is so necessary to both their Happiness. Besides, the Risque run of a Discovery, which at least ruins a Woman's Reputation, and destroys the Husband's Quiet; nay, where Virtue does not Intirely give way, if it warps but ever so little, the Consequence is shockingly fatal: for tho' the good Man, suspicious of the Wife's Chastity, the Wife of the

---

[103] Mandeville's unsentimental and almost clinical description of the irreversibility of a prostitute's career ties in with the recurrent theme (previously noted) of the harlot's progress. His extended passage on the stages of her career seems to reflect an early seventeenth-century proverb, "Once a whore, always a whore."

Gallant's Constancy, and the Gallant of the Husband's Watchfulness, by being a Check upon each other, may keep the Gate of Virtue shut; yet then even all Parties must be attended with a never-ceasing Misery, not to be imagin'd, but by those who too fatally *feel it.*

The Crime of debauching young *Virgins* will appear much greater, if we consider that there is much more Mischief done, and the Temptation to do it much lessen'd by the fear of getting Children; which, in most Circumstances of Life, does a Man a deal of Prejudice, and keeps at least three Parts in four of our sober Youth from gratifying this violent Passion. Besides, the Methods that are [11] Necessa-|ry to be taken, before a Man can have such an Action in his Power, are in themselves Criminal; and it shows a certain Baseness of Mind to persuade a Woman, by a thousand solemn Vows and Protestations, into such a good Opinion of you, and Assurance of your Love to her, that she trusts you with all that is dear and near to her; and this with no other View but the Gratification of a present Passion, which might be otherwise vented, than at the certain Expence of her Ruin, and putting her under the Necessity of leading the Life of a *Publick Courtezan.*

From this general Consideration of Whoring, it is evident, that tho' all the several Species of it proceed from the same Cause, our natural Love and Passion for Women, yet they are very different in their Natures, and fully as distinct Crimes as those which proceed from our Love to Money, such as Murder, Shoplifting, *&c.* And I hope I have said enough to prove, that the Publick Part of it is by far the least Criminal, and least Detrimental to the *Society*; which of itself is a sufficient Motive for the *Legislature* to confine it to that Channel. I shall now proceed farther, and show, as I before propos'd, that the incouraging of publick Whoring, will not only prevent most of the mischievous Effects of this Vice, but even lessen the Quantity of Whoring in general, and reduce it to [12] the narrowest Bounds which it can possibly be contain'd in.

When I talk'd of encouraging publick Whoring, I would be understood to mean, not only the erecting *Publick Stews*, as I at first hinted, but also the endowing them with such Privileges and Immunities, and at the same time giving such Discouragement to private Whoring, as may be most effectual to turn the general Stream of Lewdness into this common Channel.

I shall here lay down a Plan for this Purpose, which, tho' it may well serve to illustrate this Point, and make good the Proof of my present Argument, would doubtless receive infinite Improvement by coming through the Hands of a *National Senate*, whose august Body, being compos'd of *Spirituals* as well as *Temporals*, will, I hope, take into Consideration this important Affair, which so nearly concerns both.

The Plan I would propose, is this: Let a hundred or more Houses be provided in some convenient Quarter of the City, and proportionably in every Country Town, sufficient to contain two Thousand Women: If a hundred are thought sufficient, let a hundred *Matrons* be appointed, one to each House, of Abilities and Experience enough to take upon them the

Management of twenty Courtezans each, to see that they keep themselves neat **[13]** and decent, and entertain Gentlemen after a civil and obliging Manner. For the encouragement of such *Matrons*, each House must be allow'd a certain Quantity of all sorts of Liquor, Custom and Excise free; by which Means they will be enabled to accommodate Gentlemen handsomely, without that Imposition so frequently met with in such Houses. Besides the hundred abovemention'd, there must be a very large House set apart for an Infirmary, and Provision made for two able Physicians, and four Surgeons at least. Lastly, there must be three Commissioners appointed to superintend the whole, to hear and redress Complaints, and to see that each House punctually observes such Rules and Orders as shall be thought Necessary for the good Government of this Community. For the better Entertainment of all Ranks and Degrees of Gentlemen, we shall divide the twenty Women of each House into four Classes, who for their Beauty, or other Qualifications may justly challenge different Prices.[104]

The first Class is to consist of eight, who may legally demand from each Visitant Half a Crown. The second Class to consist of six, whose fix'd Price may be a Crown. The third Class of four, at half a Guinea each. The remaining two make up the fourth Class, and are design'd for Persons of the first Rank, who can afford to Pay a Guinea for the Elegancy of their **[14]** Taste.[105] To defray the Charges of this Establishment, will require but a very moderate Tax: For if the first Class pays but forty Shillings Yearly, and the rest in Proportion, it will amount to above ten thousand Pounds a Year, which will not only pay the Commissioners Salaries, Surgeons Chests, and other Contingencies, but likewise establish a good Fund for the Maintenance of Bastard-Orphans and Superannuated Courtezans.

For the better Government of this *Society*, it will be necessary that the Mistress have an absolute Command in her own House, and that no Woman be suffer'd to go abroad without her Leave. No Woman must be suffer'd to lie in within the House, nor any young Children admitted under any Pretence. No Musick or Revelling to be allow'd in any Room, to the Disturbance of the rest. No Gentlemen disorderly or drunk, to be admitted at an unseasonable Hour, without the Consent of the Mistress: And, in case of Violence, she must be empower'd to call the Civil Aid.[106]

---

[104] Roger Thompson (*Unfit for Modest Ears*, pp. 62–63) describes the different ranks in the hierarchy of whores that were known to exist in the later seventeenth century, from the King's mistresses down to the "street-walkers, bulkers and drabs, who solicited in the red-light areas or taverns. . . ."

[105] Some American readers may need to be told that in the English monetary system preceding the current one (in which a pound is now equal to 100 pence), a shilling consisted of twelve pence and twenty shillings made a pound. A crown, in Mandeville's time, was a coin worth five shillings.

[106] Mandeville certainly knew the regulations of the medieval stews on the Bankside in Southwark, published in Stow's *Survey of London*. See the excerpt below reprinted from *A Collection of Chirurgical Tracts* (1740), Appendix I.

For the *Society*'s Security in Point of Health, it must be order'd, That if any Gentleman complains of receiving an Injury, and the Woman, upon Search, be found tainted, without having discover'd it to the Mistress, she shall be stripp'd and cashier'd. But if a Woman Discovers her Misfortune before any **[15]** Com-|plaint is made against her, she shall be sent to the *Infirmary*, and cured at the Publick Charge. No Woman that has been twice pox'd shall ever be re-admitted. *Note*, That three Claps shall be reckon'd equivalent to one Pox.

But as no *Society* ever fram'd a compleat Body of Laws at once, till unforeseen Accidents had taught them Foresight, we shall refer the farther Regulation of these Laws, with whatever new ones shall be thought necessary, to the *Wisdom of the Legislature*.

The *Publick Stews* being thus erected and govern'd by good and wholesome Laws, there remains nothing to compleat this Project, but that proper Measures be taken effectually to discourage all other Kinds of Whoring whatsoever. And here it is to be hoped, that those worthy *Gentlemen* of the *Society* who have hitherto distinguish'd their *Zeal* to so little Purpose, will now exert themselves where they have so good a Prospect of Success; for altho' a poor Itinerant Courtezan could not by any Means be persuaded to starve at the Instigation of a *Reforming* Constable, yet a little *Bridewell* Rhetorick,[107] or the Terrors of a Transportation, will soon convince her that she may live more comfortably and honestly in a *Publick Stew*. If there are any so foolish as to love Rambling better, or who are not qualify'd to please Gentlemen according to Law, they ought to be transported; for *Bridewell*, **[16]** as it is now manag'd, only makes them poorer, and consequently lays them under a greater Necessity than ever of continuing Whores.

Let us now suppose, for Brevity sake, that the *Publick Stews* are as much as possible favour'd and encourag'd, and that all the other Branches of this Vice have the utmost Rigour of the Laws exerted against them.

It now remains for me to show what Benefit the *Nation* would receive thereby, and how this Project would prevent or in any Degree alleviate those Mischiefs which I have mention'd to be the necessary Consequences of this Vice. As for any Objections that may be rais'd against me, either *Christian* or *Moral*, I shall refer them to the Close of this Discourse.

First then, I say, the *Nation* would receive a general Benefit by having such a considerable Number of its most disorderly Inhabitants brought to live after a regular civiliz'd Manner.[108] There is, one Year with another, a

---

[107] By "*Bridewell* Rhetorick," Mandeville means the specific kind of "persuasion" that inmates of that prison experienced. The harsh living conditions and forced labor required of the prisoners should persuade them to seek a better way to earn wages.

[108] The phrase "general Benefit" is probably as close as Mandeville gets to reminding his readers of his famous subtitle, *Private Vices, Publick Benefits*. Would sexual commerce with a courtesan in one of the newly-erected, state-owned and state-supervised brothels still be considered "private vice"? That becomes problematic, but the speaker seems convinced that his proposal, if realized, would produce various public benefits.

certain Number of young Women who arrive gradually, Step by Step, at the highest Degree of Impudence and Lewdness. These Women, besides their Incontinence, are commonly guilty of almost the whole Catalogue of immoral Actions: The Reason is evident: They are utterly abandon'd by their Parents, and thereby reduc'd to the last **[17]** De-|gree of Shifting-Poverty; if their Lewdness cannot supply their Wants, they must have Recourse to Methods more criminal, such as *Lying, Cheating, open Theft, &c.* Not that these are the necessary Concomitants of Lewdness, or have the least Relation to it, as all *lewd Men of Honour* can testify;[109] but the Treatment such Women meet with in the World, is the Occasion of it.

Those Females, who either by the Frigidity of their Constitutions, a lucky want of Temptation, or any other Cause, have preserv'd their Chastity; and the Men, in general, Chaste or Unchaste, are so outrageous against these Delinquents, that they make no Distinction: all of them are branded with the same opprobrious Title, they are all treated with the same Contempt, all equally despis'd; so that let them be guilty of what other Crimes they please, they cannot add one Jot to the Shame they already undergo. Having thus remov'd the Fear of worldly Reproach, which is justly esteem'd the greatest *Bulwark of Morality*, it is no wonder if these Women, insensible of Shame, and prick'd on[110] by Want, commit any Crimes, where they are not deter'd by the Fear of corporal Punishments. But the Case now will be quite alter'd; these Women, as soon as they have attain'd a competent Share of Assurance, and before they are pinch'd with **[18]** the Extreme of Poverty, will enter themselves in some of the above-mentioned Classes of profess'd Courtezans; where, instead of being necessarily dishonest, they will have more Inducements to Honesty than any other Profession whatsoever. The same Money defends, as well as it corrupts a *Prime Minister.* A *Churchman* takes Sanctuary in a Gown, and who dare accuse a Mitre of *Simony*?[111] Accuse a *Colonel* of Injustice, he is try'd by his Board of *Peers,* and your Information is false, scandalous, and malicious. A *Lawyer* cheats you according to Law; and you may thank the

[109] Though Mandeville devoted his last book to the subject of honor (*An Enquiry into the Origin of Honour and the Usefulness of Christianity in War*) and previously dealt with male and female honor in various other works—notably in "Remark (R.)" of his *Fable of the Bees*—this is the only passage in which he refers specifically to a "lewd" man of honor. But he previously in effect had described a lewd "man of honor" in the closing sentence of "Remark (R.)": "He must make no Attempts upon his Friend's Wife, Daughter, Sister, or any body that is trusted to his Care, but he may lie with all the World besides." (*Fable*, I, 223, ed. Kaye)

[110] The most famous use of this phrase in English literature occurs in Shakespeare's *King Henry the Fourth, Part One* (V.i.130–132), where Falstaff, after playing dead, says "Well, 'tis no matter; honour pricks me on. Yea, but how if honour prick me off when I came on?" Mandeville alludes to this famous speech on honor not only here but elsewhere in *A Modest Defence.*

[111] The mitre in this case stands for a Bishop of the Church of England. Another example of synecdoche (a part standing for the whole) appears earlier in the "Dedication," where a gentleman has a "bog-house" removed from his garden with the result that "every Nose in the Family was convinc'd of his Mistake."

Physician, if you live to complain of him. *Overreaching* in Trade, is *prudent Dealing*; and *Mechanick Cunning*, is stiled *Handicraft*.[112] Not so fares the poor Courtezan; if she commits but one ill Action, if for Instance, she should circumvent a Gentleman in a *Snuff-Box*, she can hardly escape Detection; and the first Discovery ruins her; she is banish'd the *Publick Stews*, mark'd out for Infamy; and can have no better Prospect than a Transportation. On the other hand, the Motives to Honesty will be as great here as any where: It is natural for Mankind to regard chiefly the good Opinion of those with whom they converse, and to neglect that of Strangers; now in this Community, Lewdness not being esteem'd a Reproach, but rather a **[19]** Commendation, they will set a Value on their good Name, and stand as much upon the Puncto of Honour, as the rest of Mankind; being mov'd by the same commendable Emulation, and deter'd by greater, or at least more certain Punishments. Besides this Reformation in Point of Honesty, the Publick will receive another Benefit in being freed from those nocturnal Disorders, Quarrels, and Brawlings, which are occasion'd by vagrant Punks, and the Number of private Brothels dispers'd throughout the City, to the great Disturbance of its sober Inhabitants.

We have already mention'd the *French Disease* as one of the worst Attendants upon Lewdness, and with good Reason; for in the Enjoyment of this Life, Health is the *sine qua non*: And this Distemper has one Thing in it peculiarly inveterate, as if it came out of *Pandora*'s worst Box:[113] there is no other Disorder, but what at some Age, or in some particular Constitution, will abate of itself without the Application of Medicines; but this is such a busy restless Enemy, that unless resisted, he is never at a Stand, but gathers Strength every day, to the utter Disquiet of the Patient. Now it is so evident that the *Publick Stews*, when well regulated, will prevent the

---

[112] The frauds or cheats of the different professions and trades was one of Mandeville's favorite themes. He used it previously in *The Grumbling Hive* (1705), the poem that grew into *The Fable of the Bees*:

> . . . others follow'd Mysteries,
> To which few Folks bind 'Prentices . . .
> As Sharpers, Parasites Pimps, Players,
> Pick-pockets, Coiners, Quacks, South-sayers,
> And all those, that in Enmity,
> With downright Working, cunningly
> Convert to their own Use the Labour
> Of their good-natur'd heedless Neighbour.
> These were call'd Knaves, but bar the Name,
> The grave Industrious were the same:
> All Trades and Places knew some Cheat,
> No calling was without Deceit.   (Kaye's edition, I, 19–20)

[113] "Pandora's worst box": accounts of this myth generally mention only one box given by Zeus to Pandora (the first woman, in Greek myth) with instructions not to open it. Her curiosity causes her to disobey and as a result all of the evils known to humanity escape from the box. Thus the tale of Pandora, like the story of Eve in the Hebrew Scriptures, associates the origin of evil with womankind. For the earliest account of Pandora, see Hesiod's *Works and Days*.

Spreading of this Plague, that a prolix and tedious **[20]** Proof of it would look like Declaiming. As this Disease has its Spring and Source entirely from publick Whoring, and from thence creeps into private Families; so it likewise receives continual Supplies and Recruits thro' the same Channel: When this Source is once dry'd up, the Nation will naturally recover its pristine Health and Vigour: And this cannot fail to happen, if due Care be taken to keep the *Stews* free from Infection; for what young Fellow will be so industriously mad, as to take pains to run his Head into an Apothecary's Shop, when he may with so much Ease and Conveniency, and without the Fear of a *Reforming Officer*, both secure his Health, and gratify his Fancy with such a Variety of Mistresses.

'Tis true, the keeping of the *Publick Stews* so very safe will appear a difficult Task, at first Sight, but not so if we consider the Case a little nearer. This Disease is propagated reciprocally from the Woman to the Man, and from the Man to the Woman; but the first is the most common for several Reasons: We are not like Cocks or Town-Bulls; who have a whole Seraglio of Females entirely and solely at their Devotion; on the contrary, one industrious pains-taking Woman, that lays herself out that Way, is capable of satisfying several **[21]** rampant Males; insomuch, that a select Number of Women get a handsome Livelihood by being able to oblige such a Number of Customers. Now, if but a few of these Women are unsound, they can infect a great many Men; whereas these Men have neither Power nor Inclination to infect the like Number of Women. I say, Inclination; for a Woman, to raise Money for the Surgeon's Fee, may counterfeit Pleasure when She really receives Pain; nay, she may even venture to complain of being hurt: for the Man will attribute the Pain he gives her, either to her Chastity, or his own Vigour; not dreaming, perhaps, that he has molested a *Shanker*. This a Female may do, as being only passive in the Affair, but a Man must have real Fancy and Inclination before he is qualify'd to enter upon Action: And how far this Fancy to Woman may be cool'd by a stinging *Gonorrhæa*, I leave the experienc'd Reader to judge; and whether a Man won't rather employ his Thoughts upon his *round* Diet,[114] how to digest two at Night, and three in the Morning; what Conveyance to find out, when poach'd Eggs grow Nauseous, and how to preserve his Linnen from being speckled; with a Thousand other Particulars that occur to a Man in this Distress: but these are sufficient, with the

---

[114] In the 1740 edition of *A Collection of Chirurgical Tracts* by William Beckett, the publisher Curll smuggled "The Natural Secret History of Both Sexes" (*A Modest Defence* under a new title) into the contents of that volume. On p. 21 of this disguised reprint of Mandeville's pamphlet, after the words "*round Diet*," an editor added "*i.e.* Pills," a meaning that readers of the 1724 edition had to infer by themselves. This anonymous "correcter" of the text evidently thought that it was more desirable to name the thing outright rather than to burden the reader with personally discovering the meaning of Mandeville's playful circumlocution.

assistance of **[22]** a *Cordee*,[115] to *bridle* any moderate Passion. So that from the whole we may safely draw this Conclusion; That since the Men are so seldom guilty of transgressing in this Kind, the spreading of this Distemper must be owing to the Neglect of Cure in the Women.[116] Now the *Publick Stews* will be so regulated, that a Woman cannot possibly conceal her Misfortune long; nay, it will be highly her Interest to make the first Discovery: so that whatever Damage the *Society* may sustain at first, when Claps are most current, it will be soon repair'd, and this Distemper, in Time, entirely rooted out. But of this enough.

The next Thing that comes to be consider'd in this Vice, is the Expence it occasions, and the Neglect of worldly Business, by employing so much of our Time and Thoughts; for let a Man have ever so much Business, it can't stop the Circulation of his Blood, or prevent the Seminal Secretion: for Sleeping or Waking, the *Spermaticks*[117] will do their Office, tho' a Man's Thoughts may be so much employ'd about other Affairs, that he cannot attend to every minute Titillation. A Man of Pleasure, indeed, may make this copulative Science his whole Study; and, by Idleness and Luxury, may prompt Nature that Way, and spur up **[23]** the Spirits to Wantonness: but then his Constitution will be the sooner tired; for the Animal Spirits being exhausted by this Anticipation, his Body must be weaken'd, and his Nerves relax'd; neither will his irregular effeminate Life assist them in recovering their former Force. Besides, those Parts which more particularly suffer the Violence of this Exercise, are liable to many Accidents; and Men of Pleasure, though otherwise pretty healthy, are often troubled with Gleets[118]

---

[115] "Cordee" is a variant of "chordee," from the French. The OED gives its first appearance in English as 1708, when it appeared in Motteux' translation of Rabelais. It signifies an abnormal condition, "a painful inflammatory downward curving of the penis." At the website of the University of Michigan's Department of Urology, one finds this relevant information: "Hypospadias is a birth defect found in boys in which the urinary tract opening is not at the tip of the penis. Bending of the penis on erection may be associated with this and is known as chordee. Hypospadias occurs in about 8 of 1000 male births." See http://www.um-urology.com/patients/hypospadias.html. Mandeville seems to be saying that venereal disease and certain abnormalities of male sex organs will go far in reducing sexual desire, but he does not tell us whether, or how, these two conditions are related.

[116] Mandeville concludes that since males with VD would tend to avoid sexual activity, the burden of guilt for transmitting VD would therefore fall upon the prostitutes themselves. Of course he has no intention of examining the deeper economic and social structures that placed prostitutes in their unfortunate condition in the first place. Though he elsewhere reveals an incipient feminism with respect to the talents and rationality of women, he (or the persona he created here) seems entirely incapable of imagining a viable society free of prostitution. See M.M. Goldsmith's edition of Mandeville's contributions to *The Female Tatler* in his *By a Society of Ladies* (1999).

[117] According to the OED (second ed., 1989), "spermatics" as a plural noun means "the spermatic vessels" and examples of this usage before 1724 are recorded for 1690 and 1719.

[118] A gleet is a morbid discharge of slimy liquid from an animal or human being; or, a discharge of purulent matter from the urethra. (*The Oxford Universal Dictionary on Historical Principles*, third edition revised, 1955.)

and Weaknesses, either by a former Ulceration of the *Prostrates*,[119] or else some violent Over-straining, which occasions this Relaxation. These Men, 'tis true, will talk very lusciously of Women, but, pretend what they please, they can never have that burning Desire which they had formerly, when their Vessels were in full Vigour. The Truth is, their Lust lies chiefly in their Brain, kept alive by the Impression of former Ideas, which are not so easily rubb'd out as the Titillation which created them; and this Passion comes to be so diminish'd, that, in time, it changes its Residence from the *Glans Penis* to the *Glandula Penealis*.[120] A Man of Business, on the contrary, or one who leads a sober regular Life, will seldomer be attack'd by these wanton Fits, but then they will come with double the Violence; for though it is a **[24]** common received Opinion, that the longer a Man refrains, the better he is able to refrain, yet it is only true in one Sense, and amounts to no more than this: That if a Man has been able, for such and such Reasons, to curb this Passion, for Instance, a Month, he will, if the Same Reasons hold, and without an additional Temptation, be able to curb it a Month longer; but, nevertheless, he may have Desires much stronger than a Man who, for want of these Motives to Abstinence, gratifies them every Day. If there are some Men of a particular Constitution, whose puny Desires may be easily block'd up with the Assistance of *three small Buttons*; or else endow'd with such an extraordinary Strength of Reason, that they can master the most *rampant* Sallies of this raging Passion; I heartily congratulate their happy Conquest, but have nothing more to do with them at present, the *Publick Stews* not being design'd for such: I am here speaking of those Men of Business, who, notwithstanding their Abstinence or the Regularity of their Lives, are sometimes prevailed upon to quench these amorous Heats; and, I say, in such Men the Passion is much stronger than in Men of Pleasure, and that their Abstinence contributes to heighten the Violence of the Desire, and make it the more irresistible: **[25]** for the Fancy not being cloy'd with too frequent Enjoyment, presently takes fire; and the *Spermaticks*, not being weaken'd with forc'd Evacuations, are in their full Vigour, and give the Nerves a most exquisite Sensation: so that upon the

---

[119] The term "prostrates" indicating a gland or male organ, as the text implies, appears neither in the *Oxford Universal Dictionary* nor in the online *Oxford English Dictionary*; nor is it listed in *The Physical Dictionary*, a popular medical dictionary in the seventeenth and eighteenth centuries, written by the Dutch physician Steven Blankaart (Stephen Blancard, 1650–1702). "Prostrates" reappears in the London 1740 edition of *A Modest Defence*, attributed (falsely) to Colonel Harry Mordaunt and printed for T. Read. Mandeville was probably referring to the prostate gland. "Prostrates" may have been a variant of "prostate" in his time, or it may be a typo.

[120] From the penis to the pineal gland. Mandeville alludes to Descartes' hypothesis that the pineal gland is the place in the body most likely to be associated with the soul. The fullest development of Descartes' view of the pineal gland as the soul's seat (or place of contact with the body) is found in his last work, *Les Passions de l'âme* [The Passions of the Soul] (1649). In this passage Mandeville once again displays his philosophical wit. The learned punning in this pamphlet, which is one more aspect of its deliberate rhetorical showmanship, seems to go beyond Mandeville's previous practice in this vein of humor.

least toying with an alluring Wench, the Blood Vessels are ready to start; and to use *Othello's* Words, *The very Sense aches at her.*[121]

Now what shall this Man do, when he has once taken the Resolution to make himself easy? He must either venture upon the Publick, where, it is Odds, he may meet with a Mischance that will either drain his Pocket, and make him unfit for any Business, at least without Doors; or else he must employ both his Time and Rhetorick, and perhaps too his Purse, in deluding some modest Girl; which, besides the loss of Time in carrying on such an Intrigue, is apt to give the Head such an amorous Turn as is quite inconsistent with Business, and may probably lead a Man into After-Expences, which at first he never dreamt of.[122]

Now, to remedy all these Inconveniencies, the *Publick Stews* will be always ready and open, where a Man may regulate his Expences according to his Ability, from Half a Crown to a Guinea; and that too without endangering his health: and besides, which is chiefly to be consider'd, if **[26]** a Man should be overtaken with a sudden Gust of Lechery, it will be no Hindrance to him even in the greatest Hurry of Business, for a ready and willing Mistress will ease him in the twinkling of an Eye, and he may prosecute his Affairs with more Attention than ever, by having his Mind entirely freed and disengag'd from those troublesome Ideas which always accompany a wanton Disposition of the Body. But to proceed:

Another ill Consequence of Whoring, is the Tendency it has to dispeople a Nation; and that both by the Destruction of Bastard Infants, and by ruining young Mens Constitutions so much, that, when they marry, they either beget no Children, or such as are sickly and short-liv'd. The first of these, indeed, is almost unavoidable, especially in modest Women, who will be guilty of this Cruelty as long as Female Chastity carries that high Reputation along with it, which it really deserves:[123] However, in common

---

[121] Misquoted from Shakespeare's *Othello, the Moor of Venice,* IV, ii, 69. The full passage runs as follows (lines 67–69):

> O thou weed,
> Who art so lovely fair and smell'st so sweet
> That the sense aches at thee, would thou hadst
> ne'er been born!

Following this outburst Othello accuses Desdemona of having played the whore. In citing this Shakespearean passage Mandeville alludes not only to his main subject, whoring, but also to his discussion of defects and pitfalls in marriage.

[122] George Lillo's domestic tragedy, *The London Merchant, or, The History of George Barnwell* (1730) depicts the gradual destruction of the main character, the young apprentice George Barnwell, through his immoderate attachment to the prostitute Sarah Millwood, who leads him astray. As in Mandeville's account, his amorous obsession interferes tragically with the "business" or laboring side of his life.

[123] Ten years earlier, in "Remark (C.)" of his *Fable of the Bees*, Mandeville anticipated this argument by noting that a modest and law-abiding woman who became pregnant out of wedlock could well be driven by her overpowering shame to murder her bastard infant, but would love and cherish any future children she had in a lawful marriage. See *Fable* ed. Kaye, I, 75.

Women, it may and will be, in a great measure, prevented by this Scheme; for every profess'd Courtezan, that is legally licens'd, will have an Apartment allotted her in the Infirmary when she is ready to lie in, and will be obliged to take care of her Child; by which means a considerable Number of Infants will be reared up, that **[27]** otherwise might probably have perish'd. Besides, there are a great many ordinary Girls, such as Servant-Maids, who are chiefly mov'd to this Action, by the fear of losing their Services, and wanting Bread. Now this handsome Provision that is made for them, will be a great Inducement for such to enter themselves in the *Stews*, rather than commit such an unnatural Action, especially when the Discovery is Death.

Let us now consider the Affair of Matrimony. Since the World is now no longer in a State of Nature, but form'd into several Societies independent of one another, and these Societies again divided into several Ranks and Degrees of Men, distinguish'd by their Titles and Possessions, which descend from Father to Son; it is very certain that Marriage is absolutely necessary, not only for the regular Propagation of the *Species*, and their careful Education, but likewise for preserving that Distinction of Rank among Mankind, which otherwise would be utterly lost and confounded by doubtful Successions.[124] And it is no less certain and indisputable, that all Sorts and Kinds of Debauchery whatever are Enemies to this State, in so far as they impair the natural Vigour of the Constitution, and weaken the very Springs of Love.

[28]   This necessary Passion is, indeed, of such a ticklish Nature, that either too much or too little of it is equally prejudicial, and the *Medium* is so hard to hit, that we are apt to fall into one of the Extremes. We are naturally *furnish'd* with an extraordinary *Stock* of Love; and, by the *Largeness* of the Provision, it looks as if Nature had made some Allowance for *Wear and Tear*. If young Men were to live entirely chaste and sober, without blunting the Edge of their Passions, the first Fit of Love would turn their Brains Topsy-turvy, and we should have the Nation Pestered with Love Adventures and Feats of Chivalry: By the time a *Peer's* Son came to be Sixteen, he would be in danger of turning Knight-Errant, and might possibly take a Cobler's Daughter for his *Dulcinea*; and who knows but a sprightly young *Taylor* might turn an *Orlando Furioso*, and venture his Neck to carry off a Lady of Birth and Fortune.[125] In short, there are so many

---

[124] A more famous restatement of this principle is attributed to Samuel Johnson. See James Boswell's *Life of Johnson* (Oxford Standard Authors edition, 1960), 601; for other editions, see the entry for Tuesday, March 28, 1775. Johnson later admitted to Boswell that Mandeville "opened my views into real life very much" (p. 948; Wednesday, April 15, 1778), but we have no documentary evidence to prove that Johnson had ever seen this passage in Mandeville's pamphlet.

[125] Dulcinea was the object of Don Quixote's amorous desire; Cervantes' masterpiece appeared in 1605 and was widely translated and reprinted. Ludovico Ariosto's *Orlando Furioso* (1516) was composed as a continuation of Matteo Maria Boiardo's unfinished poem, *Orlando Innamorato*, begun by Boiardo in 1480. The lady pursued by Orlando (Roland) is Angelica, daughter of the King of Cathay. Orlando went mad upon learning that she had wed Medoro.

Instances every day of these ruinous disproportion'd Matches, notwithstanding our present Intemperance, that we may justly conclude, if the Nation was in a State of perfect Sobriety, no Man could answer for the Conduct of his Children.

It must, indeed, be confess'd, as Matters now stand, the Excess of Chastity is not so **[29]** much to be fear'd as the other Extreme of Lewdness, tho' there are Instances of both; and many Fathers, now living, would gladly have seen their Sons fifty times in a *Stew*, rather than see them so unfortunately married. The other Extreme is equally, or rather more dangerous, as it is more common; for most young Men give too great a loose to their Passions, and either quite destroy their Inclination to Matrimony, or make their Constitutions incapable of answering the Ends of that State.

To avoid therefore these two dangerous Extremes, we have erected the *Publick Stews*, which every considerate Man must allow to be that Golden Mean so much desired: For, in the first Place, we avoid the Inconvenience of too strict a Chastity. When a Man has gained some Experience by his Commerce in the *Stews*, he is able to form a pretty good comparative Judgment of what he may expect from the highest Gratifications of Love; he finds his Ideas of Beauty strangely alter'd after Enjoyment, and will not be hurry'd into an unsuitable Match by those romantick chimerical Notions of Love, which possess the Minds of unexperienced Youth, and make them fancy that Love alone can compleat the Happiness of a married State. But this **[30]** will be so readily granted, that I shan't insist upon it farther.

In the next Place, the *Publick Stews* will prevent the ill Effects of excessive Lewdness, by preserving Mens Constitutions so well, that although they may defer Matrimony some time for their special Advantage, yet they will have a sufficient Stock of Desire left to persuade them, one time or other, to quit the Gaiety of a Single Life: And when they do marry, they will be able to answer all the Ends and Purposes of that State as well, and rather better, than if they had lived perfectly chaste.

This may seem a bold Proposition, but the Proof of it is nevertheless obvious. However, to proceed methodically, there are three Ways by which lewd young Men destroy their natural Vigour, and render themselves impotent: First, By Manufriction, *alias* Masturbation.[126] Secondly, by too frequent and immoderate Enjoyment. And, Lastly, By contracting Venereal Disorders, as Claps or Poxes.

---

[126] Masturbation was commonly thought to be extremely debilitating and dangerous, both physically and spiritually. The basis for its sinfulness in the Judaeo-Christian Scriptures is the story of Onan, who spilled his seed (Genesis 38). (Some indeed have argued that the sin of Onan is not precisely masturbation but closer in fact to *coitus interruptus*.) A key text on that issue was *Onania; or, The Heinous Sin of Self-Pollution, and all its Frightful Consequences in Both Sexes, Considered.* (about 1710, and many later editions). Mandeville would certainly have known it. His critique of masturbation includes major objections voiced in *Onania*. For a useful description of *Onania* see the following website: http://www.gayhistory.com/rev2/events/1710.htm. See also Thomas Laqueur's *Solitary Sex.*

The first lewd Trick that Boys learn, is this Manual Diversion; and when they have once got the knack of it, they seldom quit it till they come to have actual Commerce with Women: The Safety, Privacy, Convenience, and Cheapness of this Gratification are very strong Motives, and chiefly [31] persuade young Men to continue the Practice of it.

If these *Onanites* were so abstemious as to wait the ordinary Calls of Nature, this Action, however unnatural, would be no more prejudicial, when prudently managed, than Common Copulation; but, instead of this, they are every Day committing *Rapes* upon their own Bodies; and though they have neither real Inclination nor Ability to attack a Woman, yet they can attack themselves, and supply all these Defects by the Agility of their Wrists; by which means they so weaken their Genitals, and accustom them to this violent Friction, that, tho' they have frequently Evacuations without an Erection, yet the common and ordinary Sensation which Females afford to those Parts, is not able of itself to promote this Evacuation: so that they are impotent to all Intents and Purposes of Generation.

To put a Stop therefore to these clandestine Practices, and prevent young Men from laying *violent Hands* upon themselves, we must have recourse to the *Publick Stews*, which cannot fail to have the desired Effect: For which of these private Practitioners can be so brutish, as to prefer this boyish, solitary Amusement before the actual Embraces of a fine Woman, when they can [32] proceed with the same Convenience, Safety, and Privacy in the one, as well as the other.

In the next Place, Men are often weaken'd, and sometimes contract almost incurable Gleets by too frequent and immoderate Enjoyment. This seldom or never happens but in private Whoring, when some particular Mistress has made such a strong Impression upon a Man's Fancy, that he exerts himself in an extraordinary Manner beyond his natural Ability, and thereby contracts a Seminal Weakness, which is generally more difficult to cure than a virulent Running. Now this Danger will be pretty well remov'd by the Encouragement given to *Publick Whoring*, which, as I shall show more particularly hereafter, will divert Mens Minds, and turn their Thoughts very much from private Intrigues: And it will be readily granted me, that no such Excess is to be fear'd in *Publick Stews*; where a Man only acting out of a general Principle of Love to the whole Sex, will be in no Danger of proceeding any farther than he is prompted by Nature, and the particular Disposition of his Body at that time.

As for the third Cause of Impotency, the Venereal Disease, we have already prov'd that this Institution of the *Stews* [33] is the best and surest Remedy against it; and shall only observe here how happily this Project provides against the various ill Effects of Lewdness, in whatever Light we consider them.

Thus, I think, the first Part of my Proposition pretty well clear'd, *viz*. That the *Publick Stews* will preserve Mens Constitutions so well, that they will have a sufficient Stock of corporal Ability, and consequently Inclination left to persuade them, sooner or later, to enter into the Marriage-State.

I say farther, that these Men, having thus preserv'd their Constitution, will answer all the Intents and Purposes of that State, rather better than if they had lived perfectly chaste.

When a Man and a Woman select one another out of the whole Species, it is not merely for Propagation; nay, that is generally the least in their Thoughts: What they chiefly have in View, is to pass the Remainder of their lives happily together, to enjoy the soft Embraces and mutual Endearments of Love; to divide their Joys and Griefs; to share their Pleasures and Afflictions; and, in short, to make one another as happy as possible. As for Children, they come of Course, and of **[34]** Course are educated according to their Parents abilities.

Now all these Enjoyments depending upon the mutual Affection of these two, Man and Wife; whenever this Affection fails, either in the Woman or the Man, that Marriage is unhappy, and all the good Ends and Designs of this State entirely frustrated. To give the Women their Due, they must have the Preference in Point of Constancy;[127] their Passions are not so easily rais'd, nor so suddenly fix'd upon any particular Object: but when this Passion is once rooted in Women, it is much stronger and more durable than in Men, and rather increases than diminishes, by enjoying the Person beloved. Whether it is that Women receive as much Love as they part with, and that the Love they receive is not entirely lost, but takes Root again by Conception; whereas what a Man parts with never affects Him farther, than just the Pleasure he receives at the time of parting with it; or whether this Difference is owing to the different Turn of Mens Fancies, which are more susceptible of fresh Impressions from every handsome Face they meet, or perhaps that their Heads are so much employ'd in worldly Affairs, that they only take Love *en passant* to get rid of a present Uneasiness, whereas Women **[35]** make it the whole Business of their Lives: Whatever the Reason is, I say, it is experimentally true, that a Woman has but a very *slippery Hold* of a Man's Affections after Enjoyment. Let us see therefore which of these two, the chaste or the experienc'd Man, will be least liable to this Failure of Affection, and consequently which of the two will make the best married Man.

---

[127] Mandeville's opinion that women are more constant or faithful in marriage than men can be read as another piece of evidence to support the view that he was a feminist or proto-feminist. The issue by his time was centuries old. In addition to the male infidelities of Aeneas (in the Dido episode), Jason (who abandoned Medea) and Theseus (who abandoned Ariadne), there is also the passage in Ovid's *Art of Love* (Book III, lines 28–36) which states that man is always inconstant and deceptive while women are guilty of such behavior far less often. Mandeville was anticipated by the French physician Nicolas Venette in his treatise *Conjugal Love Reveal'd, In the Nightly Pleasure of the Marriage Bed and the Advantages of that Happy State* . . . The Seventh Edition (translated from the French; London, n.d. [1720?]). In Chapter XI, "Whether the Women are more constant in Love than the Men," Venette decides in favor of the women. The same judgment that women are more constant in love appears in Judith Drake's *An Essay in Defence of the Female Sex* (1696; New York, 1970, 114–115). Another instance of female constancy that Mandeville certainly knew is the story of Inkle and Yarico in Steele's *Spectator* paper, no. 11, March 13, 1711. (Almost a century later the theme of women's constancy reappeared at the end of Jane Austen's novel, *Persuasion*.)

The first great Cooler of a Man's Affections after Marriage, is the Disparity of the Match. When a Man has married entirely for Love, and to the apparent Detriment of his worldly Affairs, as soon as the first Flash of it is over, he can't help reflecting upon the Woman as the Cause, and, in some Sense, the Author of his Misfortunes: This naturally begets a Coldness and Indifference, which, by Degrees, turns to an open Dislike. Now it is these sort of Marriages that chaste Men are always in danger of falling into, as I have already proved; neither is there any effectual Way to convince a Man of this Folly, and secure him against it, but by giving him some Experience in Love-Affairs. Again, as chaste Men seldom marry for any thing but sheer Love, so they have framed to themselves such high extravagant Notions of the Raptures they expect to possess in the Marriage-Bed, that they are mightily shocked at **[36]** the Disappointment. A chaste unexperienc'd Man is strangely surprized, that those bewitching Charms should make such a faint Impression upon him after a thorow Perusal; he can scarce believe that the Woman is still possessed of the same Charms which transported him formerly; he fancies he has discover'd abundance of little Faults and Imperfections, and attributes his growing Dislike to this Discovery, not dreaming that this Alteration is entirely in himself, and not in the Object of Desire, which remains still the same. The Truth is, when a Man is full fraught with Love, and that his Pulse beats high for Enjoyment, this peccant Love-Humour falls down upon the Eye, which may be observ'd at such a time to be full brisk and sparkling: 'Tis then the Beauty of every Feature is magnified by coming through this false Perspective. and *Parthenope*[128] is no less than a Goddess. But when this dazzling Humour is drawn downwards by a Revulsion, as in the Case of Marriage, a Man's Eyes are perfectly open'd; and though they may look languid, sunk, and environ'd with blueish Circles, yet he actually sees much better than before; for *Parthenope* will now appear to him a Mortal, such as she really is, divested of all those false Glosses and Appearances.[129]

[37]   The chaste Man is surprized at this Change; he is apt to lay the Fault upon the Woman, and generally fixes his Affections on some other Female, who, he imagines, is free from those Faults: then farewell happy Wedlock. The experienc'd Man, on the contrary, has try'd several Women; he finds they all agree in one Particular, and that after a Storm of Love there always succeeds a Calm: When he enters into Matrimony, he is prepar'd against any Disappointments of that Nature, and is ready to make Allowance for those Faults and Imperfections which are inseparable from Human Kind.

---

[128] From the Greek "parthenos" meaning maiden or virgin, and "ops," face. Parthenope was one of the deadly sirens whose sweet singing enticed Odysseus and his men on their homeward voyage. In another legend connected with the founding of Naples, the siren Parthenope is washed ashore in the bay of Naples after having tried to drown herself for love of Odysseus.

[129] Jonathan Swift took such unveiling much further in his poem "The Lady's Dressing Room" (1732).

This is so true, that Women have establish'd a Maxim, that Rakes make the best Husbands; for they are very sensible how difficult it is to monopolize a Man's Affections; that he will have his Curiosity about those Affairs satisfied one time or other: And tho' this Experience is useful before Marriage, it is very dangerous afterwards.[130]

Besides, to compleat the Happiness of the Marriage-State, or indeed to make it tolerably easy, there must be some Agreement in the Temper, Humour, and Disposition of the two Parties concern'd. If, for Instance, the Man can't endure the Sight of a *Metropolis*, and the Woman can't enjoy herself out of it; if the Man is grave, serious, and **[38]** an Enemy to all jocular Merriment, when his Wife is a profess'd Lover of Mirth and Gaiety, these two can never agree; Differences will arise every Day, and Differences in Wedlock are as hard to reconcile as those in Religion: We may guess at the Reason from a parallel Instance.

After the Revocation of the Edict of *Nantz*,[131] several Protestant Gentlemen were shut up in the *Bastile* at *Paris*, where they liv'd constantly together for a considerable Time: They made an Observation, during their Stay there, That whenever the least Difference or Dispute happen'd amongst them, it was never reconciled till some time after their Enlargement; because, said they, altho' we were Yoke-Fellows in Affliction, yet never being out of one another's Company, our Animosities were always kept up warm, for want of a little Absence to cool them. It is the same Case with Matrimony; and People ought to be particularly careful to chuse a Wife as nearly of their own Temper as possible.

Now this Consideration never enters into the Head of a chaste unexperienc'd Man; he is so infatuated with personal Love, that he imagines his whole future Happiness depends upon the Possession of such a Shape, or such a Composition of Features; when he is disappointed in this, how much will it **[39]** add to his Chagrin, to find himself yoked for Life to a Woman whose Temper is quite opposite to his own, and consequently whose Satisfaction is quite inconsistent with his? We may guess the Sequel; separate Beds, separate Maintenance, and all the whole Train of Conjugal Misfortunes. In short, let us consider Matrimony under what View we please, we shall still find that the experienc'd Man will make the best Husband, and answer all the Ends of Marriage much better than a Man who lives perfectly chaste to his Wedding-Day.

---

[130] The view that "reformed rakes make the best husbands" became proverbial by the mid-eighteenth century, turning up in texts by Richardson, Wollstonecraft, and (later) Anne Bronte. Perhaps the most famous instance in Restoration drama is Mirabel, in Congreve's *The Way of the World* (1700). A recent search in the *OED.* showed no example of "reformed rake" in the entry for "rake." Mandeville's sentence above implies but does not include the term "reformed."

[131] The Revocation of the Edict of Nantes in 1685 by the government of King Louis XIV inaugurated a new era of suffering, persecution, and often exile for French Protestants, called Huguenots. A published source for this anecdote has not yet been found.

Thus, we see, by this happy Regulation of the *Publick Stews*, that Whoring, instead of being an Enemy to Matrimony, will advance and promote the Interest of it as much as possible.[132]

We come now to the last great Point propos'd, *viz.* that this Project of the *Publick Stews* will prevent, as much as possible, the debauching of modest Women, and thereby reduce Whoring to the narrowest Bounds in which it can possibly be contain'd.

To illustrate this Matter, we must step a little back to consider the Constitution of Females, while they are in a State of Innocence; and when we have taken a View of the Fortifications which Nature has made to preserve their Chastity, we shall find out **[40]** the Reason why it is so often surrender'd, and be the better able to provide for its Defence.

Every Woman, who is capable of Conception, must have those Parts which officiate so framed, that they may be able to perform what ever is necessary at that Juncture. Now, to have those Parts so rightly adapted for the Use which Nature design'd them, it is requisite that they should have a very quick Sensation, and, upon the Application of the *Male-Organ*, afford the Woman an exquisite Pleasure; for without this extravagant Pleasure in Fruition, the recipient Organs could never exert themselves to promote Conception as they now do, in such an extraordinary Manner: The whole *Vagina*, as one continu'd *Sphincter*, contracting and embracing the *Penis*, while the *Nymphæ* and adjacent Islands have their particular Emissions at that critical Minute, either as a Vehicle to lubricate the Passage, or else to incorporate with the Masculine Injection: Add to this, that the *Fallopian Tubes* put themselves in a proper Posture to receive the impregnating Fluid, and convey it, as is suppos'd, to the *Ovaria*.[133] Now it is hard to imagine, that so many alert Members, which can exert themselves in such a lively Manner on this Occasion, should be at all **[41]** other Times in a State of perfect Tranquillity; for, besides that Experience teaches us the contrary, this handsome Disposition would be entirely useless, if Nature had not provided a prior Titillation, to provoke Women at first to enter upon Action; and all our late Discoveries, in Anatomy, can find out no other Use for the *Clitoris*, but to whet the Female Desire by its frequent Erections; which are, doubtless, as provoking as those of the *Penis*, of which it is a perfect Copy, tho' in Miniature.[134]

---

[132] Another in the line of paradoxes that Mandeville assembles for the reader's delectation. He would call this "a seeming paradox."

[133] The famous Italian anatomist Gabriel Fallopius (or Gabriello Fallopio, 1523–1562) discovered the tubes that connect a woman's ovaries to her uterus. He also first named the clitoris, the placenta, and the vagina. Some believe that he also "discovered" the clitoris, but that remains uncertain.

[134] For a detailed account of the shape, position, and functions of the clitoris, see Jane Sharp's *The Midwives Handbook. Or the whole Art of Midwifry discovered. . . .* (London, 1671), 43–47. Mandeville would surely have known this book.

In short, there requires no more to convince us of the Violence of Female Desire, when raised to a proper height, but only to consider, what a terrible Risque a Woman runs to gratify it. Shame and Poverty are look'd upon as Trifles, when they come in Competition with this predominating Passion. But altho' it must be allow'd, that all Women are liable to these amorous Desires, yet, the Variety of Constitutions will make a considerable Difference; for as in some Men the *Olfactory, Auditory,* or *Optick* Nerves, are not so brisk and lively as in others, so there are some Women who have the Nerves of their *Pudenda* more lively, and endow'd with a much quicker Sensation than others. Now, whether this Difference is owing to the Formation of the Nerves, or to the different [42] Velocity of the Blood circulating thro' those Parts, or whether it is owing to the different Quantity, or perhaps Acrimony, of that Fluid which is separated from the Blood by the *Nymphæ,* and other titillating Glands: I say, from whenceso-ever this Difference proceeds, according to the Degree of this Sensation, we may venture to pronounce a Woman more or less in their own Nature Chaste.

To counterballance this violent natural Desire, all young Women have strong Notions of Honour carefully inculcated into them from their Infancy. Young Girls are taught to hate a *Whore,* before they know what the Word means; and when they grow up, they find their worldly Interest entirely depending upon the Reputation of their Chastity. This Sense of Honour and Interest, is what we may call artificial Chastity; and it is upon this Compound of natural and artificial Chastity, that every Woman's real actual Chastity depends.[135]

As for Instance, some Women are naturally more Chaste, or rather, to speak properly, less Amorous than others, and at the same time have strict Notions of Honour. Such Women are almost impregnable, and may be compar'd to Towns strongly fortify'd both by Art and Nature, [43] which, without Treachery, are safe from any sudden Attacks, and must be reduc'd by long and regular Sieges, such as few Men have the Patience or Resolution to go thro' with.

Other Women, again, have the same Value for their Reputation, and stand as much upon the Puncto of Honour; but then they are naturally of a very sanguine amorous Disposition. A Woman of this Class may not unjustly be compar'd to a Town well garrison'd, but whose mutinous unruly *Inhabitants* are strongly inclin'd to revolt and let in the Enemy. Such Women, it's true, by extraordinary Care and Vigilance may suppress these Mutinies; and Honour may for a long while keep Inclination under, but yet they are never perfectly safe; there are certain Times and Seasons, certain

---

[135] Distinguishing between the natural and the artificial passions was an important exercise for Mandeville and others who were concerned with the history and structure of the passions. In Remark (R.) of his *Fable* he offers this analysis of artificial courage: "The Courage then which is only useful to the Body Politick, and what is generally call'd true Valour, is artificial, and consists *in a Superlative Horror against Shame, by* Flattery *infused into Men of exalted* Pride" (Ed. Kaye, I, 210).

unguarded Hours, when Honour and Interest are lull'd asleep, and Love has got the entire Ascendant.[136] Besides, altho' we allow Love and Honour to be pretty equal Combatants, nay even granting, that in a *Pitch'd Battel*, when they have muster'd up all their Forces, Honour will have the Advantage, and quell Inclination; yet, in the Course of a long *Civil War*, it is Odds but Love one Time or other obtains a Victory, which is sure to be decisive: for Inclination has this unluckly [*sic*] Advantage over **[44]** Honour, that, instead of being weaken'd, it grows stronger by Subjection; and, like *Camomile*, the more it is press'd down and kept under, the sturdier it grows;[137] or, like *Antæus*, it receives fresh Vigour from every Defeat, and rises the Brisker the oftener it is thrown.[138] Whereas Honour once routed never rallies; nay, the least *Breach* in Female Reputation is irreparable; and a *Gap* in Chastity, like a *Chasm* in a young Tree, is every day a *Widening*. Besides, Honour and Interest require a a long Chain of solid Reasoning before they can be set in Battel-Array; whereas Inclination is presently under Arms, the moment Love has pitch'd his *Standard:* For, as we find that the least wanton Glance of a Lady's Eye quickly alarms a Man's Animal Spirits, and puts the whole Body Corporate into an unruly Ferment; so, doubtless, the Female Imagination is at least equally alert: and in such a sudden Scuffle betwixt Love and Honour, it is ten to one but the Enemy *enters*; for the *Gate* of Chastity, like the *Temple of Janus*,[139] always stands *open* during these Conflicts. It must indeed be granted, that if the Loss of Honour was immediately to succeed the Loss of Chastity, the Virtue of these Women would be much stronger than it is; but they flatter themselves with the Hopes of Secrecy, and fancy that they have **[45]** found out an Expedient to purchase Pleasure without the Expence of Reputation; by this means Honour is reconciled to Inclination, or at best made to stand Neuter; and then the Consequence is very obvious. In short, a wanton

---

[136] In the sixteenth and seventeenth centuries the conflict between love and honor was exploited widely in poems, plays, novels, and paintings. It would have been remembered as a popular commonplace by Mandeville's literate contemporaries.

[137] The allusiveness of Mandeville's text continues to surprise us. The most famous appearances of this account of the camomile occurred first in Lyly's *Euphues* (1579; p. 46 in the Arber reprint) and later in Shakespeare's *I Henry IV*, II, iv, 440–441 (1598). Lyly's "euphuistic" style is parodied by Falstaff, who plays Prince Hal's father King Henry IV in this scene. Falstaff cites Lyly's line as "the camomile, the more it is trodden on the faster it grows." Since Mandeville names. Falstaff later in this pamphlet, it seems likely that he was alluding here to this passage in *I Henry IV*.

[138] The son of Poseidon, the sea god, and of Gaia, goddess of the earth, Antaeus fought with and always conquered visitors to his land, so long as his feet were in contact with his mother Earth. But he was finally vanquished by Heracles, who discovered his secret and crushed him while he was elevated above the earth.

[139] The gates of the Temple of Janus in the Roman Forum were said to be opened for war and closed in times of peace. Janus, the ancient god of doorways, gates, and beginnings, is mentioned in many Roman works including Virgil's *Aeneid*; see Book VII, lines 601ff. *Janus bifrons*, or Janus with two heads represents the door looking before and behind. Mandeville would have learned the essential facts about this god early in his classical education, but it is relevant to note here that this image appears in the first page or two of Montaigne's essay III, 5, "On Some Verses of Virgil," from which Mandeville silently borrowed various passages for use in this pamphlet.

Woman of Honour may withstand a great many Attacks, and possibly defend her Chastity to the very last; but yet she is every day in danger of being surpriz'd, and at best will make but a very precarious Defence.

A third Sort of Women, the very Reverse of the preceding, have neither Honour nor Inclination; that is to say, they have neither the one nor the other to an equal Degree with the rest of the Sex. These Kind of Women who put a slighter Value than ordinary upon their Characters, are generally, in their Circumstances, either above the World or below it; for when a Woman has her Interest and Fortune depending upon her Reputation, as all the middle Rank of Womankind have, she is a Woman of Honour of course. Interest, indeed is inseparable from Female Honour, nay, it is the very Foundation of it; and Honour and Interest, when they are consider'd as Guardians to Chastity, are synonimous Terms. The bare Puncto of Honour, when abstracted from Interest, would prove but a small Rub to Women in their eager **[46]** Pur-|suit of Pleasure: Thus we see the Conduct of a Maiden Lady, how much more Circumspect it is whilst her Fortune in Marriage is depending, than afterwards, when that Point of Interest is secured by a Husband; for all marry'd Women are above the World, in so far as they are out of the Reach of any Suspicions or Surmises, or even a Probability of Incontinence; and since they are not liable to be detected by Pregnancy, there's no other Sort of Conviction able to prejudice them, but downright ocular Demonstration: Which seems to be the Reason why so many of them take such Liberties, as if they were of *Falstaff*'s Opinion, when he said, *Nothing but Eyes confutes me.*[140] Female Honour, therefore, being so nearly ally'd and closely annex'd to worldly Interest, we must confine this Class of Women to two Sorts: First, those whose Fortunes are independent, and above being influenc'd by the Censure of the World; and, secondly, those who are so far below the World, that they either escape its Censure, or else are incapable of being hurt by it. The first Sort lie under this Disadvantage, that let their natural Chastity be ever so great, the smallest Spark of Desire is capable of being blown up and rais'd to a considerable Pitch; whereas, when a Woman is once arriv'd to **[47]** Ma-|turity, that Portion of Honour which she has acquir'd, is with Difficulty preserv'd, and at best is incapable of any Improvement. The second Sort are equally liable to have their Passions rais'd, however low they may be naturally, and besides lie under this farther Disavantage, that tho' they can't promote their Interest by preserving their Chastity, yet, if they have the least Spark of Beauty, they will find their Account sufficiently in parting with it. The Virtue, indeed, of this Class of Women, seems chiefly

---

[140] Misquoted from Shakespeare's *The First Part of King Henry the Fourth*, V, iv, 125. Falstaff says, "Why may not he [Hotspur] rise as well as I? Nothing confutes me but eyes, and nobody sees me." He then stabs the corpse of Hotspur in the thigh, intending to claim later that he was the one who slew Hotspur. For Mandeville, the most important words uttered by Falstaff were probably those that appear a few lines earlier in this play, comprising Falstaff's brief disquisition on the shortcomings of honor (V, i, 127–139) and concluding with "Honour is a mere scutcheon—and so ends my catechism."

to depend upon the Degree of Beauty which they stand possess'd of; for if they have Charms sufficient to provoke young Men to be at any tolerable Pains and Cost, their Chastity can never hold out long, but must infallibly surrender.

The fourth and last Kind of Women we shall mention, are those who have a very moderate Share of Honour, join'd to a very amorous Constitution.

The Virtue of these Women is entirely defenceless; and, as soon as a Man has removed that little timorous Coyness, which is natural to young Women in their first Attempts, he may proceed with Confidence, and conclude the Breach to be practicable; for whatever Resistance he meets with afterwards, will only enhance the Pleasure of Conquest. Most Women, indeed, let them **[48]** be ever so fully resolv'd to comply, make as great a Shew of Resistance as they can conveniently counterfeit; and this the Sex would pass upon the World for a kind of innate Modesty: but it is very easily accounted for.

As soon as Women have entertain'd any Degree of Love, they make it their whole Study to raise and maintain an equal Degree of Passion in the Men; and they are very sensible how far the bare Appearance of Modesty will prevail to render them amiable. The Pain they suffer in smothering their Desires, is fully recompenced by that secret Pleasure which a Lover's Eagerness gives them, because they esteem it a Proof both of the Sincerity and Violence of his Passion. A Woman is not,[141] without some Reason, afraid, lest a Man's Love should diminish after Enjoyment, and would gladly bribe his After-Love, by the great Value she seems to put upon her Chastity before she makes him a Present of it.

Besides, not to mention the actual Pleasure a Woman receives in Struggling, it is a Justification of her in the Eye of the Man, and a kind of *Salvo* to her Honour and Conscience, that she never did fully comply, but was in a manner forced into it. This is the plain natural Reason why most Women refuse to *surrender* upon **[49]** Trea-|ty, and why they delight so much in being *storm'd*.[142]

Having thus taken a cursory View of the Sex, in their several Classes, and according to their several Circumstances, we may conclude, preferring Truth to Complaisance, that by far the greater Part of Womenkind hold their Virtue very precariously; and that Female Chastity is, in its own Nature, built upon a very *ticklish* Foundation.

---

[141] This punctuation was carried over, without change, from the first edition, 1724A. The comma after "not" seems misplaced. It clearly belongs after the preceding word "is," thus allowing an easier comprehension of the double negative "not without." This correction was in fact introduced into the 1740 edition falsely attributed to "the late Colonel Harry Mordaunt" (London: T. Read), p. 34.

[142] Almost three centuries after this work first appeared, this paragraph will surely be troubling to modern sensibilities because we understand how close the belief that women enjoy being "stormed" is to the notion that women enjoy being raped. Such blatant sexism and *machismo* do not appear in Mandeville's other writings: these terms seem to apply rather to his created persona, and not to the author himself.

Hudibras has ludicrously plac'd the Seat of Male-Honour in the Posteriors, whereby it is secur'd from any Attack in Front; but Female-Honour, notwithstanding the apparent Safety of the Situation, like a Debtor's House upon the Verge of two Counties, is liable to be attack'd both Ways; *à parte ante, & à parte post.*[143]

That the Seat of Honour in Females has this double Aspect, like *Janus bifrons*,[144] and consequently that it is two Ways accessible, has already been taken notice of by almost all the *Writers* upon this Subject; but it is worth remarking here, that *Lycurgus* had an Eye to it when he modelled the *Spartan* Petticoat; for tho' the Warmth of the Climate obliged the Women to be very open in that Part of their Dress, insomuch that, if we believe *Plutarch* in his Comparison of *Numa* and *Lycurgus*, the **[50]** Habit which the Maidens of *Laconia* wore came but to their Knees, and was open on both Sides, so that as they walked their Thighs appear'd bare; yet this wise *Lawgiver* would not permit them to make the least Aperture, either in the fore or hind Part of that Garment; rightly judging, that those two sacred *Avenues* to a Maid's Honour ought to be guarded with the utmost Caution.[145]

For this same Reason the upright Posture of the Body has always been esteem'd the most decent; and it has ever been the Mode, in all Countries, for Ladies to cursey instead of bowing: for though a Female-Bow might seem a modest and coy Reclension of the Body, with regard to the Person saluted, yet it would occasion a very indecent Projection to those who should happen to be behind; especially since that dangerous Fashion of *Postern Plackets* has crept into the *European* Petticoat.[146]

---

[143] Mandeville alludes to the following passage in Samuel Butler's rollicking satirical poem *Hudibras* (1663–1678):

> But Hudibras gave him a twitch,
> As quick as lightning, in the breech,
> Just in the place where honour's lodg'd,
> As wise philosophers have judg'd.
> Because a kick in that place more
> Hurts honour than deep wounds before.
>   (Part II, Canto iii, lines 1065–1070)

Mandeville was strongly attracted to Butler's poem over the decades. He uses the same verse form, rhyming octosyllabic couplets, in *The Grumbling Hive; or, Knaves Turn'd Honest* (1705). Other examples are his translation of Scarron in *Typhon* (1704) and his collection of poems, *Wishes to a Godson* (1712). Before quoting a couplet from *Hudibras* in his medical treatise—*A Treatise of the Hypochondriack and Hysterick Passions* (1711, 1715, 1730)—Mandeville called its author "the incomparable Butler" (1711 ed., p. 94), and he again named him and quoted from *Hudibras* in his *Enquiry into the Origin of Honour . . .* (1732, p. 134).

[144] Mandeville mentions Janus earlier on p. **[44]** of the 1724B text.

[145] The source for this well-known passage about Lycurgus's dress code for Spartan females is Plutarch's *Lives of the Noble Grecians and Romans*; see the translation by John Dryden et al., revised by Arthur Hugh Clough (1864; New York: The Modern Library, n.d.), p. 95. Mandeville referred to passages from Dryden's Plutarch at least six times in his *Fable of the Bees*.

[146] "Postern" means a back door, an entrance other than the honorable one. "Plackets" are slits in women's skirts or petticoats leading to inner pockets. Mandeville's reference is obviously bawdy, as are Laurence Sterne's references to the placket-holes in women's clothing, in his *Tristram Shandy* (1759–1766).

But to return to our present Argument, the Design of which was to prove the following *Syllogism*.

The only way to preserve Female Chastity, is to prevent the Men from laying Siege to it: But this Project of the *Publick Stews* is the only Way to prevent Mens laying Siege to it: Therefore this **[51]** Pro-|ject is the only Way to preserve Female Chastity.[147]

The former Part of the Proposition is, I hope, sufficiently proved. It is, indeed, evident, from the bare Consideration of the Nature of Females, that if the Men are suffer'd to go on, as they now do, in the Pursuit of Pleasure, there is no possible Way can be found out, effectually, to secure the Virtue of any one Woman of any Rank, or in any Station of Life. If a Woman is handsome, she has the more Tryals to undergo, if homely, and for that Reason seldom attack'd, the Novelty of the Address makes the greater Impression: If she is married, it is odds but there's a Failure at home, and habitual Pleasures are not easily foregone, especially when they may be enjoy'd with Safety: If a Maid, her unexperienc'd Virgin-Heart is capable of any Impression: If she is rich, Ease and Luxury make the Blood run mad; and Love, if high-dieted, is ungovernable: If poor, she will be the easier bribed, when Love and Avarice jointly must be gratified.

In short, to sum up all, there is in the Passion of Love a certain fatal *Crisis*, to which all Womenkind are capable of being wrought up: The Difference of Virtue consisting only in this, that it is very hard to work a virtuous Woman up to this **[52]** *Crisis*, and requires a very unlucky Concurrence of Circumstances: Whereas a Woman without a good Stock of Virtue, must have an unaccountable series of good Fortune if she escapes. But, virtuous or not virtuous, when this Passion is once rais'd to the *critical* Height, it is absolutely irresistible.

Since therefore Female Virtue cannot effectually be secured, but by preventing the Men from laying Siege to it, it remains for us to examine, if this Prevention can be effected by any other Method than that of erecting the *Publick Stews*; and whether or no the *Publick Stews*, when erected, will have the desired Effect.

That young Men, in a good State of Health, have their Desires towards Women much stronger, and more violent, than for the Enjoyment of any thing else in this Life, is a Truth not to be contested. And it is likewise as certain, that young Men will gratify these Desires, unless the *Legislature* can affix such a Penalty to the Commission of the Fact, that the Apprehension of the Penalty may give their Minds more Uneasiness, than refraining from the Gratification.

Now there are but three Things which Men fear in this Life, *viz*. Shame, Poverty, and bodily Pain, and consequently but three **[53]** Sorts of Punishments which the *Legislature* can inflict. The first of these, indeed,

---

[147] Here again Mandeville continues to indulge his taste for paradoxes. How can it be that a system of state-controlled brothels will actually support female chastity? And are his answers persuasive?

might be omitted; for Shame is so very little in the power of the Laws, that it hardly deserves the Name of a Penalty. If the Pillory, and such like infamous Punishments, are more terrible for the Shame that attends them, than for the bodily Pain, it is not because such a Posture of a Man's Body, with his Neck through a Hole, is in itself ignominious, or that any Law can make it so; but because it publishes to the World, that a Man has been proved to commit such a certain Action, in its own Nature scandalous, which he is asham'd to have thus publickly made known. The truth is, Honour and Dishonour being only the different Opinions of Mankind, as to the Good or Evil of any Action;[148] and these Opinions in the Mind arising, as Dr. *Cl——ke*[149] well observes, from the natural Fitness or Unfitness of the Actions themselves, cannot be alter'd or determin'd by any *Secular Force*. And that they are entirely out of the Power of the *Legislature*, is evident in the Instance of Duelling; where a Man often receives Honour for a Breach of the Law, nay is forced to break it in Defence of his Honour.[150]

[54]   The utmost Scandal, therefore, which the Laws can affix to any Action, is to make a full and open Publication of the Fact: Now it is evident that this Publication cannot have a sufficient Influence over Mens Minds to deter them from Wenching, a Crime which meets with so favourable a Reception in the Eye of the World, that young Men are not asham'd to boast of it.

We must have recourse then to a Fine, or Corporal Punishment, or perhaps both. If it is a Fine, it must be one of these three sorts; either a certain determinate Sum for every Offence, or, to make it fall more equally, such a certain Portion of a Man's whole Substance, or else it must be such a Sum as the Jury shall think sufficient to repair the Woman's Damages. The first is impracticable because of its Inequality, with regard to Mens different Fortunes. The second would punish none but Men of Fortune. And the third, in many Cases, would be impossible; for Women are often ruin'd by such as have it not in their power to make them amends. But granting that a Fine could be so happily contriv'd as to affect all Men

---

[148] This formulation of the relativity of good and evil expresses a commonplace idea, but Mandeville could well have been thinking of Montaigne's essay I, 14: "That the taste of good and evil depends in large part on the opinion we have of them."

[149] The language of the fitness and unfitness of things was commonly associated with the writings of Mandeville's English contemporary, Dr. Samuel Clarke, D.D. (1675–1729), particularly his second set of Boyle lectures, *A Discourse concerning the Unchangeable Obligations of Natural Religion, and the Truth and Certainty of the Christian Revelation* (1706). Francis Hutcheson, one of Mandeville's contemporary detractors and critics, also quarreled with Clarke's use of "the fitness of things." Henry Fielding satirized this expression by placing it in the mouth of the Deist Mr. Square, in *The History of Tom Jones* (1749).

[150] In the last two decades of his life Mandeville expressed his views on duelling in different works. He ridiculed the "man of honor" and disapproved of duelling, but he apparently did not think that it ought to be entirely outlawed because it had the function of keeping would-be bullies in check. See his *Fable* (ed. F.B. Kaye), I, 219–220; II, 83, 87–98; see also his *Enquiry into the Origin of Honour and the Usefulness of Christianity in War* (1732), 63–83, and numbers 52 and 84 of the periodical *The Female Tatler* (1709–1710), edited by M.M. Goldsmith in *By a Society of Ladies*.

equally in their several Stations of Life; and let us suppose this Fine considerable enough, for so it must be, to deter any moderate-spirited Man: yet
still we lie under a manifest Dilemma as to the Point of **[55]** Proof; for if
the Proof is to depend upon the Evidence of Eye-Witnesses, none but
Fools will be convicted; and let a Man be ever so indiscreet, he that swears
to *rem in re*[151] must have good Eyes, and be a good Swearer withal. If, on
the other hand, a Man is to be convicted upon the sole Evidence of the
Woman, we run into greater Inconveniencies: for either a Woman is to be
recompenced for the Injury she has received, or not; if not, there is no
modest Woman of common Sense, but will chuse much rather to conceal
her Weakness, than expose it in publick Court so much to her own
Prejudice; and this too upon the sole Motive of doing Prejudice to a Man,
for whom, in all probability, she still retains an Affection: So that no Man
would be accus'd but by such sort of Women as the Law can never intend
to favour or countenance.

And if the Woman is to receive this Fine, either in part or the whole, by
way of Reparation, not to mention its being an actual Encouragement to
transgress, this Recompence would only be a Means to promote a
Multitude of false Accusations; for what Man could live with so much
Circumspection, that a Woman might not often have an Opportunity to
accuse him of such a Fact, with very probable Circumstances, when there
is no Opportunity of detecting the Fallacy. **[56]** This Difficulty, indeed, is
not to be got over; and the Objection lies equally strong against all sorts of
Corporal Punishment, Death itself not excepted. For if there are so many
false Indictments for *Rapes*, where a Woman receives no Benefit by the
Prosecution, where she is liable to such cross Examinations, and where the
Possibility of the Fact is so much doubted, that a Woman is generally
discountenanc'd, and must bring a Number of probable concurrent
Circumstances before she can gain Credit: I say, if notwithstanding these
Discouragements, there are so many malicious Prosecutions for *Rapes*, that
the Benefit of the Law in general is much disputed, what may we expect
in the present Case, where a Woman has nothing to do but acknowledge
that she was over-persuaded, and then all Difficulties vanish? Besides, if
such a Law was made, setting aside that the Remedy would be worse than
the Disease, it is much to be question'd if it prov'd any Remedy at all: For
what Fine can we propose as sufficient to deter Men, when there are so

---

[151] Legal Latin, the literal meaning of which is "the thing in the thing." Anyone alert to the
sexual bantering that courses through *A Modest Defence* should easily recognize the bawdy insin-
uation. In the law courts the phrase was directly used as a substitute or circumlocution for "the
penis in the vulva." Thus we find in the famous jurist Sir Edward Coke the following examples:
"So as there must be *penetratio*, that is res in re, either with mankind, or with beast, but the least
penetration maketh it carnall knowledge." And, "Although there be *emissio seminis*, yet if there be
no penetration, that is, *res in re*, it is no rape. . . ."See Coke's *Third Part of the Institutes of the Laws
of England*, [1644] 4th ed., 1670, Ch. X ("Of Buggery, or Sodomy"), p. 59 and Ch. XI ("Of
Rape"), p. 60. I wish to thank Rutgers Law librarian Paul Axel-Lute for supplying this reference.
It also occurs, in part, in Todd C. Parker's *Sexing the Text*, 12.

many that squander away their whole Fortunes upon this sole Gratification? And what Corporal Punishment, on this side Death, can we find out equivalent to a *Pox*, which they every day run the Risque of?

[57]   But no such Law, as yet, has been so much as propos'd, altho' Whoring has been a very obvious Mischief ever since Laws were in Being; therefore, without farther Argument, considering the Wisdom of our *Legislature*, that such a Law never has been made, ought to be sufficient Reason for us to judge it impracticable.

Since the Torrent of Lewdness, then, is too strong to be opposed by open Force, let us see if we can find out an Expedient to divert it by Policy, and prevent the Mischief tho' we can't prevent the Crime.

Most *Authors*, who have writ of Government, have chose to express their Sentiments by comparing the Publick Body with the Body Natural; and Mr. *Hobbes*, in his *Leviathan*, has carry'd the *Allegory* as far as it will go.[152] To make use of it in the present Instance, we may look upon *Whoring* as a Kind of Peccant Humour in the Body-Politick, which, in order to its Discharge, naturally seizes upon such external Members as are most liable to Infection, and at the same time most proper to carry off the Malignity. If this Discharge is promoted by a Licence for *Publick Stews*, which is a Kind of legal Evacuative, the Constitution will certainly be preserv'd: Whereas, if we apply Penal Laws, like violent Astringents, they will only drive the Disease back into **[58]** the Blood; where, gathering Strength, and at last assimilating the whole Mass, it will break out with the utmost Virulence, to the apparent Hazard of those sound Members, which otherwise might have escaped the Contagion. As we may observe in a *Clap*, where Nature of her own Accord expels the noxious Humour thro' the same Passages by which it was at first receiv'd; but if we resist Nature in this Discharge, and repel the Venom by too hasty an Application of *Stypticks*, the Disease then turns to a *Pox*, seizes the Vitals, and, to use *Solomon*'s Words *like a Dart, strikes thro' the Liver*.[153] But, leaving, *Allegory* as more proper for *Rhetorick* or *Poetry*, than such serious Debates, since this Project of the *Publick Stews* is the only Expedient now left for the Preservation of Female Chastity, the Question is, Whether or no this Expedient will really answer the End propos'd?

---

[152] At the beginning of the "Introduction" to his *Leviathan* (1651), Hobbes compares the commonwealth or political state to an "artificial man," and uses the figure of the body-politic frequently thereafter.

[153] Proverbs 7: 23. At this point Mandeville applies this famous dart image to the pain resulting from an improper treatment of the clap. In Proverbs 7 the image is part of a larger cluster signifying the ensnaring wiles and dangers of the harlot who seduces a young man "with her much fair speech" (verse 21). He goes to her "as an ox goeth to the slaughter" (v. 22) "till a dart strike through his liver" (v. 23). This precise passage is employed in an earlier description of harlotry in *Aristotle's Master-Piece*, a popular sex manual that first appeared in 1684 and was frequently reprinted for more than a century. In that anonymous work this passage from Proverbs is cited precisely where the dangers of harlotry are reviewed. See *Aristotle's Master-Piece* (London, 1698), p. 45. Mandeville would certainly have known this work, and he may have borrowed this biblical image from it.

To prove the Affirmative, requires no more but that we look into our-selves, and examine our own Passions; for Love ever was and will be the same in all Men, and in all Ages. The first amorous Emotions that young Men feel, are violent; they are plagued with a Stimulation, which raises a vehement Desire: The Passion is strong, but then it is general; it is lust, not Love: And therefore the natural Impatience of *Lust* will prompt them **[59]** to take the speediest way for present Gratification, and make them prefer the ready and willing Embraces of a Courtezan, before the doubtful and distant Prospect of enjoying a modest Damsel, whose Coyness will cost so much Pains, as well as Time, to overcome; and, when overcome, may probably occasion a future Uneasiness, and give them more Trouble after Enjoyment than they had before.

Besides this, if their first Affections should happen to be engaged to a particular Object, which is very rare; and that this particular Object was in their power to compass, which is still rarer; yet there is naturally in Young-men a certain secret Shame, which attends their first Sallies, and prevents their declaring a private Passion, 'till it grows so violent, that they are forced to give it vent upon the Publick; and by that means, get into a regular Method of making themselves easy, without doing their Modesty any Violence.

But tho' the natural Bent of Men's Minds inclines them to an easy Purchase of Pleasure in their first Amours, yet publick Whoring lies at pres-ent under so many Disadvantages; the Publick Women, for want of good Regulation, are so infamous in the Principles and Practice; the Places of resort so vile, and so scandalously imposing in the common Expence, and lying under the Lash of the **[60]** *Civil* Power, so pester'd with the merce-nary Officiousness of *Reforming Constables*; and which is worst of all, the Plague of *Claps* and *Poxes* is so inevitable, that Men contrary to their Inclinations are often forc'd to enter upon private Intrigues, either without trying the Publick, or after meeting with some Misfortunes in the Tryal.

Now if we see daily so many Young Men who prefer the publick Commerce under all these Disadvantages, what Success may we not expect from this happy Establishment of the *Stews*, when the Young Women's Behaviour will be regulated after a civil decent Manner; when the Houses of Entertainment will be so Commodious, and the Expence of Accommodation so reasonable; when the horrid dread of *Claps* is entirely removed; and when the Laws, instead of disturbing such Assemblies, will be employ'd in their Protection, to give them the greater Countenance and Encouragement; surely we may hope for a thorough Reformation.[154]

But if these Considerations should not prove fully effectual, and some Men should be so obstinate as to persist in private whoring, notwithstand-ing these Inducements to the contrary; we must then have recourse to *Legal*

---

[154] The phrase "thorough Reformation" resonates with centuries of English and Continental Protestant history; it commonly appears in the writings of Luther and other reformers.

Force, and drive those who are too resty[155] to be led: For tho' the Laws can't prevent Whoring, they may yet regulate it; **[61]** the *Quid* is not in their power, but the *Quomodo* is.[156] A Man must Eat, but he may be directed how to Eat. The strongest Curb can't stop an unruly Horse, but the weakest will serve to turn him: And the smallest Stream is not to be obstructed, tho' we can change the Course of the greatest River.[157] So Love, tho' ever so unruly and headstrong in the general, changes the particular Object of its Passion with the smallest Circumstance; and legal Penalties are no trifling dissuasives, when the Laws don't command Impossibilities.

This Argument indeed, of Compulsion, is in a manner Supernumerary, and thrown in, as it were, *ex abundanti*:[158] For the *Publick Stews* under this regular Oeconomy, will have so much the Advantage of private Whoring, whether we regard the Ease and Conveniency of Enjoyment, or the Beauty and Variety of Mistresses, that Men's natural Inclinations will sway them sufficiently without this Superfluous Constraint. If there is any fear of Success, the Danger lies on the other Side; and indeed we have some colour of Reason to apprehend, lest the whole Body of Lewdness being turn'd upon the Publick, there should want a sufficient Supply of young Women to recruit the *Stews*; which, by that Means may run into a sudden Dis-repute, and lose a **[62]** Cha-|racter that will be difficult to retrieve. But however plausible this Objection may seem at first Sight, we shall find, upon a nearer View, that it only serves to make the Excellence of this Scheme the more manifest.

As there is constantly in the Nation, a certain Number of young Men, whose Passions are too strong to brook any Opposition: Our Business is to contrive a Method how they may be gratify'd, with as little Expence of Female Virtue as possible. But the Difficulty lies in adjusting this Matter, and gaging our young Men's Affections so exactly, that the Modesty of one

---

[155] The *OED* second edition online sends us to "restive a. 3" for the definition of "resty": "3. Of horses: Refusing to go forward; stubbornly standing still; obstinately moving backwards or to the side when being driven or ridden; hence, resisting control, intractable, refractory." In using "resty" here Mandeville may also have been recalling both his "Dedication"(p. iii, above) in which he reports that an ancient philosopher "compares Lewdness to . . . a head-strong young Colt," and his "Preface" (p. *xv*, above) in the first apostrophe: "*Speak* Hibernian Stallion. . . ." Comparing sexually active young men to horses was, by Mandeville's time, an established commonplace in European literature. One should recall that horses were then much more frequently seen, and smelled, not only in rural places but in towns and cities as well. Completely reversing the centuries-old association of horses with fiery lust, the Houyhnhnms in Swift's *Gulliver's Travels* are depicted as being fully rational and in complete control of their sexual instincts.

[156] "The what" and "the how."

[157] This sentence, interestingly, brings together the three dominant metaphors for the power of sexual appetite employed by Mandeville in this work: food and hunger; the wild stallion; and the stream or unstoppable river. Each of these figures is a powerful force of nature that cannot (or should not) be repressed or removed, and each therefore requires intelligent management or regulation.

[158] From, or out of, abundance or superfluity. This common phrase occurs in the Vulgate version of the New Testament in Luke 21: 4 and 2 Corinthians 9: 1.

Woman may not be sacrific'd, more than is absolutely necessary for the Preservation of the rest.[159]

The Gallants of this age, indeed, are not quite so sturdy as that Rampant *Roman* Emperor who deflower'd ten *Sarmatian* Virgins in one Night;[160] but what we want in Constitution, we make up in the Nicety of our Palates; as a squeamish Stomach requires the greatest Variety of Dishes: And some of our Youth are grown such perfect *Epicures* in Venery, that they can relish nothing but *Virgins*: They destroy, it is true, a great deal of Beauty, by browsing only upon the buds.

But we ought not to judge of these Men's Abilities by the Number of Women they **[63]** de-|bauch, no more than we should measure the Goodness of a certain curious Gentleman's Appetite by his bespeaking several Dozen of young Pigeons, when he only regal'd upon the Rumps: Neither is it intirely from a Wantonness of Fancy, or a Luxurious Taste of Pleasure, that Men indulge themselves in making this Havock, but chiefly for their own personal Safety. Young Girls are so giddy, thoughtless, and unexperienc'd, and withal so fond of the Sport, at their first setting out, that they seldom escape a Taint; and a Man is not safe in being constant: Nay, some Men are afraid of venturing even after themselves. By this Means several likely Women, that might do the Publick signal Service, are in a short time render'd useless: And, by a modest Computation, we are put to the Expence of as many virtuous Women in one Year, as might reasonably serve the Nation six.

Now, the *Publick Stews* will regulate this Affair so precisely, and with such critical Exactness, that one Year with another, we shall not have one Woman employ'd in the Publick Service more than is absolutely necessary, nor one less than is fully sufficient.

When this Project is first set on foot, the vast Choice and Variety there is at present of these Women, will give us an **[64]** Op-|portunity of making a very beautiful Collection; and will, doubtless, for some Time, occasion a considerable Run upon the Publick; so that *Private Whoring*, the only Nursery of our Courtezans, may probably remain too long neglected: For the whole Body of our incontinent Youth, like a standing Army,[161] being

---

[159] One can scarcely believe that the reasoning in this paragraph is meant to secure the reader's assent or approval. Are we to think that there are only two classes of women, the modest and the immodest, and that the latter group consists of those employed as prostitutes? Will the state "sacrifice" one modest woman because of its need to increase the ranks of licensed or approved prostitutes by one? Is there a bank or fund of national modesty that can be manipulated in this manner by calculating politicians who wish to keep that fund as large or as full as possible? Considering the absurdity of this "political arithmetic," should we continue to think that Mandeville seriously recommended state sponsorship and regulation of prostitution?

[160] Emperor Proculus (280–281 A.D.). Here again Mandeville borrows a passage from Montaigne's *Essais*, Book III, ch. 5 ("On some verses of Virgil"): in the Donald Frame translation (Stanford, 1958, 1968), p. 649; the Florio translation (Modern Library edition), p. 769; the Pléiade edition, p. 955.

[161] The phrase "standing army," which Mandeville exploits for its bawdy possibilities, was the focus of a pamphlet war (now called the "standing army controversy") which peaked between 1697 and 1699 during the reign of King William III. It continued to reverberate in the decades that followed. See Lois G. Schwoerer, "*No Standing Armies!*"

employ'd in constant Action, there cannot well be spar'd a sufficient Detachment to raise the necessary Recruits.

But however true this may be, we shall thereby suffer no Inconvenience; for if the Supplies of young Women, which we may reasonably expect from the Northern and Western Parts of these Kingdoms, or from such Places as are remote and out of the Influence of this *Scheme*: I say, if these Supplies should not prove sufficient to answer the greatness of the Demand, and that the Reputation of the *Stews* upon this Account, should begin to flag, why then the worst Accident that can befall, is a gradual Relapse into our former State of *Private Whoring*; and this no farther than is just necessary to recruit the *Stews*, and thereby make them retrieve their former Character: For every Woman that is debauch'd more than is barely necessary, only brings so much additional Credit and Reputation to the *Stews*, and in some measure atones for the Loss of her own Chastity, by being a Means **[65]** to preserve that of others; so that whenever the Tide of private Lewdness runs too high, and exceeds the just and ordinary Bounds, it must of Course, by encouraging the *Publick Stews*, immediately suffer a proportionable Ebb: That is to say, it must be reduced again so low, that there will remain but just a sufficient Quantity to supply the *Stews*: which is as low, as in the Nature of the Thing is possible.[162]

I might here lavish out Encomiums, and take Occasion to dwell upon those many Advantages that will accrue to the *Nation* by this admirable Scheme; but shall only take Notice of this peculiar Excellence, which it has above all other Schemes, that it necessarily executes itself.

But since the necessity of debauching a certain Number of young Women, is entirely owing to the Necessity of supplying the *Publick Stews*; a Question may very reasonably arise, whether this Project might not be vastly improv'd, even to the total Extirpation of *Private Whoring*, by an Act *for encouraging the Importation of foreign Women*.[163] This, I must confess, deserves a serious Debate: for, besides the Honour of our Females, which would be preserv'd by such an Act, it might bring this farther Advantage; That whereas most of our estated Youth spend a great Part of their **[66]** Time and Fortunes in travelling Abroad, for no other End, as it seems by most of them, but to be inform'd in the *French* and *Italian* Gallantry; they would then have an Opportunity of satisfying their Curiosity in foreign

---

[162] Though the speaker had previously stated that stern legal measures to curtail private whoring would have to be in force in order for his proposal to succeed, he now informs us that the survival of some private whoring will be essential for the replenishment of the new public stews, whenever necessary. He seems to imply that private whoring can never be completely eliminated.

[163] Mandeville knew that the pattern of the hypothetical legislation he has just named was commonplace. Earlier laws with similar language did exist, as in this example: "An Act for encouraging the Importation of Naval Stores from America" (1704 and later dates). The law that Mandeville contemplates anticipates the current worldwide trafficking in women and children for sexual and economic exploitation, a practice that is outlawed and discouraged by most modern nations.

Amours, without stirring out of *London*. But I shall leave the Decision of this Matter to abler Pens, well knowing, that a Truth of this Nature, which carries so much the Air of Novelty, will require much better Authority than mine to warrant it.

Let it suffice for the present, that I have fully prov'd what I at first propos'd in this Treatise: That *Publick Whoring* is neither so criminal in itself, nor so detrimental to the *Society*, as *Private Whoring*; and that the encouraging of *Publick Whoring*, by erecting *Stews* for that Purpose, will not only prevent most of the mischievous Consequences of this Vice, but even lessen the Quantity of *Whoring* in general, and reduce it to the narrowest Bounds which it can possibly be contain'd in.

After what has been said, it may, perhaps, appear somewhat odd to talk of Religious Objections, as if either Christianity or Morality could possibly object against a Scheme, which is entirely calculated for the Welfare and Happiness of Mankind. But since a **[67]** great many Men amongst us have entertained such whimsical Notions of Religion, as to imagine, that in some Cases, a Law may be unjust and wicked, tho' it evidently promotes the Publick Good; as if the right Enjoyment of this Life was inconsistent with our Happiness in the next: I say, since many Men of Understanding have suffer'd themselves to be possess'd with this mistaken Principle, I shall, as briefly as may be, answer such objections as can, with any colour of Reason, be offer'd.

First then, I expect to be attack'd with that old moral Precept, of *Not doing Evil that Good may come of it*.[164] This may be answer'd with another old Saying, equally authentick, and more applicable to the present Purpose, that *of two Evils we ought to chuse the least*. The Case is this: A private Member of a *Society*, may, doubtless, commit a Crime with a Design to promote the Good of that *Society*, which was partly the Case of *Felton* against the Duke of *Buckingham*; and this evil Action may possibly answer the Goodness of the Intention, but is universally condemn'd as an unwarrantable Presumption; and falls justly under the Censure of doing a certain

---

[164] The very old precept of "not doing evil that good may come of it," as Mandeville surely knew, is found in the New Testament in Romans 3:8 where the principle "Let us do evil, that good may come" is positively rejected. It gained new significance when Machiavelli posited his political maxim that the ends justify the means. Its later uses in the writings of Karl Marx ensured the survival of this doctrine as a living concept for all later writers on political theory. In proposing non-virtuous solutions to the problems of controlling the spread of syphilis and eliminating (or at least reducing) infanticide, Mandeville can be accused of thinking that in these instances the ends do justify the means, but his taking such a position does not at all turn him into a proto-Marxist. He also tried to avoid being associated with that formula by casting his entire proposal as "the lesser of two evils." It is barely possible that Mandeville was remembering the presence of this precept in an earlier work of whore fiction, *The London Jilt*, in which the whore (a first-person narrator) says (95–96), "Here it might be objected, that we must never do any mischief that good may come thereof, but my Maximes were wholy different from this, and I was very little concerned whether they were conformable or not with the Prophane or holy Philosophy."

Evil, for the Prospect of an uncertain Good.[165] But as to the *Legislature*, there is a wide Difference; for they, and they only, are **[68]** en-|trusted with the Welfare of the *Society*: This Publick Welfare is, or ought to be, the whole End and Scope of their Actions; and they are fully impower'd to do whatever they judge conducive to that End. If their Intentions come up to this, they are certainly in their Consciences acquitted: But as to the World, their Actions, that is, their Laws, are judg'd good or bad, just or unjust, according as they actually prove beneficial or detrimental to the *Society* in general: And therefore it is the grossest Absurdity, and a perfect Contradiction in Terms, to assert, That a *Government* may not commit Evil that Good may come of it; for, if a Publick Act, taking in all its Consequences, really produces a greater Quantity of Good, it must, and ought to be term'd a good Act; altho' the bare Act, consider'd in itself, without the consequent Good, should be in the highest Degree wicked and unjust.[166]

As for Instance: A Ship performing Quarantine, and known to be infected, is sunk by a Storm; some of the Crew, half drown'd, recover the Shore; but the moment they land, the *Government* orders them to be shot to Death; This Action, in itself, is no less than a downright unchristian and inhuman Murder: but since the Health and Safety of the Nation is secured by this severe Precaution, it is no Wonder, if we allow **[69]** the Action to be not only justifiable, but in the strictest Sense of Morality Just.[167]

---

[165] King Charles I's favorite courtier, George Villiers, Duke of Buckingham, was assassinated by an English soldier named John Felton on August 28, 1628 at Portsmouth. To the general public Felton appeared to have committed a heroic and beneficial deed, but the law required Felton's life and he was accordingly hanged on November 29, 1628.

[166] Mandeville was well aware that his defense of state needs (or "reasons of state") as a more compelling basis for political actions than biblical or Christian commandments was a position that many Christians rejected. His entire sentence here contains ambiguities and debatable concepts that beg for further analysis and clarification. How can anyone measure the results of legislation, a "public act," "taking in all its Consequences," and conclude with confidence that the results in general are either good or evil? Mandeville, moreover, knew well that human actions often have unintended and unforeseen consequences. We can sense here anticipations of nineteenth-century Utilitarianism with its felicific calculus and greatest happiness principle. To avoid admitting that there may be flaws in his argument, Mandeville makes his point swiftly, without stopping to consider its problematic implications.

[167] This example of murderous violence arising from a quarantine is not merely hypothetical and fortuitous: it relates to the active fear of many Britons in the early 1720s that the epidemic of the plague in the French port city, Marseilles, would spread to their own country. Defoe reported in 1721 that 315 persons attempting to escape from a quarantined section of the city of Toulon were shot. See Paula R. Backscheider, *Daniel Defoe: His Life*, 489. Mandeville's example here illustrates the state's decision to commit a "lesser evil" in order to avoid a potentially greater one, the spreading of the plague throughout the nation. Whether this example of extreme evil is comparable to the legislation that Mandeville recommends on behalf of state-sponsored prostitution is an open question. Is the deplorable state of "private whoring" (as he described it) really equivalent to the bubonic plague? It is hard to know how Mandeville would have answered this question, but it is quite clear that he is intent upon demonstrating the vital role of the state in securing the welfare of its citizens. (For a somewhat earlier reference to the plague of Marseilles, see his *Fable*, ed. Kaye, I, 384.)

Another Objection, or rather the same set in a stronger Light, is, That altho' the Welfare and Happiness of the Community is, or ought to be, the only End of all Law and Government, yet since our spiritual Welfare is the *Summum Bonum* which all Christians should aim at, no Christian Government ought to authorize the Commission of the least known Sin, tho' for the greatest temporal Advantage.

To this Objection, I answer, That it is universally allow'd as one of the greatest Perfections of the Christian Religion, that its Precepts are calculated to promote the Happiness of Mankind in this World as well as the next; if so, then it is a direct Arraignment of the Lawgivers infinite Wisdom, i.e. a Contradiction to assert, that, in Matters of Law and Government, the Publick Breach of any Gospel Precept can possibly be for the temporal Good of any *Society* whatever: And therefore we may with Confidence affirm, that no sinful Laws can be beneficial, and *vice versa*, that no beneficial Laws can be sinful. Now we have already given sufficient Proof of the Benefit the *Publick* would receive by licensing the *Stews*, and therefore ought to conclude such Licence lawful; but lest the apparent Wickedness of the *Stews*, **[70]** should be objected against this general Reasoning, it is fit that we examine this Matter a little nearer.

Fornication is, no doubt, a direct Breach of a *Gospel* Precept, and is therefore a Sin; but this Sin, barely as such, concerns the *Government* no more than the Eating of Black-puddings, equally prohibited in the same Text.[168] The Reason is this: The Sin consists in a full Intention to gratify a Lustful Desire; which Intention the *Legislature* cannot possibly prevent: penalties indeed may deter Men from gratifying their Desires, at the Expence of the Publick, but will rather increase than lessen the Desires themselves. If it is argu'd, that the Sin of the Intention is aggravated by being put in Execution, so much the better for our Purpose; for then the Argument stands thus:

Since the Sin of the Intention is entirely out of the *Legislature's* Power, the utmost they can do, with regard to this Sin, is, to prevent its being aggravated by actual Commission.

[71] But the *Publick Stews*, as we have already prov'd, will prevent as much as possible this actual Commission.

Therefore the *Publick Stews* will prevent as much as possible this SIN.[169]

---

[168] Acts, c.15. v.29. *That ye abstain from Meats offer'd to Idols, and from Blood, and from Things strangled and from Fornication: from which if ye keep yourselves*, ye do well. Fare ye well (Mandeville's footnote).

[169] The practice of using false logic deliberately in order to elicit laughter is centuries old and especially visible in academic and intellectual circles. In this paragraph Mandeville not only gives us a ridiculous syllogism but also adds one more paradox to a work in which paradoxes are used both for serious and for playful ends. In this instance the entire paragraph is offered as a joke because every reader knows very well that recourse to prostitutes in public stews (or anywhere else) does not limit fornication but increases it. It is an interlude of jesting and is as far removed from earnestness as anything in this book.

Another Branch of this Objection, without which the Objection itself would be of no Force, is, that the authorizing of *Publick Stews* is a Publick Encouragement for People to Whore.

If by People are meant those in the *Stews*, I hope it will be thought no Crime to encourage such People, rather to confine themselves to the Practice of one Vice, than live by committing a Thousand; especially when that one Vice is what they would really practise, whether they were encourag'd or not.

But if any imagine that this particular Licence would be a general Encouragement to the whole *Nation*, they are certainly mistaken. For, as to the Men, they are already as bad as they can be; if any Thing cures them, it must be *Satiety*; Let them have full and free Leave to take a Surfeit of unlawful Love, and they will soon learn to prefer the Chaste Embraces of Innocence before the bought Smile of Harlots loveless, joyless, unindear'd casual Fruition.[170]

[72] It is a right Observation, that Restraint does but whet a Man's Passions instead of curing them. ——— *Exuperat magis, ægrescitque medendo.* Æn.12.[171] And a late ingenious Author, who study'd Mankind, speaking on the Subject, has these Words: *To put down* Publick Stews, *is not only to disperse Fornication into all Parts, but, by the Difficulty, to excite wild and wanton People to this Vice.*[172]

---

[170] Without any hint to the reader, Mandeville appropriates a famous passage from Book IV of Milton's *Paradise Lost* and silently weaves it into the texture of his prose. The passage actually begins with IV, 750–751:

Hail wedded Love, mysterious law, true source
Of human offspring. . . .

Fifteen lines later Milton tells the reader that true love resides in the undefiled marriage bed, and

. . . not in the bought smile
Of harlots, loveless, joyless, unendeared,
Casual fruition . . .   [IV, 765–767]

This identification was previously noted by T.G.A. Nelson in "Women of Pleasure," 187. Nelson correctly observes that "Mandeville, though he dwells, as does Milton, on the sordidness of casual unions, offers no rhapsody on sex within marriage." Mandeville's use of these lines from Milton is a bit more complicated and ironic because, even while accepting Milton's condemnation of "the bought smile / Of harlots," Mandeville (or his invented persona) recommends a surfeit of fornication with harlots as a reliable pathway to marriage—something that Milton would never have accepted.

[171] Virgil, *Aeneid* Book XII, line 46: "exsuperat magis aegrescitque medendo" ("Grows all the stronger, all the sicker, with the cure,"—Frame's translation). Mandeville could have found this in any Latin edition of Virgil, but he probably found it in Montaigne's *Essais*, Book III, ch. 12 ("Of Physiognomy"): in Frame's edition, p. 796; in the Florio translation (Modern Library), p. 942; in the Pléiade edition, p. 1168. Montaigne quotes this line in the context of his deploring the civil war that has come to his estate.

[172] Here Mandeville quotes directly from Montaigne's "Apology for Raymond Sebond," *Essais*, II, 12: in Frame's translation, p. 440; in Florio's (Modern Library), p. 528; in the Pléiade edition, p. 658.

It was observ'd at *Rome*, that in the full Liberty of Divorces, there was not a single Instance of one in fifty Years: And that *Cato* long'd for his Wife again as soon as she was in another's Possession.[173]

The Master of Love says positively, *Quod licet ingratum est, quod non licet acrius urit.*[174] And *Martial* speaking to a married Rake, *B. 3. Ep.* 68. says,

> *Cur aliena placet tibi, quæ tua non placet uxor?*
> *Nunquid Securus non potes arrigere?*[175]

I prithee tell me why a Wife
    Thy am'rous Fancy never warms?
What! without Danger o'thy Life,
    Cannot thy Cod-piece stand to Arms?

[73]   And again, *B.1. Ep.*74.

> *Nullus in urbe fuit tota, qui tangere vellet*
> *Uxorem gratis, Caeciliane, tuam*
> *Dum licuit: sed nunc, positis custodibus, ingens*
> *Turba fututorum est. Ingeniosus homo es.*[176]

There's no Man, Caecil, in the Town,
    Would, *gratis*, have enjoy'd thy spouse;
But now thou are so jealous grown,
    Lord! what a Croud about the House!
You've lock'd her up, t'increase her Value:
In short, you are a cunning Fellow.

---

[173] Mandeville continues to quote from Montaigne, this time from II, 15—"That our desire is increased by difficulty." See Frame, p. 464; Florio, p. 555; Pléiade edition, p. 692. It thus appears that, among the authors that Mandeville borrowed from in composing this pamphlet, Montaigne was his major source, but perhaps second to his own "Remark (H.)" published ten years earlier.

[174] The "Master of Love" is Ovid; the quotation is from his *Amores* (or *Love Books*), Book II, Elegy xix, line 3: "What is permitted, we scorn; we more eagerly pursue what is forbidden." Mandeville probably found this in Montaigne's essay II, 15 ("That our desire is increased by difficulty"): Frame, p. 466; Florio, p. 558; Pléiade edition, p. 695.

[175] These lines from Martial's *Epigrammata* [*Epigrams*], Book III, no.70 (in modern editions; not 68 as Mandeville has it) appear in Montaigne, II, 12, "Apology for Raymond Sebond." See Frame, p. 441; Florio, p. 528; Pléiade edition, p. 659.

[176] In Martial's *Epigrammata* [*Epigrams*], Book I, no. 73 (not 74, as given by Mandeville). See Frame, p. 441; Florio, p. 528; Pléiade edition, p. 659. In both cases the English verse translations are most likely by Mandeville himself. In one of his earliest publications, *Some Fables after the Easie and Familiar Method of Monsieur de la Fontaine* (London, 1703), he included his own translation of two of La Fontaine's fables. The two translations here reflect his proclivity for the "low" style of burlesque poetry, of which Butler's *Hudibras* is one of the best examples. More of his erotic poetry in this vein appeared in his pamphlet *Wishes to a Godson, with other Miscellany Poems* (London, 1712). Mandeville's

The *Publick Stews* will not encourage Men to be lewd, but they will encourage them to exercise their Lewdness in a proper Place, without disturbing the Peace of the *Society*, and with as little Detriment to themselves as possible. And, as to the Women, there's not the least Shadow of Encouragement: For no modest Woman ever lost her Maiden-head with the dismal Prospect of becoming a *Publick* **[74]** *Cour-|tezan*: And if a Woman is not modest, the licensing of the *Publick Stews* is no more an Encouragement for her to practise, than the allowing a certain Number of Hackney-Coaches every *Sunday* is an Encouragement for the rest to ply; when the very Licence, to some, expresly implies a Prohibition of the rest.

Having now sufficiently proved the Institution of the *Publick Stews* to be a Political Good, and answer'd all the religious Objections against it; I shall conclude with observing, That I have the Authority of *Italy*, the most Politick Nation in the World, to back me in the first Part of my Argument; and the Opinion of *Holland*, one of the strictest Reformed Churches, to vindicate me in the second;[177] and that we ourselves enjoy'd the Benefit of this Institution till we were depriv'd of it by the over-hasty Zeal of our first Reformers in the sixteenth Century.

The *Publick Stews* were antiently kept in *Southwark*, if not by an express Licence from the Government, at least by an open Permission; though we have most Reason to believe the first, since they paid regular Taxes both to the *Lord-Mayor* of the City, and to the Bishop of the See.

[75] We do not find that they were ever molested 'till the 25th of *Edward* the Third, when, in the Parliament at *Westminster*, at the Request of the *Londoners*, says *Daniel*, [1] an Act pass'd, obliging all Common Whores to distinguish themselves, by wearing Hoods striped with divers Colours, or Furs, and their Gowns turn'd inside out.[178]

---

translations of Martial here reinforce the view that, in addition to any serious social and medical reforming that the author appears to support, his essay is intended as a literary showpiece, a space in which he exploits the comic possibilities of classical learning, including history, logic, and rhetoric.

[177] Mandeville's claims that both Italian political authority and Dutch Reformed religious thought support his argument would raise any reader's eyebrow. There may be a grain of truth in his remark, but these claims are probably part of the fun he is having with the forms of academic logic. In his medical treatise his spokesman is Philopirio or "lover of experience." Mandeville's medical practice proceeds empirically, and it certainly does not involve curing by means of Aristotelian syllogistic logic. The very fact that the success of his case for public stews depends on his skill in handling deductive syllogistic logic should make his readers suspect that something is amiss. However, granting him his pleasure in playing with the ancient forms of rhetoric and logic, most readers will continue to regard his core proposal to regulate and clean up the public stews as the central message of his pamphlet.

[178] See Samuel Daniel, *The Collection of the Historie of England*, By S.D. London, Printed by Nicholas Okes, dwelling in Foster-Lane for the Author, 1618, 205. A photographic reprint of this edition was published by Scholars' Facsimiles and Reprints (Delmar, New York, 1986). Mandeville's historical sketch should not be taken as authoritative and it is certainly incomplete. Ruth M. Karras reports, with supporting documentation, that "At least as early as 1277, the city

This, indeed, was but a Trifle to what they suffer'd thirty Years after by *Wat Tyler*'s Rebellion.

In the fifth of *Richard* the Second, *Wat* marched up from *Dartmouth*, with a true Spirit of Reformation, fully resolv'd to burn and destroy every thing that oppos'd him: If the Archbishop's Palace at *Lambeth* could not escape, there was little Mercy to be expected for the *Stews*; besides, Whoring was not the least of *Wat*'s Grievances: He began his Rebellion by killing a Collector of the Poll-Tax for being a little too brisk upon his Daughter; and his Antipathy to the *Stews* was still encreas'd, by the *Lord-Mayor's* shutting the City-Gates, and denying him Entrance; for he could not revenge the Affront more effectually, than by cutting off so large a Branch of his Lordship's Revenue.[179]

In short, everything concurred to the Destruction of the *Stews*, and demolished they were.

[76]   This Action, however, lost *Tyler* his Life; for *Will. Wallworth*, the then Lord-Mayor, was the very Man that struck him first off his Horse in *Smithfield*: For which the King knighted him, gave him a hundred Pounds Pension, and added the Dagger to the City-Arms.[180]

Whilst Whoring was in this unsettled Condition, the *Bishop* thought it a good Opportunity to ingross the whole Profit of licensing Courtezans, which occasion'd them fresh Trouble; for *John Northampton*, who succeeded *Walworth*, either piqued at the Bishop's invading his Right, or out of a real reforming Principle, for he was a follower of *Wickliff*, commenced a severe Persecution.[181] He had his Spies and Constables in every Street, to apprehend Strollers; and such Women as were neither handsome nor rich enough to bribe his Officers, were carried through the Streets in great Pomp, with their Hair Shorn, and Trumpets and Pipes playing before

[London] prohibited any 'whore of a brothel' from living within the walls. . . . [and] In 1310 Edward II ordered the mayor and sheriff of London to abolish brothels, which were harboring thieves and murderers." See Karras, *Common Women*, 14–15. On sumptuary legislation introducing a dress code for whores, see p. 21. Her entire first chapter, "Prostitution and the Law," is relevant to these closing pages of Mandeville's pamphlet.

[179] Most accounts of Wat Tyler's rebellion (the Peasants' Revolt of June 1381) do not include details of his attack upon the stews. This month-long revolt of peasants from Essex, Kent, and East Anglia, protesting the recent imposition of a poll tax that was unacceptable to the poorer classes, came to an end in London. After taking many lives including those of the Chancellor Archbishop Simon of Sudbury and the Treasurer, Sir Robert Hales, Wat Tyler was killed by London's mayor William Walworth and others loyal to the young King Richard II. A few leaders of the rebellion were captured and beheaded, but most of the peasants were allowed to return to their homes and a general amnesty was declared in December of that year.

[180] E.J. Burford (*Bawds and Lodgings*, p. 78) notes that "when Walworth stabbed Wat Tyler to death, he surely had in mind less his loyalty to the King than the fact that Tyler had burnt down his whorehouses and released the whores from bondage."

[181] John Wyclif (or Wycliffe, or other variants; ca 1328–1384), the most important ecclesiastical reformer in England before the Reformation, is also famous for having been the leading translator among those who produced the so-called Wyclif bible, the first translation of the Latin of the Vulgate into Middle English.

them. All this he did contrary to the express Commands of the Bishop, who had several Bickerings with him upon that Head.[182]

This great Reformer *John Northampton* was, from his troublesome Temper, nick-nam'd *Cumber-Town*; and as he succeeded *Tyler* in the Work of Reformation, so he had like to have met with as bad a Fate: **[77]** For two Years after he was found guilty of High-Treason, without making the least Defence; had his Goods confiscated, and was condemned to perpetual Imprisonment a hundred Miles from *London*: Accordingly he was sent to *Tentagil-Castle* in *Cornwall*.[183]

This dreadful *Cumber-Town* being removed, the Stews had leisure to re-settle themselves under the Protection of the Church; and enjoyed an almost uninterrupted Tranquillity for an hundred and fifty Years.

We find, indeed, an Act passed at *Westminster*, in the 11th of *Hen*. the 6th, that no Keepers of *Stews*, or *Whore-Houses*, in *Southwark* should be impannelled upon any Jury, or keep a Tavern in any other Place.[184]

But the most sensible Blow they ever felt, was the Invasion of the *French-Pox*. The Spaniards had brought it from the Islands of *Florida* to *Naples*, and the Army

---

[182] According to G.M. Trevelyan, "One day a dense mob, headed by the Mayor himself, marched across London Bridge, raided the stews and pilloried a number of the unhappy occupants. . . . The real motive, as churchmen complained, was to protest against ecclesiastical jurisdiction by an open usurpation of the Bishop's privileges. Perhaps the Mayor was also aiming a blow at Walworth by exposing his discreditable property [i.e., his share in the stews]." (*England in the Age of Wycliffe*, 1909, p. 280.) The repressive and punitive measures taken by John of Northampton and his officers against strollers (presumed to be harlots) appears to fit easily into Mandeville's conclusion. But it also adds a bonus of symmetry to the entire essay because the activities described in this passage closely resemble those of the "Gentlemen of the Societies" described by Mandeville in his dedication. Moreover, John of Northampton's conflict with William of Wykeham, the Bishop of Winchester, reflects the conflict between church and state that is mentioned or alluded to in the confutation section and elsewhere in this discourse.

[183] In an online review of the political struggles in London in the 1380s, we learn that Robert Cumberton was the brother of John of Northampton and that the surname Cumberton was sometimes used to refer to Northampton as well as to other family members. See Stephen Alsford's informative website:

www.trytel.com/~tristan/towns/florilegium/government/gvpoli24.htm.

This information differs from Mandeville's remark that "Cumber-Town" was John of Northampton's nickname and that it was associated with his "troublesome Temper." John of Northampton, a loyal follower of John of Gaunt and of Wycliffe, served as Lord Mayor of London, after Walworth, from 1381 to 1383. Thereafter his enemy Sir Nicholas Brembre became Lord Mayor. John of Northampton was eventually ruined by Brembre through a charge of treason. After noting the relationship of Wat Tyler and John of Northampton to the stews and whores of Southwark, Mandeville apparently thought that details of the murder of Wat Tyler by Walworth and the conviction and imprisonment of John of Northampton would be useful. The speaker, either Mandeville or his invented persona, almost delights in their having had unfortunate conclusions to their careers, as fitting punishments for their interference with the peaceful operation of the Southwark stews.

[184] The most famous reference to the Southwark stews in the time of Henry VI is probably the line that the Duke of Gloucester speaks to Henry Beaufort, Bishop of Winchester, in Shakespeare's *1 Henry VI* (I, iii, 35): "Thou that giv'st whores indulgences to sin."

of *Charles* the 8th, when he conquer'd that Kingdom in the Year 1495, transmitted it into *France*, from whence it had a very quick Passage into *England*; for there was an Act passed in the latter end of *Henry* the 7th's Reign, for expelling out of the *Stews* all such Women as had the Faculty of burning Men.[185]
[78]   However, we find they still continued in good Repute in the Reign of *Henry* the 8th,[186] and yielded a considerable Revenue to the *Bishop* of *London*; for *Bucer*, in one of his Books against *Gardiner*, taxes him with it as an heinous Crime, that he should receive most of his Rents out of the *Publick Stews*.[187]

After this terrible Accusation, we may easily guess what Quarter our *Stews* met with at the Reformation. But now *Bucer* has got his ends; the *Stews* are destroy'd; those publick Nusances are demolish'd; Whoring is attack'd on all hands without Mercy; and what then? Why, truly, by mere

---

[185] This account of the transfer of syphilis from the New World to Europe was well known in Mandeville's time. In 1530 it appeared in Fracastoro's poem called *Syphilis; Sive, de morbus Gallicus* (i.e., *Syphilis; or, The French Disease*). Mandeville would have known many accounts of the origins and spread of syphilis, including the opening chapter of John Marten's *Gonosologium Novum* (1709). For accounts of the ongoing debate about the origins of syphilis, see the articles by the late Stephen J. Gould and Kevin P. Siena, listed in our bibliography below.

The act for removing those women from the stews who had the power to "burn" men (i.e., infect them with venereal disease) is reported by John Stow in his *Survey of London* (1603): "No stewholder to keepe any woman that hath the perilous infirmitie of burning, nor to sell bread, ale, flesh, fish, wood, coale or any victuals, &c." Stow, however, assigns this legislation to the eighth regnal year of Henry II, or 1161; see the edition of Stow by C.L. Kingsford (Oxford: Clarendon Press, 1908,1971) II, 55. For Stow on the regulation of the stews, see further the next footnote and the extract reprinted from *A Collection of Chirurgical Tracts* (1740), below.

[186] In *A Collection of Chirurgical Tracts* by William Beckett, a posthumous collection published by Edmund Curll (London, 1740), Curll quietly included a reprint of *A Modest Defence*, which he now attributed to Luke Ogle, Esq. with a new title, "The *Natural* Secret History of *both Sexes*." Among the minor changes made in this text is the inclusion of a new footnote precisely at this point. The footnote reads as follows: "In the latter end of *March* (Anno Reg. Hen. VIII. 36) 'the *Stewes* on the Bank-side of the *Thames*, in *Southwark*, was put down, by the King's Commandment, which was proclaimed by sound of Trumpets, no more to be privileged, or used as a common Bordell, but the Inhabitants of those Houses, to keep good and honest Rule, as in all other places of the Realm.['] Stow's Chron. P. 591." The date commonly assigned for this event is 1546. The *English Short Title Catalogue* lists the following title for the Elizabethan John Stow (who also wrote the popular *Survey of London*): *The summarie of Englyshe chronicles. . . . Vnto 1598.* London: R. Bradocke, 1598. (Information on medieval English prostitution contained in *A Collection of Chirurgical Tracts* is listed further.)

[187] The Continental reformer Martin Bucer (1491–1551), in one of his later responses to charges and aspersions cast upon him by Stephen Gardiner, Bishop of Winchester, accused Gardiner of savoring the sweetness "of the luker, which he receaued out of the fylthye commune brothel-houses or stewhouse[s]" i.e., rents from the Bankside properties owned for centuries by the Bishops of Winchester. This passage appears on (unnumbered) p. 105 of Bucer's *The Gratulation of the mooste famous Clerke M. Martin Bucer . . . Translated out of Latin in to Englishe.* [London, 1549]; Pollard and Redgrave STC (second edition), no. 3963. Since Mandeville usually cited his quotations and references to rarer works from more recent secondary sources such as Bayle's *Dictionnaire historique et critique*, we might guess that he found this information not in the 1549 source named above but in a more recent account of events in the English Reformation.

dint of Reforming, we have reduced Lewdness to that pass, that hardly one Batchelor in the Kingdom will lie with a Woman, if he is sure that she's not sound; and very few modest women will suffer a Man to get them with Child, unless he makes a Promise to marry. In short, the Truth is, we are at this present Writing as bad as we can be; and I hope I have fairly shown how we may be better.[188]

FINIS.

---

[188] Mandeville's concluding remark is deliberately ambiguous: what precisely does he mean by "bad" and "better"? We can easily guess that the speaker does not mean the "bad" and "better" of common morality or religious instruction. The voice or persona at the end seems to suggest yet again the character of a rake or debauchee, revealing the same traits that the reader encountered in the opening paragraph where this rakish personality accuses "the Gentlemen of the Societies" of "stopping up those *Drains* and *Sluices* we had to let out our Lewdness." (See our extended remarks in "Authorship," listed further.)

[The next four paragraphs comprise the anonymous "Answer" that was added to *A Modest Defence* in its first reprinting, dated 1725. The printer is no longer identified as "A. Moore near St. Paul's" but as "A. Bussy in Ivy-Lane." Original page numbers are again inserted here in bold type and within brackets, but now the year is given with the page number, as in this example: **[1725:58]**. Speculations on the authorship of the "Answer" will appear in a footnote.]

[1725:58]   *ANSWER*

If ever a publick Temptation was publickly laid in the way of every Man, that is dispos'd to be vicious, this Book, which is call'd *A Modest Defence of Publick Stews*, &c. is such in the most palpable and flagrant degree that ever the Press was debauch'd with. The Title, in plain English, is *A Modest Defence of the most impious Immodesty*; a Title not more absurd and senseless than the Subject is obscene and shameless. The Author seems to have aped that superlative Composition, lately publish'd with the Title of *Private Vices, Publick Benefits*; or it may be, both these Books come from one Hand, for the same pernicious Spirit runs alike thro' each of 'em.

While I admir'd at his unparallel'd Impudence, in Dedicating it to the *Gentlemen of the Societies*, I own, I could not help smiling, when a serious Friend of mine wish'd some of our Right Reverends would Answer this mischiveous [sic] Tract, call'd the *Modest Defence*. To confute such a Libel as this Paragraphically wou'd be raking in a Lay-stall, and making the Stink the more unsufferable. I doubt not, but the chaste Author if [read, of] it longs for nothing so much as an Answer, that it may enlarge the Demand for his Book, and enable him to pay off some of his Scores at the *Gin-Shops*. But I shall not trouble my self, or the World, with any other, than the following, which I humbly presume, will be thought the fittest, as well as the concisest Answer that such a vile Performance deserves.

[1725:59] The Gentlemen to whome that mis-called *Modest Defence*, is inscrib'd are certainly in *Best of Causes*; and notwithstanding all that abominable Sneer, in that very modest Dedication, they seem hitherto to have prosecuted the laudable Ends they have in view by the best Means, and purest Intentions. 'Tis owing to these Gentlemen that so many notorious Houses of Lewdness have been shut up, so many Advocates for it silenc'd, and that even our Plays are writ with much more Modesty and acted with more Decency. And if the bashful Author of *the Modest Defence*, &c. will but send his Name, and that of his Garret, to any of the Gentlemen here treated of, he may depend on a speedy Answer.

What follows is a Summary Account of the Usefulness and Success of certain *Societies*, who have been the greatest Instruments in supressing Vice in general, and that sort of it in particular, which that graceless Writer of the *Modest Defence* has so much labour'd to promote.[189]

---

[189] In a critical essay following his translation of this work into Italian, Dario Castiglione speculates that the reprinting of *A Modest Defence* in 1725 with the "Answer" and the annual report of the SRMs was probably a contrivance or scheme by the publisher for legitimizing that reprint. See Castiglione's translation, *Modesta difesa delle pubbliche case di piacere* (1989), p. 10. Reasons for believing that Mandeville had no part in the 1725 edition of *A Modest Defence* are presented in the Notes on the Text. See further remarks on authorship in the Commentaries.

[In 1740, seven years after the death of Mandeville, the notorious publisher Edmund Curll surreptitiously included a reprint of *A Modest Defence* in *A Collection of Chirurgical Tracts* that were "Written and Collected" by William Beckett, a recently deceased physician. This last phrase presumably allowed Curll to add *A Modest Defence* to this collection attributed to Beckett. The title page gives no hint whatever that this collection of medical pieces would also include Mandeville's piece on the stews. Only those who had had previous acquaintance with earlier printings of this work would have recognized it under its new title, which is first seen in the table of contents as "*The Natural* Secret History *of both Sexes. By* Luke Ogle, *Esq.*" Only when one arrives at the title page for this work inside the book does one see its subtitle: *or, A Modest Defense of Public Stews. With an Account of the Present State of Whoring in these Kingdoms.* This work, a fairly faithful reprint of Mandeville's *Modest Defence*, is followed by an appendix describing earlier English regulations on whores and brothels. It appears to have been added as a supplement to Mandeville's concluding historical survey of regulations and ordinances concerning the stews in England.]

From A Collection of Chirurgical Tracts (*London: E. Curll, 1740*)

APPENDIX
NUMBER I.

RICHARD RAWLINSON, L.L.D. and R.S.S. in his Account of *Southwark*,[190] informs us, that next to the *Bear-Garden* on the Bank–Side was formerly the BORDELLO, or STEWES, so called from several Licensed Houses for the Entertainment of Lewd Persons, in which were Women prepared for all Comers. They were subject to several Laws and Regulations, and their Manner of Life and Privileged Places, received several Confirmations from the Crown.

In 1162, King *Henry* II, in a *Parliament* held at *Westminster*, passed an Act, confirming several Ordinances, Statutes, and old Customs observed in that Place, amongst which the following are remarkable:

That no *Stew-Holder* or his Wife, should lett or stay any single Woman to go and come freely at all Times when she listed.

[190] See *Aubrey's* Natural History and Antiquities of *Surrey, 8vo*. Vol. V. p. 221 (footnote added to this 1740 edition).

[78]   No *Stewholder* to keep any Woman to board, but she to board abroad at her Pleasure.

To take no more for the Woman's Chamber than *fourteen* Pence.

Not to keep open his Doors upon the Holy-days.

Not to keep any single Woman in his House on the Holy-days, but the *Bailiff* to see them voided out of the Lordship.

No single Woman to be kept against her Will, that would leave her Sin.

No *Stew-Holder* to receive any Woman of Religion, or any Mans Wife.

No single Woman to take Money to lie with any Man, except she lye with him all Night, till the Morrow.

No Man to be drawn or enticed into any *Stew-House*.

The *Constables*, *Bailiffs*, and others, were every Week to search every *Stew-House*.

No *Stew-Holder* to keep any Woman that hath the perillous Infirmity of *Burning*, nor to sell Bread, Ale, Flesh, Fish, Wood, Coal, or any sort of Victuals.[191]

Anno 1345, Stews were licenced by King *Edward* III. Anno 1381, these Stew-Houses belonged to *William Walworth*, Lord-Mayor of *London*, who let them out to some *Flemish* Women, and soon after they were plundered by *Walter Tyler*, and the rebellious *Kentishmen*, when **[79]** proba-|bly they were put down, and again suffered, and afterwards confirmed by *Henry* VI. In 1506, King *Henry* VII. for some Time shut up these Houses, which were in Number *Eighteen*, and not long after renewed their Licence, and reduced them to *Twelve*; at which Number they continued till their final Suppression by Sound of Trumpet, in 1546, by King *Henry* VIII, whose tender Conscience startled at such scandalous and open Lewdness. The single Women who were Retainers to, or Inmates in, these Houses, were excommunicated, not suffered to enter the Church while alive, or if not reconciled before their Death, prohibited Christian Burial, and were interred in a Piece of Ground called the *Single-Women's Church-Yard*, set a-part for their Use only. These Houses were distinguished by several Signs painted on their Fronts, as, a *Boar's-Head*, the *Crane*, the *Cardinal's Hat*, the *Swan*, the *Bell*, the *Castle*, the *Cross-Keys*, and the *Gun*.

---

[191] This list of regulations and the paragraphs that follow were extracted from John Stow's *A Survey of London*, published in 1603 and often reprinted. See the edition of Stow's *Survey* by Charles Lethbridge Kingsford, 54–55.

Regulated stews, recommended (1).
[An anonymous article from
The Gentleman's Magazine,
vol. 19 (July 1749), pp. 314–315.]

From the OLD ENGLAND, July 15.
Of the Sailors' demolishing Baudy houses.
Licens'd Stews recommended.
[*See* Hist. Chron. July 1]

THO' the Sailors are in no wise to be justified for this unlucky intermeddling out of their element, yet a great deal may be said in extenuation of the guilt of making reprisals among the pestiferous receptacles of aggregate filth and iniquity. It must be owned to be a very hard case, that, when an honest devotee to *Neptune* is seduced to pay his vows to the altar of *Venus*, he should be robbed in the midst of his devotion, while his attention is engaged in honour of the Goddess; and before he can recollect his scattered senses, loses sight of the thief forever, or perhaps dares not resist, or even murmur, for fear of being knocked on the head.—This naturally prompts a man to avenge his own cause; and, since he can't obtain justice, take it in such a manner as he can. After a hapless drudge has been toss'd upon the ocean in the service of his country, for perhaps a great many years, to be ensnared into a house of destruction, with all that he has painfully earned for such a series of time in his pocket, and to be robbed of all at last, is not only a very great hardship upon the sufferer, but a high reflection upon the government of a nation that permits such nests of pyratical seducers. [*whose power, as described by the* wise man, *he shews, and goes on:*]

The prevalence of these alluring *degenerates*, is so well known to all the nations on the continent, more especially maritime countries, that they have wisely restrained greater vices by *lesser*, in erecting public stews for the gratification of inordinate passions, under proper regulations of behaviour, price, and entertainment.—These, it seems, it is no discredit to frequent.

The guest has nothing to apprehend from ill usage either in his amorous dalliances, or table regales. He sleeps in peace and safety, and knows his pockets are sacred against the approach of unhallow'd fingers. These are not novelties, for we read of them among the antients, not as iniquitous tolerations, but, on the contrary, so very commendable, that we find *Cato*, with all his inflexible virtue, recommending the frequenting of the stews, as a laudable practice, to a young man whom he surprized just coming out of one of them; insinuating, it was much better to see him there, than in attempting the honour of his neighbour's family. There is no doubt of these places having been considered by the antients, as well as the moderns, as so many protections to the chastity of their wives and daughters.

We not only find Roman Catholic countries, but those of protestants too, licensing such houses, and drawing considerable taxes out of them for the public benefit.—Our prejudices *too long* prevailed against falling in with the other countries, in erecting Hospitals for *Foundling Children*; but, having ventur'd to break the ice of obstinacy and folly, we now experience the public utility of such an hospital, and wonder we grew no sooner wise, for the benefit and preservation of human kind.[192]

I shall be rallied by the wags of the town, as growing wanton in my old age, and becoming an advocate for establishing the propagation of vice and immorality, according to law. Perhaps too some over-nice constitutions may join them with their serious reflections against me. To the first I answer, that they will have no reason to complain of a regular accommodation of this kind, as it will contribute not a little to lessen their expences, and allay the anguish of imaginary apprehensions and real pains. Surgeons, apothecaries, and *some justices*, indeed, may have reason to stir up an opposition to a project that may hurt their trade. The art also of picking pockets imperceptibly may be lost, for want of practice, among the women, under the regulation of the price and behaviour; but then these poor creatures will be less exposed to the brutal buffetings of rakes and bullies, to correction in *Bridewell*, and involuntary visits to our plantations abroad.—The scandalous connivance at brothel houses, and the methods used to furnish them with fresh supplies of women, is too shocking to be mentioned! It is high time for reformation, and monstrously shameful that it should be so long delay'd, 'till an act of the suffering *mob* should point out the necessity of it, at the expence of liberty, and perhaps of life.

---

[192] The Foundling Hospital established in 1739 by Captain Thomas Coram was supported by Hogarth, Handel, and other artists; it also had a royal charter. Though the original building no longer exists, the work of the Coram Foundation is still carried on. Similar charities later appeared.

Regulated stews, recommended (2).
[From (Anonymous), Reflections Arising from the Immorality of the Present Age . . . (London, Printed for M. Cooper . . . 1756).]

[p. 51]   That Brothels are already but too public, may seem, and even has been censured as, a grievance of no trivial consequence, and yet we see them so far tolerated, as to be (if you'l admit the expression) publickly connived at, not in an obscure recess, or private place, but in the midst, the heart of our Metropolis; and though nothing would discountenance their present ill effects so much, as being brought under some proper regulations, with what contempt, nay with what fury, would any serious proposition be received, to establish them by law; the odious appellation of A PUBLIC STEW carries so harsh an inuendo with it, that people would be persuaded to believe, an institution of such a nature little better than an open violation of all laws, both human and divine; witness the wrong constructions and unmeaning sarcasms that are still daily vented against that glorious one, the Foundling-House, and we should therefore have books and ballads, prints and news papers, exhibited against such a design, with as much virulency and indignation, as were lately against the memorable *Jew bill*, when, at the same time, the cause of Virtue might be as much out of the question in the clamour against the one, as was, perhaps, that of Christianity, amongst most of the opponents to the other.

Give me leave, however, to carry the reflection a little further.

[52]   I shall pass over the many particular advantages resulting from such an institution, they having been so fully treated of, in a certain Pamphlet published some years ago, as to make any thing I could say of that head impertinent,[193] but as a very principal benefit might accrue from such

---

[193] [Here follows the footnote inserted at this point in the 1756 text:] "A treatise to prove the reasonableness and benefit of public whoring, by a toleration of public stews, by Col. H. Mordaunt, in 1743." This reference to "Col. H[arry] Mordaunt" and to the year 1743 strongly suggests that *A Modest Defence* is the pamphlet meant by this anonymous author. This author may have erred in recalling the exact title and date, or perhaps he was deliberately being inaccurate. A search for the title in this footnote yielded no positive result.

an establishment, which was either looked over by that judicious author, or purposely omitted, who (though I acknowledge myself unequal in schemes of this nature to such an adept) seems to have formed his plan as much with a view to private pleasure, as for the promoting a public benefit; and since the still permitting ladies of the town (the softest appellation I can give them) openly to haunt our chief assemblies, and brazen in the very face of quality, seems a nuisance which even that piece, elaborate as it is, has not considered as an evil, I shall confine my sentiments on such a scheme only to that particular.

The prevailing taste in the article of dress is raised so high, that any thing in the Attire, which may visibly denote a modest woman, is reckoned ungenteel, because it is commonly out of fashion, few of our new-invented modes being perfectly conformable to the rules of decency, it being a fundamental laid down by most of our modern belles, *to look as engaging as they can*† [† Vide *Guardian*, No. 10]; but though custom and fashion goes a great way in sanctifying every thing, the observation of a certain modern **[53]** Author seems just, when he tells us, that any thing in the attire, which has an effect too alluring, cannot be said to be strictly decent; and if we consider the source from whence most of our modern whims are taken (I mean those inviting allurements, the short pettycoats, the tristed [twisted?] hat, the dangling ribbands, with a long &c. we shall find it would be palpably inconsistent with the design of their first institution, to expect they should be so; and if those, whom we cannot but acknowledge to be really modest women, will not forbear catching these inticing airs from wretches, who for their daily bread are compelled to hang out such *Signs*, and stretch every action to the outside of modesty, what wonder that the whole promiscuous throng of females in general, pass under the common censure of light, wanton, and fantastic? Or, how can women of virtue expect to have that difference [i.e., deference] paid them they deserve, when they cannot by any means be distinguished from Hirelings and Prostitutes?[194] [etc.]

---

[194] Our anonymous author seems to be recommending Mandeville's proposal for regulating the public stews, and while doing so he adds a "public benefit" that Mandeville did not mention or emphasize, namely, that a new system of regulated stews would restore dress codes that would enable the public to distinguish easily between a prostitute and a woman of virtue and modesty.

Commentaries

Audience

Mandeville's critics in his own time and toward the twentieth century frequently characterized his writing as coarse and vulgar. If we include the anonymous *Modest Defence* in the list of his works then those terms might apply to parts of this work. Yet in a famous passage in which he specifies the audience for whom he is writing, he takes an elitist position, attempting to separate himself from hoi polloi and their vulgarity:

> But as nothing would more clearly demonstrate the Falsity of my Notions, than that the generality of the People should fall in with them, so I don't expect the Approbation of the Multitude. I write not to many, nor seek for any Well-wishers, but among the few that can think abstractly, and have their minds elevated above the Vulgar. If I have shewn the way to worldly Greatness, I have always without Hesitation preferr'd the Road that leads to Virtue.[195]

His elitist posture is also visible when he argues that large and powerful nation-states require vast numbers of poor, uneducated workers to labor as drudges. On the other hand, he had some unkind words for members of the nobility and aristocracy, especially Anthony Ashley Cooper, the third Earl of Shaftesbury.

Mandeville knew that *A Modest Defence*, or at least its bawdy passages, would appeal to readers who were interested in sex and prostitution. His classical quotations and allusions, however, were aimed at a smaller group, those who had received a classical education (usually at a university) and were highly literate—and virtually all in this group were males. Some of these university-educated males became educators, quite a few became clergymen, others became MDs, while yet others entered the legal profession to become barristers and eventually judges. Many readers in these groups would have recognized Mandeville's aims as a rhetorician.

---

[195] From "Remark (T.)" of his *Fable of the Bees* (ed. F.B. Kaye, I, 231).

Predictably the clergy, theologians, and avid supporters of Christianity would find his pamphlet repulsive. He provokes them in various ways. He aims his ridicule at the deceased Bishop Burnet and at Dr. Samuel Clark, but is careful not to provide every letter in their names. He is even more careful when he merely alludes to Bishop Gibson's sermon on masquerades to the SRMs without naming him. He knew that many clerics were attracted to heretical or irreligious texts which permitted them to display their skills in published controversy. In general one could expect them to denounce anyone who recommended a policy of tolerating fornication.

Though he had earned his MD and reportedly practiced medicine, there is no reason to think that in *A Modest Defence* he had something new to say to his fellow physicians. Yet if he could not teach them something new and important, he might at least try to amuse them. It is possible that a reaction or response to this work by an eighteenth-century physician may be discovered, but meanwhile I know of none.

There are surely other callings or groups of individuals who might have been attracted to his pamphlet, but a particularly important subset of these readers would be those whom the author appears to address directly, and these readers fall into two groups. The first and most obvious group consists of those to whom he dedicated his *A Modest Defence*, the "gentlemen" of the Societies for the Reformation of Manners (the SRMs). A few of them may have had university training, but most of them would not have been highly literate. The sophisticated syntax and complex wit of his dedication would have been too difficult for many of those so-called gentlemen to grasp.

When we move beyond Phil-Porney's Dedication and Preface to his main essay, we gradually realize that Mandeville is now addressing the nation's legislators (see pp. [12] and [15]). We would identify them as MPs, members of Britain's Parliament, but for whatever reason he refers to them simply as legislators and speaks almost always of "a National Senate." In the only passage where he uses the word "Parliament" (p. 75 of the 1724B edition), he refers to a Parliament in the reign of Edward III. He may have avoided addressing living members of Parliament for prudential reasons. Although he used two pseudonyms, "A Layman" and "Phil-Porney," his critics would have been sufficiently aware of his true identity. In any event, he seems to suggest that his proposal is being presented to members of the highest assembly in the land. It is clear that these legislators were his intended audience and that he addressed his proposal to them.

That practically all members of these groups would have been males leads us to wonder how many women had read this book. I have not seen a single reference to it by any woman writer in that century. Any admission by a woman that she had read it could well have marked her as immodest.

It is interesting to consider, furthermore, that a very specific audience, the Middlesex Grand Jury, did not "present" this pseudonymous work as a public nuisance, as it had done the previous year with the third edition of Mandeville's *Fable of the Bees*. Was his support of state-regulated prostitution less annoying or less dangerous than his attack on the supporters of the Charity-schools movement? It is reported that the SRMs were not universally admired by members of the clergy or by all holders of public offices, and for that reason there may not have been sufficient outrage to generate a new presentment. Furthermore, the composition of the Grand Jury itself had changed.[196]

By mid-century there were distinct signs that the taste of the nation was in the process of changing and that attitudes toward prostitution and harlots were also changing. In the emergent "age of sensibility" the new wave of writers on this subject, stimulated in part by a religious revival, published plans and then set up charitable institutions to help prostitutes who wished to abandon their former employment and return to virtuous living. This change of taste or attitude may explain why in that century there were no further reprints of *A Modest Defence* in English after 1745.

Anonymity and the Question of Authorship

Because we lack external evidence to demonstrate that *A Modest Defence* was unquestionably written by Bernard Mandeville, MD, every reference to him as the author of this work, as we already have stated, should be taken to mean that he probably or most likely did write it.

In 1724 and 1725 the only overt signs of authorship in these three editions are the names "A Layman" and "Phil-Porney." In the 1740s two rival editions appeared, one attributing this work to Colonel Harry Mordaunt and the other attributing it to Luke Ogle. The name Luke Ogle, with its possible suggestion of ogling in an erotic context, was not just another invented name designed to complement that of "A Layman." The name belonged to a dissenting clergyman with the title Vicar of Berwick on Tweed, who was ejected from his congregation in 1661 following the Restoration of King Charles II to the throne. He continued to preach after his ejection but was hounded and opposed by the authorities. He died in 1696.[197]

As for the pseudonym Colonel Harry Mordaunt, one can say that there were various other Mordaunts in English history. A Harry Mordaunt, Esq. is referred to as a "superviser of the forest" in a communication sent by Thomas Thynne to Robert Harley, first Earl of Oxford, around June 1712.[198] But in the decade ending in 1740 the most famous person bearing this surname was undoubtedly Charles Mordaunt, third Earl of Peterborough and first Earl of Monmouth (1658–1735), an older contemporary of Mandeville. Opposing King James II, Mordaunt as an early whig

---

[196] See W.A. Speck, "Bernard Mandeville and the Middlesex Grand Jury," 362–374.

[197] For more details about his life see *Calamy Revised: Being a Revision of Edmund Calamy's Account of the Ministers and Others Ejected and Silenced*, 1660–1662, by A.G. Matthews (Oxford: Clarendon Press, 1934), 372.

[198] See *A Catalogue of the Letters and Papers of Robert Harley* ... University of Nottingham Library.

in Holland plotted to have him removed. He accompanied the future King William III to England in 1689 and became a Privy Councillor and first lord of the treasury. He later became disaffected with King William and was imprisoned for a short period. After William's death in 1702, Mordaunt, who inherited the earldom of Peterborough in 1697, resumed his political activities in the new reign of Queen Anne and served his nation as a military leader in Spain during the War of the Spanish Succession. A dispute about the quality of his service brought him home and, having deserted the whigs for the tory faction, he was vindicated by the House of Lords in 1711. With the accession of King George I and the return of the whigs to power in 1714, he was again excluded from holding public office and spent the remainder of his life in retirement. His friendship with Alexander Pope began around 1722 and continued until his death. It thus seems possible that whoever associated "Colonel Harry Mordaunt" with the authorship of Mandeville's pamphlet also wished to link the third Earl of Peterborough with the pornographic content of this work. By the twentieth century it was eventually accepted that neither Ogle nor Mordaunt nor a third candidate named George Ogle could have been the true author of *A Modest Defence*.

The best case for regarding Mandeville as the author was published in 1921 by F.B. Kaye, the doyen of Mandeville scholars in the last century.[199] Kaye's review of earlier attributions of this work to Mandeville includes the "answerer" who retorted to *A Modest Defence* in a postscript to the 1725 edition of that work.[200] Kaye failed to mention, however, that George Bluet, one of the earliest critics of Mandeville, had also attributed *A Modest Defence* to him. After reviewing some later positive attributions and dismissing those who tried to assign this essay to George Ogle, Kaye noted that the German scholar Paul Sakmann in his book on the Mandeville controversy (1897) had made a persuasive case for Mandeville's authorship. The strongest piece of evidence for authorship used by Sakmann and Kaye is the close relationship of "Remark [H.]" to *A Modest Defence*. Kaye concluded that

> The extraordinary parallels in the argument, the identity of style, the tradition ascribing the book to him, and the absence of anyone else who could be thought to have written it, make me positive that the book is by Mandeville.[201]

A decade after Kaye affirmed Mandeville's authorship, a Dutch scholar, Johannes H. Harder, argued that the author was probably the person in whose name *A Modest Defence* had been registered at the Stationers'

---

[199] F.B. Kaye, "The Writings of Bernard Mandeville," 419–467.

[200] Kaye apparently accepted the anonymous "Answer" to Mandeville's essay as an authentic reply, overlooking the possibility that Mandeville or his bookseller added that questionable reply merely in order to stimulate sales.

[201] Kaye, "Writings," p. 456.

Company (in compliance with the copyright statute of 1710), one Lawrence Le Fever (or LaFever). Harder's objection was soon demolished by Ronald S. Crane, who agreed with Kaye that Mandeville was the probable author.[202]

Professor Crane's support of Kaye's attribution of *A Modest Defence* to Mandeville was a strong stamp of approval and thereafter Kaye's attribution was accepted by almost all writers who have dealt with that work. A modern authority on Mandeville, M.M. Goldsmith, takes a more cautious position by remarking that it was "possibly written by Mandeville."[203] Because we still lack any external documentary evidence that Mandeville wrote this book, the case for his authorship is to that extent weakened. Some of its passages seem to reflect the language and point of view of a trained lawyer or barrister, or at least they contain materials possibly supplied by such an expert. Nevertheless, I find Kaye's reliance upon tradition and internal evidence convincing and I believe that Mandeville did write most of this work if not all of it.[204]

Up to now our main concern under the heading of authorship has been the question of attribution: who really wrote this work? But one more point that should be made in this context is that our hidden author openly called attention to his own anonymity. Unlike the authors of many other pseudonymous writings across the centuries, our hidden author focuses our attention upon the mystery of his fatherhood by calling his pamphlet a "Foundling" that was "clandestinely dropt" at the reader's door, thus implying that it is illegitimate, that is, a bastard. In the opening sentence of his "Preface" he informs us that his printer, whom he calls a "midwife," refused "to help bring it into the world" unless the author was willing to "father" it. To dodge or avoid this requirement the author points out that "several other pious authors" including the pious authors of *Eikon Basilike* and *The Whole Duty of Man*, were also of anonymous origin. The implied question is, did the printers of those works also insist upon having the true names of the writers who fathered those texts? Mandeville thus uses the very question of his authorship to make fun of his pious antagonists.

The Early Critics of *A Modest Defence*

The most detailed analysis of Mandeville's writings in his own time was *An Enquiry Whether a general Practice of Virtue tends to the Wealth or Poverty, Benefit or Disadvantage of a People?* (1725), by George Bluet (or Blewitt). In the seven chapters of this book-length polemic, Bluet focuses mainly, as

---

[202] Johannes H. Harder, "The Authorship of *A Modest Defence*, 200–203; Ronald S. Crane, "Bernard de Mandeville," 122–123.

[203] Goldsmith, *Private Vices, Public Benefits: Bernard Mandeville's Social and Political Thought*, 149.

[204] For modern assessments and discussion of the problems of anonymity, see the listings for Robert J. Griffin in the Bibliography.

one would expect, upon *The Fable of the Bees*, but there is sufficient internal evidence in Bluet's remarks to convince us that he was also responding to *A Modest Defence of Publick Stews* even though he never names that work.

Bluet's intention was to expose Mandeville's writings as generally immoral and atheistic. Mandeville's pages, he finds, are full of faulty reasoning with many non sequiturs, misquotations, misinformation, and unacknowledged borrowing from other authors, most notably Pierre Bayle. Bluet's critical method typically involves repeating or paraphrasing a passage in the *Fable*—about Vanini, say, or Sir Paul Rycaut, or the stews— and then delivering a detailed rebuttal that concludes with what he hoped would be regarded as withering sarcasm or devastating satire, as in the following excerpt (in which the italicized words or phrases are quotations from Mandeville's *Fable*):

> It is one of his favourite Opinions, that in every Country there ought to be a Tolleration of *publick Stews*, or *Temples of Venus*. The Magistrate must connive at them, but he must not encourage them; he ought to tolerate them, but still continue to abominate them. And then from the instance of *Holland* [in "Remark (H.)"], he tells you, the Magistrates do well, to be *always squeezing them of their immoderate gains, punishing those necessary Profligates, the Bawds and Panders*, and laying them under all possible Marks of Infamy. But surely, if they do so much Service to the Publick, it should rather be the Duty of the Magistrate upon *his* Principles to erect Statues to their Honour. For the same Reasons that plead for a *Toleration*, are equally strong for all possible *Encouragement* that can be shewn them. The Reasons he gives why they should be *tolerated*, is to prevent a much greater, that of Adultery. The more Reputation therefore Stews are in, the less Occasion (according to his Scheme) there should be for Adultery. For a Toleration of these *Temples of Venus* is not, I presume, upon the same Foot with a Toleration of meer speculative Errors in Religion, which it is the Duty of the Magistrate barely to *allow of*, but not to *encourage*. As much as we have heard of *natural Rights* of late Years, I don't remember it has ever yet been gravely asserted in print, that a Liberty of Whoring comes into the Number of them. If then it be only the good Policy of the Governors (as a Means to prevent Adultery) that this Toleration is owing to, it ought to reach much further, and Whores, Bawds, and Panders, so far from being laid under particular Hardships and Discouragements, ought to be put upon the same Foot with all other worthy Promoters of the Commoneweale.
>
> . . . What a fine consistent System of *Ethics* is this! . . . . All *private Vices* are *publick Benefits*; but it is the Duty of the Magistrate upon *State Principles* to prevent Adultery, by allowing of Fornication! It would be tedious to take particular Notice of all such shuffling Passages . . . . (Bluet, *Enquiry* (1725); see pp. 91–93 and 301–302 in J. Martin Stafford's reprint collection, *Private Vices, Publick Benefits?*)

In saying that "All *private Vices* are *publick Benefits*," Bluet repeats the famous subtitle of Mandeville's *Fable of the Bees* (i.e., "Private Vices, Publick Benefits"), but he also distorts it by adding "all" and "are."[205] Bluet is correct, however, in reminding the reader that according to Mandeville the vices of individuals tend to produce "public benefit" or benefit for the society as a whole; and that prostitution was one of those vices. As Mandeville put it toward the end of *The Grumbling Hive* (1705),

> So Vice is beneficial found
> When it's by Justice lopt, and bound.

Bluet and many other defenders of the received morality would have none of this.

Although Bluet seems here to have concluded his critique of Mandeville's views on prostitution, this passage is only a brief anticipation of the nearly forty pages that he later devotes to this subject. In Section VI he ridicules the treatment of masquerades and everything else in Mandeville's "Remark (H.)." He does not name *A Modest Defence* anywhere, but one can tell from the following passage that he is also replying to that work:

> Suppose now that the Author's Project were put in Execution, and extended every where (as sure it ought to be if it be so useful a one); suppose that not only the larger *Towns* in the Country, but every *Parish* had one of these *Temples of Venus* in them, to be licensed every Year by the Justices, as Ale-Houses are now: Can any one seriously think that such a *Toleration* would promote the Cause of Chastity in either Sex? That it would *prevent* any *worse Evil* than is now committed there? (Bluet, *Enquiry* (1725); see pp. 157–158 and 344 in Stafford's reprint edition.)

Bluet must have had *A Modest Defence* in mind because nowhere in his *Fable* does Mandeville mention his proposal that the state erect and regulate new public stews. Further support for this view is the fact that he tries to equal or exceed Mandeville's abbreviated history of "tolerated Stews in *England*." Bluet mentions John Stow and Sir Henry Spelman, writers on English history, topography, and law who are not named in Mandeville's pamphlet, while also citing Daniel, whom Mandeville did name. A possible reason for

---

[205] Mandeville's original phrase, "Private Vices, Publick Benefits," was far less positive or extreme, allowing for a variety of different readings (as Francis Hutcheson correctly observed). Toward the end of his "Vindication of the Book" Mandeville himself elaborated on his initial paradox by asserting "that private Vices by the dextrous Management of a skilful Politician, may be turn'd into publick Benefits." (Kaye ed., I, 369 and 411–412). He continued to clarify the meaning of his paradoxical subtitle on p. 38 of his last piece, *A Letter to Dion* (1732), in which he replied to the inaccurate charges against him that appeared in George Berkeley's *Alciphron*.

Bluet's failure to cite the title of Mandeville's book is that he knew that he could be faulted for ascribing a pseudonymous or anonymous work, "written by a Layman," to Mandeville.

Bluet's unremitting stream of detailed refutations seems not to have achieved his desired objective, the demolition of Mandeville's arguments and the discrediting of his *Fable* on moral and philosophical grounds. If he had hoped to throttle Mandeville, he failed, because Mandevillean ideas percolated throughout the century, showing up in the works of Hume, Adam Smith, Voltaire, Rousseau, and other authors in the Enlightenment period. Bluet survives only in the shadow of Mandeville, but ironically he is perceived today as the most incisive of Mandeville's contemporary opponents.

In 1725, the same year in which Bluet's book was published, there also appeared an anonymous fifty-six page pamphlet titled *A Conference About Whoring*. This work has been described as a reply to Mandeville, yet it never mentions Mandeville's name or any work by him. It turns out to be a work of religious morality in dialogue form which yet allows for pious ejaculations by different speakers. Early in this pamphlet a wife lectures upon what the biblical Joseph would have said to Potiphar's wife, inventing for Joseph a seven-page response to her wicked proposal! Commonplaces abound, including denigration of the fallen woman and the whore, exhortations to save one's immortal soul, reasons for remaining virtuous and avoiding fornication and adultery, and the praises of lawful matrimony. On the last page of this moral tract or sermon in dialogue form, the last speaker (the husband and host) says "I have a Book in my Hand that is wrote in Defiance of [virtue]." But before he can mention the author or title or anything about it, his wife invites him and their two guests to sit down to dinner. Whether this evil book in hand was *The Fable of the Bees* or *A Modest Defence* or anything else by Mandeville, is not stated.

In 1726 a revised and expanded edition of *A Conference About Whoring* was published with a new title, *A Modest Defence of Chastity*. The London printer and vendor is no longer "J. Downing, in Bartholomew-Close near West-Smithfield," but "A. Bettesworth." In its newly added "Preface," the author informs us that this work was in fact a direct response to and critique of *A Modest Defence*

> *The following Paper was occasioned by another call'd,* A modest Defence of publick Stews; *wrote in Derision of divine and human Laws; with an Ayr and Spirit peculiar to a Person: who seems neither to fear God or regard Man. The Book is one continu'd Sneer upon Things serious and moral; tho' the very first Sentence in it avers that*——Nothing shews a greater Affectation of Wit; than treating grave Subjects with Burlesque and Ridicule.   (p. iii)

This nameless critic then informs us that he will not answer Mandeville point by point and quotes the Book of Proverbs (26:4) to the effect that "a Fool . . . must not be answer'd according to his folly." Whether the anonymous author of *A Conference upon Whoring* was the same person who added this direct attack upon Mandeville one year later is not known, but it remains one of the very few published reactions to his treatment of prostitution during his lifetime.

Another negative assessment, presumably published a few weeks after Mandeville's pamphlet first appeared, was reprinted as "Letter LXII" in volume four of *A Collection of Miscellany Letters, Selected out of Mist's Weekly Journal* (London, 1727). The *NCBEL* (II, 901) reports that "Defoe contributed to and probably edited" Mist's *Weekly Journal: or, Saturday's Post*, which suggests to us that the author of this review could well have been Defoe. This author deplores all modern writings that tend to "the Corruption of good Manners and Modesty" and in order to protect his readers from the poison of Mandeville's book on the stews he even refuses to name it!

> Let it suffice, the the plain Intent and Design of it, is, for the Propagation of Lewdness.————And take it all in all, it is such a Composition of Dulness and Wickedness, as even this extraordinary Age has not produc'd before.

This reviewer soon names the already famous (and infamous) *Fable of the Bees* which, he believes,

> has as much good and bad Reasoning in it as ever were seen in the Writings of the same Author. This Gentleman I take to be the first amongst us who has argued for a publick Toleration of Vices. He seems a great Admirer of the Policies of the Dutch; but as there is no Government without some Errors, he has (for the Ostentation of shewing his Parts) chosen to recommend the Licence which is given to publick Lewdness amongst them, imitating herein a Lawyer, who is Council for a Felon at the Bar; he knows his Client is a thorough-pac'd Rogue, and will certainly be found guilty; however, he has the Vanity of making the most of a bad Cause.   (IV, 237–238)

This reviewer correctly noted the presence of the courtroom and legal thought that suffuses this pamphlet, but he refrains from naming Mandeville and is even uncertain that Mandeville was its true author. It could have been written, he thinks, by "One of the wretched Imitators of this Author." Unlike Bluet, this author (possibly Defoe) does not probe into the logic of Mandeville's argument. Apart from condemning the pamphlet outright, he devotes most of his review to extolling the virtues of female modesty and chastity. In describing what happens when a woman loses her modesty or is no longer chaste, he remarks that "she who is given up to Shame, grows immediately regardless of all those Duties, which are the Ornaments of the Sex" and can no longer be a good wife, parent, or friend (p. 236).

One of the leading Deists of the age, Matthew Tindal, briefly referred to Mandeville's *A Modest Defence* in a reply to Bishop Gibson's *Pastoral Letter*, in 1728 and later editions. In that work Tindal quoted from the *Pastoral Letter* (p. 2) to the effect that "... *in some late Writings*, Publick Stews *have been openly vindicated.*" He responds to Gibson's charge by remarking that

> There is, indeed a Pamphlet, call'd *A Modest Defence of Publick Stews*; wherein the Author endeavours to shew, That since Men can't be made perfect, a lesser Inconvenience ought to be permitted to prevent a greater; and that *Stews*, under the Regulation propos'd, wou'd not have those ill Consequences now occasioned [7] by common Women; but whether this Gentleman is mistaken, or not, I do not see how the Cause of Infidelity is concern'd; especially since there were licens'd Stews in *Southwark* for many Ages, under the Protection and Regulation of the good Catholick Bishops of *Winchester:* And the States of *Holland*, and other Christian Countries do now tolerate such Places, to prevent greater Inconveniences; particularly that before-mention'd.[206]

By "greater Inconveniences" Tindal means the practices of sodomy and bestiality, which he had been previously discussing, naming particular instances in which Christian clergymen had been involved over the ages. Tindal's notice of Mandeville's pamphlet on the stews was on the whole either neutral or more likely even commendatory, because he mentions that Mandeville's proposal in fact reflected the actual practice of a number of countries including Holland—which is a way a saying that it was not a wild or harebrained idea. Tindal follows this up by noting that Gibson's *Pastoral Letter* also knowingly distorts the subtitle of *The Fable of the Bees* when, in Gibson's words, it states that "*Publick Vices are recommended to the Government as Publick Benefits.*"

Another negative critique of Mandeville on prostitution appeared in 1729 in a large folio volume written by John Disney, who had defended the SRMs in print about two decades earlier:

> *A View of Ancient Laws against Immorality and Profaneness; Under the following Heads; Lewdness; Profane Swearing, Cursing, and Blasphemy; Perjury; Prophanation of Days devoted to Religion; Contempt or Neglect of Divine Service; Drunkenness; Gaming; Idleness, Vagrancy, and Begging; Stage-Plays and Players; and Duelling. Collected from the* Jewish, Roman, Greek, Gothic, Lombard, *and other Laws, down to the middle of the Eleventh Century.* (By John Disney, *M.A.* Cambridge [and London] ... 1729.)

It is clear from the title of this ambitious work that Disney was continuing the anti-vice campaign begun in 1698 by Jeremy Collier in his *Short View of the Immorality and Profaneness of the English Stage* and somewhat earlier by the SRMs. Its overview of the legislation against all forms of vice in all

---

[206] [Matthew Tindal], *An Address to the Inhabitants of the Two Great Cities of London and Westminster* . . . . The second edition, with alterations and additions. (London: Printed and sold by J. Peele, 1730), pp. 6–7.

known cultures up to the eleventh century was probably designed as a historical justification, full of precedents, for the anti-vice activities of the SRMs and was addressed in part to English legislators. It is the kind of historical review that begs for a continuation into the later centuries, but we have no evidence of the appearance of any further volumes by Disney. He could not resist an opportunity to expose what he regarded as the wicked doctrines of this immoralist, but he also avoided dignifying Mandeville's principles through a lengthy refutation. The three-page rebuttal of Mandeville deftly condenses the Christian moralists' objections to the *Fable* and *A Modest Defence*, but all or most of his argument had already appeared in Bluet.

For many decades the Defoe scholars had accepted *Some Considerations Relating to the present Number of Street-Walkers* as one of his minor works, dating it at 1726. More recently this attribution has been challenged and the dating has been revised to about 1735.[207] From a number of passages in this text we can conclude that the anonymous author was aware of Mandeville's views on whoring in *A Modest Defence* and was apparently offering a solution to that social problem by steering between the extremely punitive measures of the SRMs and the toleration of public stews that Mandeville supported. This author glances at Mandeville's prose, for instance, in his remark that "publick Whoring in part destroys that End which its best Advocates contend for, that is to say, the securing of the Virtue and Reputation of the Chaste Ladies. . . ."(p. 4) The author summarizes Mandeville's closing historical survey of the laws on prostitution in these words:

> That the same [regulation of whores] was practis'd here formerly, we have Reasons to believe from some old Laws, which we find regulating the Apparel and Behaviour of Whores, and the Keepers of Stews: and from these Arguments, several warm Gentlemen would infer the Fitness and Necessity at once of tolerating Fornication, and restraining the Irregularities of Harlots.

In his statement that "our Street-Reformers, who are inclin'd to make human Weakness no Allowances, think of no Cure for Lewdness, but Amputation. . . .," the author must surely have been using the term "Street-Reformers" to mean the members of the SRMs.[208]

---

[207] In John Robert Moore's *A Checklist of the Writings pf Daniel Defoe*, second edition (1971) p. 205, this work is listed as no. 485. In Furbank and Owens' *A Critical Bibliography of Daniel Defoe* (1998), this work is excluded from the Defoe canon. Tony Henderson in his recent book *Disorderly Women . . .* accepts this de-attribution and revised date; see our Bibliography.

[208] *Some Considerations*, pp. 4–5. The "amputation" here matches Mandeville's term "lopping." Bradford K.Mudge in *The Whore's Story* (2000) devotes three pages (51ff.) to *Some Considerations*, probably because he was convinced that it was written by Daniel Defoe. Mudge, disagreeing with most scholars, evidently found this pamphlet more significant for the study of early eighteenth-century prostitution than *A Modest Defence*, which he barely names in a footnote. Furbank and Owens (as we have noted) deleted *Some Considerations* from the Defoe canon and Novak in his recent biography of Defoe is uncertain of its authenticity.

The author notes two extremes: on the one hand, Mandevillean toleration of whoring, and on the other, "all the Whippings, *Bridewels* and *Work-Houses*, which are invented as Discouragements to Vice." What he recommends as the mean between these two extremes is no more than such "Encouragements to Virtue" as the legislators should enact into law, to promote the institution of marriage. If there were more marriages, if bachelors (as in classical Greece and Rome) were pushed toward marriage more actively by fines and other social pressures, writes this author, the number of strumpets would decline. Marriage is best when it involves social equals (one of Mandeville's points) and "Next to no Marriage, Inequality in Marriage is the greatest Mischief" (p. 7), again voicing Mandeville's views. At the end of the first of his two letters to a member of Parliament, the author quite unexpectedly embraces the harsh methods of the reformers in the SRMs in order to thin the ranks of the whores:

> Let the Whipping-Post, Work-House, and Transportation, be employ'd to dissipate the present Set of Street-Walking Strumpets; and let us by gentler Allurements to Virtue, destroy the Hopes of any Succession of such miserable Sinners.   (p. 8)

Mandeville's pamphlet, too, declares war on "private whoring," but what this anonymous critic cannot and will not accept is the proposed establishment of new public stews, the Mandevillean solution. The number of indirect references to the contents of *A Modest Defence*, including the subject of marriage, suggests that this pamphlet is highly dependent upon Mandeville's. Like Mandeville's other critics, he focuses also on *The Fable of the Bees*, in which the worst are said to contribute something that benefits the public. But this author denies that "a Street-walking Whore" really produces any social good:

> Sure no body will urge, that the Consumption of Commodities and Manufactures which she helps towards, is a sufficient Atonement for the Mischief she does, and the want of that Good she is incapable of doing. . . .   (p. 6)

He is well aware that he is debunking Mandeville's famous defense of luxury consumption. Curiously, Mandeville in his pamphlet on the stews did not make use of his earlier theory of the social value of luxury consumption. As for the author's alternative proposal, greater encouragements to early marriage, the members of Parliament did not revise the English marriage system until the so-called Marriage Act was passed in 1753. Its attempt to define more rigorously the differences between licit and illicit marriages apparently made it more difficult to get married according to the new, stricter requirements for a legal marriage. But Mandeville did not foresee this legislation.

The debate and controversy continued to attract writers after Mandeville's death. One of the most notable of these later entries was composed by Saunders Welch, who recommended compassionate charitable treatment for common prostitutes, including a place of refuge or retreat for them. Welch argues that the loss of future population owing to the high percentage of barrenness in prostitutes is "no less a national than a moral evil." Mandeville had earlier brought up this same notion of depopulation as caused by sterility or incapacitation resulting from sexual overindulgence by males, either through fornication or through masturbation. He argued that moderate exposure to prostitutes in regulated brothels would ultimately produce better husbands—reformed rakes—than would those males who remained chaste until marriage. Though he does not mention Mandeville's name, Welch obviously rejects his argument for public stews. According to Welch,

> such criminal converse alienates the mind from matrimony; for it is hard to conceive that those men who have contracted habits of conversing with every woman they like, will be brought to confine themselves to one modest woman; and too many of them who do are so debilitated and weakened by disease and debauchery, that if any children are procreated by such marriage, they are too generally weakly and infected with the *Evil* and other diseases, from the corrupted state of the father's constitution. And surely the maxim that a reformed rake makes the best husband must be false, unless it can be proved, that it is a benefit to the fair sex to have, instead of a vigorous constitution, the dregs of a broken one.[209]

Those who resort to prostitutes, he argued, will pay a heavier price in many ways than those who do not, and Mandeville would probably have agreed with him, with the proviso that Welch was surely speaking of "private whoring" and not of the regulated and improved "public whoring" that he proposed as a substitute. It should be noted that Welch's case against tolerating or encouraging prostitution is based not on religious doctrine or on abstract principles of rational morality but on considerations of national interest and social utility, which is essentially the same pragmatic basis upon which Mandeville built his case for regulated stews.

It appears that in eighteenth-century England no rival program or plan for the active regulation of public houses of prostitution was ever proposed in print. Some decades after the publication of *A Modest Defence* there was a revival of printed discussions and proposals about prostitution, but the new emphasis (in proposals by Sir John Fielding, Jonas Hanway, Saunders Welch, and Robert Dingley) was not upon removing or reforming that

---

[209] Saunders Welch, *A Proposal to render effectual a Plan, to remove the Nuisance of Common Prostitutes from the Streets of this Metropolis; to prevent the Innocent from being seduced; to provide a decent and comfortable Maintenance for those whom Necessity or Vice hath already forced into that infamous Course of Life . . . .* (London, 1758); reprinted in *Prostitution Reform: Four Documents* (New York and London: Garland, 1985), pp. 13n.–14n. Welch, one of the Justices of the Peace for the County of Middlesex, was closely associated with the Fielding brothers, Henry and Sir John.

profession, but upon building the Magdalen Hospital for repentant prostitutes with the intention of improving their lives and saving their souls. In France, on the other hand, a number of writers began publishing ideal plans for building and regulating houses of prostitution. The best known of these works is *Le pornographe* (1769) by Restif de La Bretonne.[210]

Some Twentieth-Century Views on *A Modest Defence*

The first important treatment of *A Modest Defence* in the twentieth century is found in Havelock Ellis's monumental work, *Studies in the Psychology of Sex* (1906). In one of the major divisions of this multivolume work Ellis broadly reviews then current issues in prostitution and their historical background, but he completely bypasses the condemnations of harlotry in the Jewish and Christian Scriptures, remarking that when Christians gained political power, "leading fathers of the Church were inclined to tolerate prostitution for the avoidance of greater evils, and Christian emperors, like their pagan predecessors, were willing to derive a tax from prostitution."[211] Among those early church fathers, the two who stand out most for their tolerant approach to prostitution are St. Augustine and St. Thomas Aquinas. According to St. Augustine, if prostitution is eliminated from society, the world will be plagued with all kinds of lusts. Aquinas, writes Ellis,

> maintained the sinfulness of fornication but he accepted the necessity of prostitution as a beneficial part of the social structure, comparing it to the sewers which keep a palace pure. "Prostitution in towns is like the sewer in a palace; take away the sewers and the palace becomes an impure and stinking place."[212]

In order to demonstrate the transmission of this idea and its imagery to later times, Ellis quotes this passage from Robert Burton's *Anatomy of Melancholy* (1621):

> Our pseudo-Catholics . . . to keep themselves and their wives honest, make severe laws against adultery, present death; and withal fornication,

[210] See Pamela Cheek, *Sexual Antipodes*, 104ff. More about Cheek's contribution appears further.

[211] Ellis, *Studies in the Psychology of Sex*, 2 vols. (New York: Random House, 1936 [F.A. Davis Co., 1906]), Vol. 2, Part 3, p. 239.

[212] Ellis, *Studies*, vol. 2, part 3, pp. 282–283. Ellis quotes St. Augustine's Latin: "Aufer meretrices de rebus humanis, turbaveris omnia libidinibus."—from *De Ordine*, Book II, ch. iv. Ellis also identifies the precise source of his quotation from Aquinas as *De Regimine Principum* (*Opuscula* XX), Book IV, ch. xiv. Aquinas's sewer image is replicated in Mandeville's "low" comparison of the stews to a "bog-house" (i.e., outhouse) situated in a gentleman's garden. He removed the eyesore in order to improve his estate, "but it was not long before every Nose in the Family was convinc'd of His Mistake" [p. xi]. If Mandeville was aware of the Augustinian and Thomist origins of his analogy, he kept that information to himself.

a venial sin, as a sink to convey that furious and swift stream of concupiscence, they appoint and permit stews, those punks and pleasant sinners, the more to secure their wives in all populous Cities, for they hold them as necessary as Churches; and howsoever unlawful, yet to avoid a greater mischief to be tolerated in policy, as usury, for the hardness of men's hearts; and for this end they have whole Colleges of Courtesans in their Towns and Cities. . . . Many probable arguments they have to prove the lawfulness, the necessity, and a toleration of them [i.e., the stews] . . . and without question in policy they are not to be contradicted: but altogether in Religion.[213]

Whoever he meant by "Pseudo-Catholics," Burton seems to accept at least their practical compromise with the exigencies of human sexuality. Mandeville makes almost no mention of Catholicism or Catholics in his essay, but he essentially agrees with this position. Ellis, after quoting this relevant material, jumps a full century from Burton to Mandeville's *A Modest Defence*:

It was not until the beginning of the following century that the ancient argument of St. Augustine for the moral justification of prostitution was boldly and decisively stated in Protestant England, by Bernard Mandeville in his *Fable of the Bees*. . . . "If courtesans and strumpets were to be prosecuted with as much rigor as some silly people would have it," Mandeville wrote, "what locks or bars would be sufficient to preserve the honor of our wives and daughters?. . . . It is manifest that there is a necessity of sacrificing one part of womankind to preserve the other, and prevent a filthiness of a more heinous nature. From whence I think I may justly conclude that chastity may be supported by incontinence, and the best of virtues want the assistance of the worst of vices." After Mandeville's time this view of prostitution became common in Protestant as well as other countries, though it was not usually so clearly expressed.[214]

Though Ellis linked Augustine's influential sentence only with "Remark (H.)" in Part One of Mandeville's *Fable*, that should not suggest that he overlooked *A Modest Defence*. He cited this pamphlet some thirty-five pages earlier, in the context of European efforts to regulate prostitution. At this

---

[213] Part. 3, Sect. 3, Memb. 4, Subs. 2 of *The Anatomy of Melancholy* (ed. Floyd Dell and Paul Jordan-Smith, 1955), 857–858. Ellis uses this passage in his *Studies*, cited above, II, 284–285.

[214] Ellis, vol. 2, part 3, p. 285. Ellis's remark that Mandeville's *Fable* was suppressed immediately after the public became aware of his position on the stews and prostitution is inaccurate. Remark (H.) first appeared in 1714, but his *Fable* was not "presented" by the Grand Jury of Middlesex until 1723, the year in which Mandeville added his "Essay on Charity and Charity-Schools" to that work. He continued to expand his major work by adding a completely new second part to it in 1729, and in fact this work was never really suppressed.

point, immediately after citing Burton, Ellis quotes the main proposition of *A Modest Defence*, that "public Whoring . . . will not only prevent most of the ill Consequences of this Vice, but even lessen the Quantity of Whoring in general, and reduce it to the narrowest Bounds which it can possibly be contain'd in." He closes his brief exposition of *A Modest Defence* by reviewing the chief points of Mandeville's scheme.[215] Ellis sides with Mandeville against the SRMs' approach to identifying, arresting, convicting, and punishing the unfortunate women seduced into whoredom. He calls Mandeville "an acute thinker" and "a pioneer" in his advocacy of medically supervised state-regulated brothels. (Ellis, like F.B. Kaye two decades later, accepted the attribution of this work to Mandeville.) Ellis's brief but strong assertion of the pioneering nature of *A Modest Defence* set the tone for whatever positive or approbative revaluations of this work would later appear in the twentieth century.

After Ellis and Kaye, dissertations on Mandeville and the books that grew out of them always devoted some space to *A Modest Defence*, but it essentially remained out-of-print and generally unavailable (except in rare-book rooms or on microfilm) until a facsimile edition with an introduction by Richard I. Cook appeared in 1973; the introduction reappeared in an expanded version in 1975. Cook elucidates the major points including Mandeville's satiric attack on the SRMs, his plan for state-regulated stews, the connection with "Remark (H.)," and also his propensity for paradox, equivocation, irony, and ambiguity. Cook focuses primarily on the larger substantive issues, treating this work as somewhat satiric yet primarily serious in its plan for reforming prostitution. Though his title suggests that he is well aware of Mandeville's allusions to Hobbes and Swift's *Tale of a Tub*, he does not attempt to pursue the many sources of this work. Especially perceptive is his argument that Mandeville did not offer his proposal to erect public stews as a workable or practicable plan for social reform.

Most of Cook's analysis of *A Modest Defence* still holds up, though he did not attend sufficiently to the rhetorical structure and movement of Mandeville's argument. Others who deal with it generally stress its content and usually focus on the details of his new system of public prostitution. Vern Bullough does this very well, and so does Tony Henderson, but Lawrence Stone's summary is slightly flawed.[216]

To be sure, most critical treatments of *A Modest Defence* have been brief and partial. A typical instance is that of Ruth Bernard Yeazell's *Fictions of*

---

[215] *A Modest Defence* . . . (1724), p. 2; quoted by Ellis, vol. 2, part 3, p. 249. For "ill Consequences" Ellis substituted "mischievous effects," a phrase he found in Mandeville's next sentence.

[216] See the earlier quotation from Lawrence Stone in my Introduction. For typical brief treatments of *A Modest Defence*, see Vern and Bonnie Bullough, *Women and Prostitution*, 182–83, and Vern Bullough, "Prostitution and Reform in Eighteenth-Century England," 67–68. Tony Henderson provides more detailed context in his *Disorderly Women in Eighteenth-Century London*, but his treatment, like that of most others, also ignores the literary side of this work.

Modesty: Women and Courtship in the English Novel (1991). In this study she investigates the question of the natural modesty of women and reviews Mandeville's opposition to that idea. In his *Fable* and other works he argues that modesty in women is not natural or innate but the product of human invention, a combination of custom and education.[217] According to Yeazell, the views of Mandeville and Hume on modesty as a human construct gave way in the later eighteenth century to Rousseau's more influential idea of female modesty as natural and inborn. She discusses the importance of the female body in Mandeville's theory, stressing its role in the conflict "between natural appetite and artificial restraint," and she also reviews his classification of women in a range of behaviors within the extremes of chastity and amorousness. What she extracts from *A Modest Defence* is significant for her arguments regarding modesty in English fiction, but in her deliberately limited treatment of this work she ignores the sense of medical urgency behind it and avoids entirely the problems raised by his jesting or facetiousness. Since she focuses almost exclusively upon the importance of modesty in *A Modest Defence*, her readers might possibly carry away a flawed or slanted impression of Mandeville's book if they accept her partial reading of it as an account of the whole.

One might have expected a deeper analysis of *A Modest Defence* to appear somewhere in a 500-page book devoted to "sex and society in eighteenth-century Britain," but instead we find Graham J. Barker-Benfield's treatment of this work to be oddly limited.[218] He ignores the issues of prostitution and does not mention Mandeville's plan for new public stews, but uses this pamphlet to support his explication of Mandeville's views on the biological and mental equality of the sexes, and on the dangers that marriage poses for women. He notes that Mandeville in his *Virgin Unmask'd* and other works opposes the double standard, but he does not notice that this position seems to be contradicted in *A Modest Defence*.

In *Torrid Zones* (1995), another work of feminist criticism, Felicity Nussbaum uses passages from *A Modest Defence* as a springboard to a detailed discussion of John Cleland's erotic masterpiece, *Memoirs of a Woman of Pleasure* (1748–1749, later called *Fanny Hill*). She deals with Mandeville very selectively in her fourth chapter, "Prostitution, Body Parts, and Sexual Geography." In supporting an imaginative thesis on interrelationships of female sexual body parts with the colonized nations and natives located in our earth's torrid zones, she introduces three of the subjects found in Mandeville's pamphlet: his paradox that some women must be sacrificed to support the honesty or virtue of most others, his blunt review of the structures and functions of the male and female sex organs, and his use of the military metaphor of the woman's body as a besieged town. Moving from Mandeville to her discussion of Cleland's novel, she bridges the gap with

---

[217] *The Fable of the Bees* (ed. Kaye), I, 65 and 69ff.
[218] Barker–Benfield, The Culture of Sensibility, see 119–132.

this observation: "Limiting the geographical space of the transgressive female and the exotic to the torrid zones—the clitoris, the stews, and the tropics—served to locate, regulate, and colonize the sexually ambiguous and disruptive."[219]

In sharp contrast to those like Felicity Nussbaum and others who use bits and pieces of *A Modest Defence* to support their theses, Laura Mandell in her article "Bawds and Merchants: Engendering Capitalist Desires" (1992) focuses at length upon Mandeville's pamphlet. She announces at the outset that she intends to show

> how Bernard Mandeville's *The Fable of the Bees* and *A Modest Defence of Publick STEWS* engender capitalist desires. By first gendering these desires female, these texts can scapegoat the figure of woman for morally repugnant aspects of capitalist pursuits.   (p. 107)

Throughout her essay we observe an elaborate agenda in which feminist and Marxist analysis is joined with the psychohistorical and anthropological treatment of scapegoating by René Girard.

She opens the third part of her essay by observing that

> *A Modest Defence of Publick STEWS* animates the evils to be excluded from the ideal of prudent business management in the figure of the prostitute: women get (sexual) pleasure out of capitalizing, men do not; women capitalize in the service of indolence, men do not.   (117)

Using Mandeville's essay to further a larger thesis about misogyny, capitalism, and prostitution in the eighteenth century, Mandell bypasses various sections and themes that do not serve her argument, with the result that insufficient attention is paid to the work as a whole. She emphasizes the role of the businessman or merchant in relation to the "abjected" prostitute, omitting entirely the other kind of customer whom Mandeville identifies, namely, the man of honor, often a man of leisure who was more likely to indulge in sexual excesses that would weaken or even destroy his virility. Since it is difficult to link the man of honor with emergent capitalism, she ignores him and attends only to the businessman.

The pronounced medical purpose of Mandeville's proposal almost disappears in her account. She relies for her theoretical framework not only on

---

[219] Nussbaum *Torrid Zones*, 103. Though the clitoris and the bordello may suggest the heats or fires of sexuality, Mandeville merely toys with those images or uses them combatively to satirize a specific group of people. From the point of view of sexual arousal (an aim commonly attributed to works of pornography), Mandeville's piece will seem feeble when compared with works like Cleland's celebrated novel. Would not *Some Considerations Relating to the present Number of Street-Walkers* (1735?) have served as well? Or the relevant works by Venette and Marten (previously named), or *Aristotle's Master-Piece*? In any event, Nussbaum's choice seems to confirm that Mandeville's pamphlet is now being regarded as a touchstone for writings on unrepressed sexuality in that period.

Girard, but also on Julia Kristeva, whose special sense of abjection and idealizing she incorporates into her argument. Her closing sentence, interestingly, suggests a kind of polar opposition in this piece not far removed from the paradoxes that I discuss above:

> It is because *A Modest Defence of Publick STEWS* idealizes and abjects capitalist desires that real disgust with prostitutes stands in stark contrast to what appears to be real profeminist support of them.   (pp. 117–118)

Whether Mandeville personally demonstrates "real disgust with prostitutes" is debatable. How "desires" can be "idealized" and/or "abjected" I do not know, but it does seem quite clear that Mandell dislikes the capitalist merchant or man of business who wishes to relieve a momentary sexual urge and who does so by taking only a little time away from his business affairs to enjoy a whore's embrace. Mandell also seems to dislike an author who is capable of recommending such behavior as part of a solution to the problem of the evils of prostitution. She is presumably aware of the wit and sexual jokes in this work but avoids dealing with them because she finds more pressing issues that require her attention.

Much in her essay is reproduced in her book *Misogynous Economies: The Business of Literature in Eighteenth-Century Britain* (1999), but I shall not attempt here to examine in detail how she places Mandeville in a procession of authors that includes Otway, Lillo, Pope, Leapor, and Barbauld, among others. Some of her material includes "misogynous satires [that are] really about men's 'natural' hatred of women. . . ." This line of thought leads her to conclude that "turning Augustan misogyny into a literary object has reduced its literariness" (p. 34). If this generalization also refers to *A Modest Defence*, then it should be clear from my introduction above that I disagree with it. Close attention to the variety of contexts and sources of Mandeville's book, it seems to me, only reinforces our awareness of its deep "literariness." This view does not entail a rejection of Marxist or feminist analyses of its content, nor does it reject any efforts to understand how capitalism and prostitution are interrelated. But readers ought to suspect any approach that makes a part of a work stand for the whole, and one of the aims of this edition is to sharpen the reader's sense of what the whole of Mandeville's paradoxical book might be. Though she did not have this goal uppermost in her mind, Mandell's account demonstrates that Mandeville's *A Modest Defence* fully merits the detailed attention that she devotes to it.

Before Mandell's book appeared, Elizabeth Kowaleski-Wallace quoted from her article with approval and basically adopted her conclusions, adding some interesting remarks on the opposition between business and the unruly sex drive in young males. Kowaleski-Wallace's treatment of *A Modest Defence*, however, occurs in the context of women and consumerism, as the title of her book informs us: *Consuming Subjects: Women, Shopping, and Business in the Eighteenth Century* (1996).

Not every recent study dealing with eighteenth-century prostitution, erotica, or pornography acknowledges the importance of *A Modest Defence* in its time. A major study that excludes Mandeville entirely is Randolph Trumbach's *Sex and the Gender Revolution: Volume One . . .* (1998). Five of the twelve chapters in this important and controversial book, taken together, offer what is currently the most detailed historical survey of prostitution in eighteenth-century England. The absence of Mandeville from Trumbach's account may have resulted from his stronger commitment to using factual accounts of prostitutes culled from court records, newspapers, and similar documentary evidence. But we should also keep in mind that so far only volume one of a multivolume work has appeared.

Yet another partial treatment of *A Modest Defence* is Claude Rawson's essay "Mandeville and Swift," which appeared in 2001.[220] Rawson gives more or less equal space to both authors. When dealing with Mandeville he devotes most of his attention to *The Fable of the Bees*, as one would expect. But it is interesting to find that in comparing these two authors he gives more space to *A Modest Defence* than to most other works by Mandeville, apart from the *Fable*. Rawson reminds us that Mandeville referred to Swift's *Tale of a Tub* not only in his pamphlet on the stews but also in his *Letter to Dion* (1732). Though Swift must have known and been influenced by Mandeville's writings, he was quite reticent about naming him.

Rawson's thoughtful essay cannot be faulted for not delivering a full interpretation of Mandeville's pamphlet because that was never his intention. But he does provide useful insight into the interrelations of Swift's *A Modest Proposal* (1729) and Mandeville's *A Modest Defence*. In comparing these two works he notes that Swift would never have condoned the "specific operational features" of *A Modest Defence*. However, he continues, "the idea of managing an unstoppable depravity[221] so as to protect certain public decencies and stabilities was not foreign to his [Swift's] essential outlook." (73) A major difference, he finds, is that Swift's proposal is not straightforward and literal, while Mandeville's is, though he also adds (using Richard Cook's insight) that Mandeville was not trying so much to "undercut [his own] scheme as to bait the tender-minded reader."(74–75) Rawson seems to think that Mandeville is serious in offering his proposal, whereas Swift's proposal (recommending as tasty food the babies of the Irish poor) was not literally meant. My own view, as the reader already knows, is that trying to uncover the range of meanings and intentions in Mandeville's paradoxical pamphlet is a more difficult task than most readers have thought it would be.

---

[220] In *Eighteenth-Century Contexts*, ed. H.D. Weinbrot et al. (See Rawson in the Bibliography.)

[221] What is "unstoppable," in Mandeville's pamphlet, is the male sex drive. Swift may have regarded extramarital sexual activity as "depravity," but Mandeville does not use that term as a synonym for the male libido.

One might have expected to find some treatment of Mandeville in Julie Peakman's *Mighty Lewd Books: The Development of Pornography in Eighteenth-Century England* (2003), because *A Modest Defence* is in some passages overtly sexual and bawdy. However, his explicit references to prostitution, to sexual attraction, and to the sexual organs and their functions may not have seemed pornographic enough for Peakman's purposes. Or, what is more likely, in her exploration of works that are generally less familiar to researchers on sexuality, she apparently decided that Mandeville's pamphlet was already well known and widely examined.

Pamela Cheek, in *Sexual Antipodes: Enlightenment Globalization and the Placing of Sex* (2003), focuses more on prostitution than on pornography and usefully documents the influence of *A Modest Defence* on some French authors later in that century. Though it has long been known that Restif de la Bretonne relied upon Mandeville's book for ideas on regulating houses of prostitution, Cheek is the first to point out how important Mandeville's proposal on prostitution was in the emergence of a series of ideal brothel plans produced in later-eighteenth-century France. She treats these works as a genre for which Mandeville provided the model or template, and she finds that other authors in that century agreed with his view that the best way to deal with the problem of prostitution is not to attempt to stamp it out but to recognize its utility and to regulate it for the advantage of the state and its citizens.

Yet one more treatment of Mandeville's pamphlet in 2003 testifies to its growing importance for historians of sexuality. This occurs in Thomas W. Laqueur's *Solitary Sex: A Cultural History of Masturbation*, a wide-ranging analysis of changing ideas on masturbation and its representations in the literary and pictorial arts. Laqueur's "foundation" text, so to speak, is the pamphlet *Onania; or, The Heinous Sin of Self Pollution, and all its Frightful Consequences, in both SEXES Considered . . .*, which appeared "in or around 1712." According to Laqueur (p. 13), its anonymous author "actually invented a new disease and a new highly specific, thoroughly modern, and nearly universal engine for generating guilt, shame, and anxiety." Mandeville unquestionably knew this work and briefly incorporated its strictures on masturbation into some passages of *A Modest Defence*. Laqueur, knowing that he had to review Mandeville's writings on masturbation, wisely embedded his discussion within a broader survey of Mandeville's thoughts on passion-driven human nature and the social system as presented in *The Fable of the Bees*. When he gets to *A Modest Defence* proper, he elucidates Mandeville's particular reason for dealing with masturbation, namely, that the dangers of that practice suggest another reason for having state-supported brothels available to satisfy male sexual desire. Mandeville argued that recourse to the services of a prostitute is preferable to the physical abuse that young men would otherwise inflict upon themselves.

Once again we find a historian dwelling on a limited portion of *A Modest Defence* that pertains directly to his larger subject, but in this case Laqueur manages better than most others not only to convey the central concerns of

Mandeville's pamphlet but also to reveal his appreciation of the ludic or jesting dimension of that work, as in this passage:

> His infamous defense of public stews (brothels)—a commercial sexual marketplace—began with a long historical summary of evidence— page after hilarious page—that even philosophers were driven by the "irresistible force of love" and that it would be foolish to try to suppress it. Socrates confessed that even in old age he was affected by a girl's touch on the shoulder; Aristotle had a son by his concubine; Zeno was famous for his modesty because he rarely made use of boys, but he took his maidservant to bed and argued for a commonwealth of women.[222]

Laqueur savors the presence of the ludicrous in Mandeville's prose, yet he affirms the common view that Mandeville was fundamentally serious in his defense of public stews.

Some Modern Translations

One result of the worldwide expansion of Mandeville studies in recent decades is the appearance of at least three new translations of *A Modest Defence* into Italian and one into German.[223] The most informative of the Italian translations, accompanied by a useful essay, is that by Dario Castiglione (1989). Francesca Bandel Dragone's translation, reprinted in 2003, contains a page and a half of notes that barely begin to inform Italian readers of the deeper contexts and allusions that would help them to understand this work. In her recent German translation (2001), Ursula Pia Jauch makes use of some data supplied by Castiglione, but she also adds new information in her notes and interpretive essay. To satisfy the needs of the nonspecialist reader, both translators supply fundamental details about the publishing history of this work and both emphasize the importance, for Mandeville, of the self-regarding passions in understanding human motivation. Castiglione remarks that general discussions of "the passions" declined after Jaucourt's article on that subject in the Diderot *Encyclopedia*. One of the more valuable contributions of Castiglione's edition is his discovery that the first epigraph on the title page of *A Modest Defence* belongs not to

---

[222] Laqueur *Solitary Sex*, p. 285. In this last sentence, when Laqueur remarks that Zeno "argued for a commonwealth of women," he is probably misreading Mandeville's precise words (p. vii of the 1724 edition): "in his *Commonwealth* he was for a Community of Women. . . ." That is, Zeno wrote in his book on the commonwealth that women should be possessed in common by the male citizens of that state, an arrangement that is polygamous and that may sanction free love. The parallel with the Guardians in Plato's *Republic* immediately comes to mind. Raymond Stephanson calls attention to Mandeville's "humorous word-play" in his recent book *The Yard of Wit* (p. 67), but he merely glances at *A Modest Defence* in part of one paragraph.

[223] Each of these translations is listed in the Bibliography.

Seneca but to Tertullian. He identifies Montaigne's essay "On some Verses of Virgil" as a major source for Mandeville's quotations, and he also suggests that Mandeville could have known of the existence of an earlier defense of public stews mentioned in the article on Pierre Cayet in Bayle's *Dictionnaire*.

Neither Castiglione nor Jauch attempts to analyze the arrangement and progression of Mandeville's argument in any detail. Both view the work in its broader cultural setting and discuss some of its later historical connections, especially with the Marquis de Sade. Jauch also relates Mandeville's pamphlet to Hogarth's famous series of engravings, "The Harlot's Progress," to Restif de la Bretonne's *Le Pornographe* (1769), and to architectural fantasies by Claude Ledoux of structures that incorporate phallic motifs or patterns.

Prostitution: The Modern Debate

It is one of the ironies of history[224] that Mandeville's jocoserious proposal for new government-managed bordellos anticipated by 140 years the passage, by Parliament, of the Contagious Diseases Acts (1864, 1866, 1869) designed to curb the spread of venereal diseases in limited military centers. As in Mandeville's proposal, the authorities chose not to outlaw male sexual activity outside of marriage. Instead, they subjected many women, only some of whom were prostitutes, to degrading physical examinations and other forms of coercion that restricted their freedoms and civil liberties. The story of Josephine Butler's campaign against this highly discriminatory legislation has often been told. The parallel to Mandeville's position can clearly be seen in Judith R. Walkowitz's summary of the hygienic and moral inequities contained in this legislation:

> In pressuring for the medical inspection of prostitutes without imposing periodic genital examination on the enlisted men who were their clients, architects of the acts obliterated from the start whatever effectiveness as sanitary measures the acts might have had. Just as important, regulationists reinforced a double standard of sexual morality, which justified male sexual access to a class of "fallen" women and penalized women for engaging in the same vice as men.[225]

Walkowitz points out that this legislation was prompted by earlier British research which in turn was inspired by A.J.B. Parent-Duchâtelet's

---

[224] For the early history of prostitution, readers should consult the comprehensive accounts by Dufour (i.e., Lacroix), Bloch, Henriques, Sanger, and Bullough among others cited in our Bibliography.

[225] Walkowitz, *Prostitution and Victorian Society*, 3. Walkowitz at this point cites two sources: Keith Thomas's classic essay "The Double Standard" and Eric Trudgill, *Madonnas and Magdalens: The Origins and Development of Victorian Sexual Attitudes* (New York, 1976).

monumental study of Parisian prostitutes, *De la prostitution dans la ville de Paris . . .* (Paris, 1836). The major British work following upon the wave of research initiated by Parent-Duchâtelet is William Acton's *Prostitution Considered in Its Moral, Social and Sanitary Aspects . . . with Proposals for the Mitigation and Prevention of Its Attendant Evils* (London, 1857).

Shortly before Walkowitz's book was published (too late for her to cite him) appeared Alain Corbin's book *Les Filles de noce: Misère sexuelle et prostitution aux 19e et les 20e siècles* (Paris, 1978), translated (1990) as *Women for Hire: Prostitution and Sexuality in France after 1850.* Part I of this work, "The Regulationist Project and Enclosed Prostitution" reflects the earlier pattern seen in Mandeville. As in Britain, French regulationism also failed, yet, as Corbin notes, attempts to impose some form of regulation persisted. He takes the story of French prostitution up to 1975, and it is interesting to find that his index contains no mention of HIV and AIDS.

Since the latter part of the nineteenth century, arguments for and against prostitution have appeared steadily in print, in sermons, and on the lecture circuit as well. The prostitution debate warmed up considerably in the last quarter of the twentieth century with the rise of women's liberation and the renewed feminist movement that led to, among other things, the establishment of women's studies programs in universities worldwide.

Among feminists today the lines of battle in the prostitution debate essentially reveal two main groups. One group, identified as liberals, consists of those who defend and wish to legitimate prostitution by decriminalizing it, or legalizing or "normalizing" it. They base their views on grounds of civil rights, defending the individual's freedom to pursue economic gain in our free market society.[226] Their opponents, commonly described as radical feminists, include all those who regard prostitution as a continuing male or "patriarchal" assault upon women over the centuries. This male hegemony, they argue, has robbed women of their essential dignity, has treated them as objects useful for sexual gratification and has enslaved unknown numbers of them in situations of forced sexual labor.[227] These enemies of prostitution condemn it as a social and moral blight and hope to root it out of society. Presumably they will deplore Mandeville's argument for the toleration of regulated prostitution based upon the belief that it is impossible to eliminate it entirely.

Though most states in the United States continue to ban prostitution, writers who support it are as free to express their opinions as those who oppose it—a development that would have shocked and dismayed a great

[226] In his recent article "Prostitution and Sexual Autonomy: Making Sense of the Prohibition of Prostitution," Scott A. Anderson provides a useful overview of the debate. Among the liberal writers he names (see p. 749) are Martha Nussbaum, Sybil Schwarzenbach, Lars Ericsson, D.A.J. Richards, Kenneth Shuster, and Laurie Shrage. Even more recent is Laurie Shrage's electronic article "Feminist Perspectives on Sex Markets," which adds more details concerning current controversies on pornography and prostitution.
[227] Among the radicals Anderson (749–750) includes Andrea Dworkin, Catharine MacKinnon, Kathleen Barry, Carole Pateman, Sheila Jeffreys, and Evelina Giobbe.

many of Mandeville's contemporaries. Included in the group of those who argue for the legalizing and social acceptance of prostitution are many who now work or have worked in that profession. Their voices were simply not heard in Mandeville's time. The views of these contemporary sex workers are available in print and are easily found on Internet websites of groups such as COYOTE ("Call off your old tired ethics"), World Sex Guide, North American Task Force on Prostitution, PONY (Prostitutes of New York), and similar groups. The site of The International Committee for Prostitutes' Rights features the "World Charter for Prostitutes' Rights."[228] Though the authors of that document might approve of Mandeville's desire to ameliorate the working conditions and health of all prostitutes, they will probably reject actual or proposed legislation that would in any way curtail the freedom of sex workers by confining them to particular buildings, streets, or neighborhoods of any city. By advocating complete freedom of choice for any prostitute or sex worker, this charter is entirely opposed to the state regulation of whores proposed in Mandeville's pamphlet.

Thus what started out in 1724 as a bold and shocking recommendation that the state legalize prostitution will in our time appear unsatisfactory and even repulsive to those who want to see prostitution eliminated and to those sex workers who abhor the thought of imposing legal restraints on what they generally do to acquire income or wealth. The "liberals" who in the 1980s and 1990s reacted to the radicals' attacks on prostitution and pornography might sympathize perhaps with Mandeville's view that efforts to stamp out prostitution will surely fail, but they will probably agree with contemporary sex workers that they cannot accept the strict regimentation of prostitutes stipulated in his plan. Sensational as his proposal was at its inception, it is difficult to imagine that anyone today would recommend precisely that recipe for reform.

The Language of Sexuality: Mandeville's Lexicon of Sexual Terms

In this selective word-frequency list for *A Modest Defence of Publick Stews*, the number that follows a word indicates how many times this word appears in the text of the 1724B edition.

amorous 10	breach (with sexual reference) 2
bastard 4	breast-works 1
bawd 1	brothel 1
bawdy-houses 1	chaste 16

---

[228] 1985; later published in Pheterson, ed. *A Vindication of the Rights of Whores*, 40.

chastity 28
clap (=gonorrhea) 6
clitoris 1
cod-piece 1
commerce (sexual) 3
concubine (in the dedication) 3
copulation 1 (copulative 1)
courtezan 2
debauchee 1
    debauchery 1
    debauching 7
deflower 1
desire (sexual) 18
ditch 2
drain (=female sex organ) 1
ease 4 (but only once implying
    copulation)
erection (of public stews) 8
erection (of sex organ, male or
    female) 2
female 15
fornication 4
gap 1
harlot 2
honour (=female chastity,
    usually) 28
horn-works 1
immoral, immorality 2
impotency 1
    impotent 2
intrench'd, intrenchment 2
lay 11 (only two or three with
    overt sexual reference)
lechery 2
lewd (including lewdness and
    lewdly) 26
love (a complex term, often
    meaning lust or desire) 50+
lust 3
    lustful 1
maiden-head 1

male 1
manufriction 1
masturbation 1
modest, modesty (regarding sex) 21
nymphae 2
Onanites 1
pander 1
penis 3 (and "unruly member," 1)
pox (=French pox, or syphilis)
    7; pox'd 1
prostitute 1
pudenda 1
punk 1
rake 2
rampant 3
ramparts 1
rape 3
seminal 3
sex (=gender or the female sex) 7
shanker 1
sluice 1
sodomy 1
spermaticks 2
stews 59
strollers 1
surfeit (of sex) 2
tickling 1
    ticklish 3
titillating 1
    titillation 3
uneasiness (sexual urge) 3
vagina 1
venery 3
virgin 4
wanton 6
    wantonness 3
wench 1
    wenching 2
whore 4 (once as a verb)
whore-house 1
womb 1

The lexicon of sexuality in the seventeenth and eighteenth centuries is much more extensive than this list of erotic or sexual terms employed by Mandeville. It is instructive to consider some of the terms that he avoided using in this work: adultery, arse, balls, bollocks, buggery, bully, catamite, cock, coition, coitus, concupiscence, coxcomb, cuckold, cully, cunnilingus, cunt, dildo, drab, fellatio, frig, fuck, hymen, incest, intercourse, licentious, maidenhead, molly (and molly houses), nightwalker, pimp, pintle, prick, quean, semen, stones, streetwalker, strumpet, swive, tarse, tart, trull, twot, vulva, and yard.

We cannot assume that knowing Mandeville's sexual vocabulary will suddenly reveal the secrets of his engaging style, yet we can draw some conclusions from this word-frequency table. The most obvious fact about his diction is that he never descends into gross vulgarity. The anatomical terms he employs appear commonly in the medical works and books on anatomy that any medical student would have encountered in his era. His sexual metaphors and puns derive from established literary and legal traditions. His distinction between private whoring and public whoring, both of which are central to his thesis, leads to detailed definitions, but he barely mentions sodomy and does not trouble to define it.

His synonyms for "whore" include "prostitute," "courtezan" and "punk," but not "strumpet," "drab," "quean," "nightwalker" or "streetwalker." This does not mean that he never uses these absent terms. In his *Fable of the Bees* (ed. Kaye, I, 355) he speaks of "the fickle Strumpet that invents new Fashions every Week." The prevalence of "whore" and "whoring" in *A Modest Defence* confirms the report that those terms were far more current before the eighteenth century than the group deriving from "prostitute," which overtook "whore" and "whoring" and "whoredom" in the nineteenth century. It is also apparent that when Mandeville uses the terms "whore," "punk" and "prostitute" as antonyms for a chaste, virtuous, and modest woman, he exhibits the two-valued logic that one sees in many political, ideological, and religious arguments. A woman, in this perspective, is either virtuous or not, and if she is known to have lost her virginity outside of the married state, then her reputation is permanently soiled. But in fact there was a range of behaviors that could fall under the heading of "whoring," and some of them were accepted as permissible or lawful, if yet immoral. In describing the abjection of the whore Mandeville avoids entirely the shades of difference that separate casual and part-time whoring by discreet individuals from the brazen streetwalkers who did not hide the fact that they were seeking customers for their sexual services.[229]

---

[229] See Dabhoiwala, "The pattern of sexual immorality in seventeenth- and eighteenth-century London," 87 and 98–101.

While he does examine basic female sexuality, he makes no mention of menstruation, periods, menses, or menarche—but these are not faulty omissions in a work that does not aim to give a comprehensive account of female physiology. In dealing with the wider spectrum of human sexuality he says nothing about fellatio, the variations of position in sexual congress (associated with Aretino and Giulio Romano), coprophilia, necrophilia, incest, and some other sexual practices. He represents masturbation as evil and physically harmful, but in so doing he treads in the wake of the very popular pamphlet called *Onania* which had appeared about fifteen years earlier and was often reprinted. He barely alludes to pedophilia or pederasty in one sentence, but he uses neither term in this text. As for the procuress or bawd, he barely mentions her and he has nothing to say about the male procurer or pimp. Presumably his proposal, if adopted, would make deep inroads into their trade.

He could have introduced a range of "unnatural" or forbidden sexual practices into this work, but the farthest that he dares to stray from the heterosexual standard for consenting adults is his brief review of the often homosexual loves of the Greek philosophers, which involved youths as well as mature men. Adopting a rakish pose or persona, Mandeville argues that these ancient philosophers all savored the pleasures of the flesh. Yet, curiously enough, he tampers with a classical text presumably to remove a reference to homosexual attraction. As this speaker tells it, when Socrates was well on in years he was once aroused for five days by the touch of a *female*'s hand on his shoulder, but in the original text it is a male hand.[230]

His libertine pose ultimately cannot disguise the fact that he wanted heterosexuality to remain the national norm in sexual behavior. Apparently he never acknowledged the existence of homosexual attraction among his contemporaries. The excesses of a Sade would have been inconceivable to him, and just as unthinkable to him as a social reality would have been the cruelties recently reported in accounts of sexual slavery worldwide. The implication in a few of his passages is that "normal" heterosexual prostitution should be tolerated not only because it helps to preserve marriages, to protect wives, and to initiate young males into adult sexual practices, but also because it helps to keep virile males focused upon female partners and away from the attractions of gay sex. Mandeville never states the idea so bluntly, but he does seem to think along this line.

---

[230] His single reference to sodomy suggests that he disapproved of homosexual practices as unnatural or as perversions of nature. Randolph Trumbach, Rictor Norton, John Boswell, and other researchers into gay history have documented an active but often oppressed and persecuted homosexual subculture in Mandeville's era. Mandeville would certainly have been aware of it, yet in his writings he generally ignores the issues of homosexuality and male prostitution in his time.

On "the Low," including Low Humor and Bawdy

When we speak of Mandeville's propensity for "the low" we mean his attraction not only to low styles in literature such as the burlesque and doggerel (as found in Samuel Butler's *Hudibras*, one of his favorite pieces), but also his attraction to images of the lower levels of society, stressing coarseness and vulgarity in direct contrast to the elegance and refined taste cultivated by some of the wealthy and the educated. He delights in describing the uncouth, as in his account of the country booby enjoying rough handling by boatmen who vie to ferry him across the Thames. If the sublime appears anywhere in his writings, it will almost always be used in the service of ridicule, derision, or satire.

Mandeville begins his essay by sounding like a typical rake, but more often his voice is that of a learned and somewhat libertine gentleman who enjoys quoting from the major Latin authors. He composes ornate and complex sentences suggesting a high degree of rhetorical skill coupled with the politeness and delicacy that well-educated orators would display in public forums. What enlivens his prose is the contrast he cultivates between his sophisticated rhetoric—aimed at the nation's legislators—and his importation of "low" imagery and subject matter.

Now and then he peppers his sentences with unsavory similes and comparisons. He outdoes his previous efforts in this vein by comparing a prostitute to a piece of fly-blown meat in a butcher's shop; it is offered as a sacrifice to the flies in order to keep the rest of the meat untainted. In this comparison the speaker insults not only whores (tainted meat) but also their customers (carnivorous flies). And the pulling down of a bawdy-house by the "gentlemen" of the SRMs he compares to the action of the man who had an outhouse removed from his garden in order to improve the view. The predictable result—foul smells pervading his property—soon convinced him of his error in judgment.[231]

In discussing the attempts by the SRMs to rid the nation of the evils of prostitution, Mandeville accuses them of "stopping up those drains and sluices we had to let out our lewdness." We do not know whether he was aware that this comparison of whores to sewers in castles goes back to St. Thomas and St. Augustine, but by his time it had long been a commonplace, at least among the learned.

More of these low comparisons can be reviewed, but it is necessary to add, even though it seems so obvious, that Mandeville's central subject, prostitution, falls entirely within the purview of "the low," with the possible exception of the upper-class courtesans, about whom he has almost nothing to say. Discussions about the penitent prostitute Mary Magdalene

---

[231] In this comparison Mandeville emulates Swift somewhat, but he falls short of Swift's scatological imagination, or the "excremental vision" formerly ascribed to him by Norman O. Brown. The "excremental vision" may be out of favor, but there's no denying that Swift tended to use scatological imagery more often than any of his contemporaries.

would also rise above the "low" to a distinctly higher level of discourse, but Mandeville never mentions her in this book. In the scale of the reigning values of his society his chosen subject is indeed low, yet not as low as it might have been had he decided to employ the coarser language of the gutter.

Whether *A Modest Defence* deserves to be called obscene depends on which definition of that term one uses; it also depends on one's attitude toward human sexuality and other factors. Mandeville knew the term "obscene" but his preferred synonym was "lewd": he positively flaunts the lewdness of this work. When we speak of it as obscene or lewd, it is difficult not to consider two other terms having roughly the same import, pornographic and erotic. It seems unlikely that anyone in our time would be inclined to call Mandeville's pamphlet a piece of pornography in its modern sense, though it is certainly pornographic if one uses that term in its root sense of writing about prostitutes. It is quite removed from the grosser kinds of pornography excoriated by Andrea Dworkin and Catharine MacKinnon. As for the term "erotic," which we generally associate with sexual stimulation, there is actually very little of that quality in most of the pages of this pamphlet. His preferred term, "lewd," probably captures the spirit and intentions of this work best.[232]

On the whole, the lowness or baseness of Mandeville's subject matter in *A Modest Defence* may not seem shocking to a secular sensibility in the year 2006. This pamphlet will probably seem tame when compared with Cleland's *Memoirs of a Woman of Pleasure*, some works by the Marquis de Sade, or even the daily ads in our print media for sexual services in every major American city. Yet, even though it is a less erotic or inflammatory production, its central proposal will very likely appear immoral and sinful to any who consider it from a religious point of view, and to all those who think that prostitution at any social level is evil and immoral.

As for Mandeville's style in this pamphlet, we have already noted his avoidance of the vulgar terms for sexual anatomy and sexual activity. When he translates Martial's verse he prefers a lively colloquial style, but many of his sentences are of the periodic variety with multiple clauses. In keeping with the genre of the academic "declamation," he adopts a high style and sounds somewhat Ciceronian in conducting a defense. But when he wishes to satirize the hypocrisy of a series of professions, his sentences are shorter and pointed: "*Overreaching* in Trade, is *prudent Dealing*; and *Mechanic Cunning*, is stiled *Handicraft*." He enjoys the double entendres of the words "ticklish," "rampant," and some very conventional military terms applied to the battles of love.

---

[232] In "Erotica or Pornography?" (chapter 1 of her *Mighty Lewd Books*), Julia Peakman regards pornography as "one genre within a superfluity of other types of erotica, erotica being used as an overarching description for all books on sex." (p. 3). Using this distinction, we can admit perhaps that *A Modest Defence* is a piece of erotica even while we recognize that it is not highly erotic. The term "lewd" may still be the most appropriate single term to describe this pamphlet.

His punning in particular would have been regarded by many of his educated contemporaries as distinctly low. Joseph Addison and other critics of his time detested puns, but Swift and his friend Thomas Sheridan seem to have enjoyed them. In the decade preceding *A Modest Defence* readers were treated to a number of pamphlets that shamelessly cultivated punning. One of them was Swift's *A Modest Defence of Punning; Or a compleat Answer to a scandalous and malicious Paper called God's Revenge Against Punning . . .* (1716), and that was followed by Thomas Sheridan's pamphlet *Ars Pun-ica, sive Flos Linguarum: The Art of Punning; or, the Flower of Languages* (London: J. Roberts, 1719), a tongue-in-cheek or mock celebration of the art of punning from its earliest appearance in classical authors to the present.[233] Sheridan seems to be mildly castigating a vice of conversation that implies bad taste, but he clearly enjoys this low art.

Mandeville often highlights intended sexual puns by placing key words in italics, as in this sentence (p. [44]): "Honour once routed never rallies; nay, the least *Breach* in the Female Reputation is irreparable; and a *Gap* in Chastity, like a *Chasm* in a young Tree, is every day a *Widening*." Later on (p. [64]) he compares "our incontinent Youth" to "a standing Army." Such puns in *A Modest Defence* may be tired clichés, but they almost always call attention to the human sexuality that the respectable middle classes wished to hide. Very relevant here is Walter Redfern's remark that "Puns are a means of circumventing taboos, as are euphemisms, which play a similar hide-and-seek game with the listener/reader."[234] Mandeville's humor, conveyed in part through his puns, is part of his broader strategy of attacking the taboos upon open discussion of human heterosexuality. If Mandeville, who was often regarded as an immoralist in his time, jokes about sex, it should also be noted that he never tells whore jokes or prostitute jokes—he never jokes at the expense of the fallen woman.

One question we are left considering is, can we share the laughter of an author who appears to tolerate the idea and the practice of subjugating some women, virtually condemning them to a life of prostitution, in order to protect the honor and persons of most other women? To Mandeville, the campaign of our radical feminists against prostitution would have seemed to be no more than a continuation of the work of the SRMs, and his message to them would probably still be: if you can't eliminate the selling of sex, then at the very least you must take steps to control it.[235] Our

---

[233] The title page indicates that its author is "Tom Pun-sibi (*i.e.*) *Jonathan Swift*, D.D.," which turned out to be a joke. Dr. Thomas Sheridan was a close friend of Swift in Dublin; both were strongly attracted to the practice of punning as a diversion.

[234] Redfern, *Puns*, 91. Also relevant is Redfern's remark (p. 125) that "The pun can be retaliation, Parthian shot, the revenge of the disrespectful Id on the censorious Superego." This Freudian language aptly describes a major purpose of Mandeville in this work.

[235] Nadine Strossen in her recent book *Defending Pornography* (p. 192) essentially restates Mandeville's position: "If the sex industries were treated as legitimate businesses, they would be subject to a whole range of laws that would enhance the lives of the women who work in them."

current laws against prostitution criminalize it in every state in the union, with one well-known exception, yet we are aware that this profession is practiced, willingly or not, by millions of women around the globe. The social abasement and the mental and physical suffering of a great many women who have been seduced or raped or even sold into the slavery of prostitution may well provide the strongest reason for disliking and disapproving of Mandeville's pamphlet. Their suffering is no laughing matter. Still, in fairness to Mandeville, as I have argued, one should recall that most of his laughter serves the purpose of irritating the enemies of free speech, especially in the area of sexual discourse, and that in this work harlots as such are never the objects of his laughter or scorn.

Economic Aspects of *A Modest Defence*

Well before Nobelist F.A. Hayek devoted his British Academy Lecture on a Master Mind to Dr. Bernard Mandeville in 1966, historians of sociology and economics had recognized the importance of Mandeville as a precursor of David Hume, Adam Smith, Voltaire, and Rousseau, but in none of these major Enlightenment thinkers do we find any mention of Mandeville's proposal to reform prostitution. His economic thought has been the focus of various probing articles and book chapters in the last half-century, which suggests that he is at least as important in the history of economic theory as he is for early modern literary studies. From the latter part of the nineteenth century scholars have attempted to define and classify his economic thought, generally taking him to have supported either free trade (laissez-faire economics) or mercantilism, involving degrees of state regulation. Though the term "capitalism" had not yet been applied to the system of trade, consumption, and economic expansion that he favored, he is commonly regarded as a forerunner of capitalist thought—certainly a forerunner of Adam Smith—and his proposal on the public stews in particular has been viewed as an unfortunate example of capitalist and patriarchal social planning.[236]

A true contrarian, Mandeville believed that luxury consumption is beneficial to the nation and stoutly maintained this view while his critics continued to regard frugality not only as a virtue, but even as a key to the gradual amassing of one's personal fortune. In his *Fable* he approves of a whore's spending her money upon finery, which serves as one more example of private vices productive of public benefits. But that paradoxical defense of the utility of whoring to the nation is barely visible in *A Modest Defence*, except perhaps for the example of the wealthy man of pleasure who can afford to purchase the services of the most expensive courtesan in Mandeville's four ranks of whores.

---

[236] See Laura Mandell's "Bawds and Merchants: Engendering Capitalist Desires," discussed earlier.

The man of pleasure, independently wealthy and a member of the upper classes by virtue of his wealth, is contrasted in this work with the man of business, who is most of the time occupied with business matters. Of the two groups, Mandeville thinks more highly of the middle-class business-men than he does of the men of pleasure (or leisure, or honor). He argues that the man of business who does not overtax his own sexual powers will be a better husband than the often wasted and dissolute man of pleasure. The man of business has far less time for sex than the man of pleasure, a situation that works to the advantage of the former. Thus, instead of regarding prostitution merely as one facet of luxury consumption, Mandeville here stresses the role of the prostitute in catering most efficiently and eco-nomically to the recurring sexual desire experienced by males at all levels in the hierarchy of wealth.

Before publishing *A Modest Defence* Mandeville had previously defended a hands-off policy with respect to the number of workers in each trade:

> As things are managed with us, it would be preposterous to have as many Brewers as there are Bakers, or as many Woollen-drapers as there are Shoe-makers. This proportion as to Numbers in every Trade finds it self, and is never better kept than when no body meddles or interferes with it.   (*Fable*, ed. Kaye, I, 299–300)

Since this passage directly contradicts the close control over the supply of whores that Mandeville recommends in *A Modest Defence*, he may be open to the accusation of inconsistency. In his rebuttal, however, he would probably claim that prostitution is not merely another trade but that it has a special status. It requires regulation because it is harmful to the social order by spreading venereal diseases and by stimulating crime and disorderliness.

The economic implications of the speaker's proposal to erect and regulate public stews are numerous. When he writes that his plan for public stews is "self executing," that suggests an image of an economic unit or system that is self-supporting and possibly self-adjusting. The income will pay for doctors, nurses, supervisory matrons, and other personnel and oper-ating expenses. But will there never be a surplus or a profit? Is the state not permitted to profit from the sex business that it is asked to set up and oper-ate? He does not even try to persuade his readers that implementation of his proposal will result in increased employment and will also generate signifi-cant new revenues for the state. Precisely why he chose not to emphasize this potential source of revenue for the government is not immediately clear. Was the idea of the state running a lucrative and highly profitable chain of bordellos too distasteful or too vicious for him to contemplate? For whatever reason, it was a notion that he apparently preferred to avoid.

The first part of Mandeville's proposition—asserting that public whoring is less criminal and less detrimental to society than private whoring—seems quite removed from economic theory. In his claim that the new public stews "will prevent most of the ill consequences of this vice," some of those "ill consequences" will have economic import. But with his claim that the new stews will "even lessen the Quantity of Whoring in general, and reduce it to the narrowest Bounds which it can possibly be contain'd in," we find ourselves directly engaged with economic issues.

The most suspicious part of this three-part proposal is this last one: does he propose that the government micromanage the proportion of clients to whores? And if so, then how often should whores be added—monthly, weekly, or daily? (This appears to be a problem in personnel management, but that too is a part of the economics of the whole.) And what is the purpose of such micromanagement? Is it meant to insure greater profitability? That would be a normal business aim, but in this case our confident projector, an invented persona, takes pride in being able to reduce the number of women whose virtue has to be sacrificed in order to maintain the public stews. It should be noted that this fine-tuning of an economic system resembles similar instances of social calculation in Mandeville's era that are subsumed under the heading of "political arithmetic," a phrase associated with Sir William Petty, John Graunt, and Charles Davenant. In Mandeville's era the most devastating satire on political arithmetic was yet to appear—Swift's *A Modest Proposal* (1729).

In discussing issues of supply and demand relating to whores, Mandeville raises some predictable questions such as the cost of a visit to a prostitute. But he distances himself from the fiscal management of the entire operation, except to indicate that its income will support three supervisors, some medical staff, and other necessary support personnel; and that it will also cover the expenses of lying-in and the rearing of any bastards born to whores employed in the public stews. Mandeville's concern here with regulating the supply of these whores is another example of the commodification of sex in passages where he treats it as merely another product or saleable commodity. This leitmotiv runs through the entire work.

Sometimes he employs the diction of commerce or trade for purposes of wit and humor, as in this passage: "We are naturally *furnish'd* with an extraordinary *Stock* of Love; and, by the *Largeness* of the Provision, it looks as if Nature had made some Allowance for *Wear and Tear*" (p. 28). He enjoys applying the language of the tradesman or merchant to the physiology of sex, converting an organic function into a quantifiable thing or object. The cost or price of sex, then, includes not only the money charged by the whore or by her establishment, but also the customer's expenditure of a portion of his limited "stock of love" and, if he is a businessman, even his "stock" of precious time. As for the actual expense involved in seeking sexual relief, the speaker is more concerned about the cost to the male than the welfare of the female. Getting entangled with an individual young lady "may probably lead a Man into After-Expences, which at first he never dreamt of."

Yet another kind of "expense" that briefly appears in this work is the social "expense" of enrolling more chaste women into the ranks of the whores as new recruits are needed either because of increased demand or because of retirements from the workforce owing to pregnancies, illnesses, superannuation, and so forth. In this case it is not a monetary expense, but once again a figurative "expense"—a diminution of the general fund of women's honor, virtue, virginity, chastity, and modesty.[237]

Toward the end of his proposal he speculates upon the possibility of importing foreign women to add more sex workers to the state-run public stews. Mandeville knew, from biblical and classical sources, that over the centuries foreign women and children had been captured and sold or traded for use in sexual slavery.[238] He may be serious here but he does not dwell upon this issue, preferring to leave the possibility open for consideration by the nation's legislators. One reason for his not dwelling upon this afterthought may have been his awareness that such trafficking in women and children was probably too barbaric to be associated with his rational solution to the evils of "private whoring." Another explanation for his brief consideration of the possibility of importing foreign prostitutes is that he used this idea simply to pave the way for another jest: if foreign whores are imported, young British aristocrats would no longer need to take their grand tours of Europe to find exotic sexual pleasures in the major foreign countries—they could now obtain the same experiences at home! Mandeville's afterthought concerning the importation of foreign courtesans seems to be the least earnest and the least necessary feature of his general proposal.

An aspect of his argument that may be even more offensive than his bare proposal to erect and regulate the public stews is his insistence upon the need to suppress all attempts to engage in private whoring, once the new system of public stews has been implemented. From an economic perspective Mandeville's proposal plainly supports the creation of a state-owned monopoly, and to ensure its success he would have the nation's legislators criminalize private whoring, turning it into a punishable offence with the intention of eliminating it, as far as that can possibly be accomplished. He even invites the "gentlemen" of the SRMs to cooperate with his scheme by redirecting their policing activities into this new channel. Here he virtually recommends the same cruel treatment of prostitutes that Phil-Porney satirized in the Dedication: is this another example of the author's fondness for paradox and contradiction?

One imagines that the inventor of this scheme would have wanted to guarantee its success as far as is humanly possible. But would he have

---

[237] Though there are more kinds of expenditure or expense than simply the monetary kind in this work, Mandeville does not use the verb "to spend" to mean what it sometimes means in works by Shakespeare and other authors of the Renaissance, that is, the emission or ejaculation of semen.

[238] That this crime is still unfortunately very much with us here in the United States as well as around the globe can be gathered from Peter Landesman's article "The Girls Next Door" in *The New York Times Magazine*, Sunday, January 25, 2004, pp. 30–39, 66–67, 72 and 75. Mandeville's single, brief reference to sexual trafficking here suggests that he could not imagine or anticipate what in our time has become one of the most scandalous practices of organized crime.

wanted to see his proposal turned into such a stark reality? Did Mandeville himself ever approve of such a repressive totalitarian state? This is not the Mandeville that we associate with his earlier *Female Tatler* papers or the feminist tendencies visible in his *Virgin Unmask'd*. Nor does the speaker in *A Modest Defence* ever name Mandeville's "trademark," so to speak, "private vices, publick benefits." Yet one can argue that this famous subtitle of *The Fable of the Bees* is indeed reflected or mirrored in *A Modest Defence* because the plan it offers claims that the "private vice" of prostitution will be transformed not only into public vice but also into (relatively speaking) a public benefit. As for any objections to Mandeville's ambiguous defense of vice on moral grounds, we imagine him responding with a sly smile and reiterating a pragmatist's preference for the lesser of two evils.[239]

Marriage

General summaries or accounts of *A Modest Defence* have usually overlooked the importance of marriage in this pamphlet because its main subject, whoring or prostitution, is the magnet that has always attracted the reader's attention. A careful review of the entire essay should convince the reader that marriage is probably its second most important issue, and that the removal of all references to marriage from this work would seriously alter its message and intent.

The strongest point that Mandeville seems to make about marriage is that for the purpose of satisfying the sexual urges of adult men and women marriage is decidedly preferable to promiscuous sexual commerce. But the varying images of marriage in this essay reveal not one but a number of different attitudes toward it, from the cynical to the romantic or idealistic.

His earliest depiction of marriage appears in the opening Dedication, delivered in a voice that suggests a libertine speaker like the Earl of Rochester. The speaker has been admonishing the "gentlemen" of the SRMs for failing to deal effectively with the growing problems of whoring in his time

> I will now suppose, that you have given up the Men as Incorrigible; since You are convinc'd, by Experience, that even Matrimony is not able to reclaim them. Marriage, indeed, is Just such a Cure for Lewdness, as a Surfeit is for Gluttony; it gives a Man's Fancy a Distaste

---

[239] Any comprehensive discussion of Mandeville's economic ideas—unlike the cursory observations above—would have to include a review of his remarks on the division of labor. On this issue and on others Mandeville is an important precursor of the classic exposition of the advantages of this practice in Adam Smith's *The Wealth of Nations* (1776). I do not discuss the division of labor here because it seems to be entirely absent from his proposal for new public stews.

to the particular Dish, but leaves his Palate as Luxurious as ever: for this Reason **[x]** we find so many marry'd Men, that, like *Sampson*'s Foxes, only do more Mischief for having their Tails ty'd.   (1724B, pp. [ix]–[x])

In this view husbands are "incorrigible" sexual gluttons, and the married state, far from satisfying their sexual appetites, only incites them to find further satisfaction outside of the marriage bed. The tone is jocular and bawdy. The equation of sex with food, which was very old by Mandeville's time, is employed to project a negative image of marriage on the whole.

As the essay progresses, the reader encounters two further representations of marriage, both of which contradict the above quoted libertine devaluation of marriage. The first of these two positive depictions stresses the biological and sociopolitical functions of marriage, bringing us closer to issues of patriarchalism in government and family. Prostitution aims to be childless, whereas a major purpose of marriage is to replenish the population. Marriage is also the great insurer of the integrity of family lines. The legality of a marriage is of vital importance in the transmission of property and wealth, and hence of family power and influence. As Mandeville puts it,

it is very certain that Marriage is absolutely necessary, not only for the regular Propagation of the *Species*, and their careful Education, but likewise for preserving that Distinction of Rank among Mankind, which otherwise would be utterly lost and confounded by doubtful Successions.   (27)

In this unromantic passage the speaker seems utterly serious, revealing a commitment to an ordered hierarchical society that even an ardent royalist might support. Of his two passages that defend and support marriage, the first one (above) does so in the contexts of political theory and national interest: marriage is not only good for the state but absolutely necessary for its survival as one of the great nations of the earth. This view of marriage reflects one of the deepest values embedded in this essay, that of order in the state, in the family, and in individual relations. It also privileges male power and desire in accordance with the patriarchalism founded upon biblical texts.

Though one may assert the strong utility or the necessity for such a system of marriage in the modern state, that argument alone would never persuade the nation's bachelors to give up whoring and to seek out wives. There would have to be something more attractive and alluring in the wedded state for that to happen, and indeed Mandeville includes a third view of marriage here, one that can loosely be described as (according to

Lawrence Stone) companionate:[240]

> When a Man and a Woman select one another out of the whole
> Species, it is not merely for Propagation; nay, that is generally the
> least in their Thoughts: What they chiefly have in View, is to pass
> the Remainder of their lives happily together, to enjoy the soft
> Embraces and mutual Endearments of Love; to divide their Joys and
> Griefs; to share their Pleasures and Afflictions; and, in short, to make
> one another as happy as possible. As for Children, they come of
> Course, and of **[34]** Course are educated according to their Parents
> abilities.

Earlier (p. [10]) he spoke of "that mutual Love and Affection between Man
and Wife, which is so necessary to both their Happiness." In no other work
by Mandeville do we find marriage praised so highly.[241] He describes here
the highest standard of emotional and sexual fulfilment that he knows.[242] In
the hierarchy of public or social values in this work, his proposed system of
supervised brothels seems preferable to the indiscriminate "private whoring" that he deplores, but in the above passage what seems even more
desirable to him is the channeling of men's and women's sexual appetites
into marriages of mutual love and respect.[243]

Mandeville devoted far more space to marriage in his earlier book *The
Virgin Unmask'd: or, Female Dialogues Betwixt an Elderly Maiden Lady and Her
Niece . . .* (1709), in which he illustrates the numerous evils that plague

---

[240] John R. Gillis in *For Better, For Worse* (p. 14), writes that both Lawrence Stone and
Christopher Hill "are wrong in assuming a linear, continuous progression [of the conjugal ideal
of marriage] from that time [the mid-seventeenth century] to our own." Very few, he continues,
subscribed to "the idea of companionate marriage"—it "was not fully accepted, even among the
new middle classes, until the Victorian period."

[241] Curiously, his brief praise of companionate marriage may be the one moment in this work
where the double standard fades from view. A similar formulation by Defoe appeared four years
later in his conservative and rigidly moralistic book, *Conjugal Lewdness; or, Matrimonial Whoredom*
(1727; ed. M. Novak, 1967; p. 26): "Love knows no superior or inferior, no imperious
Command on one hand, no reluctant Subjection on the other. . . ." Defoe, like Mandeville,
focuses upon various defects of marriage, but his list of sexual irregularities is more specific to
marriage than is Mandeville's list. For another set of opposing views on marriage (including a set
of "wicked Arguments" for the superiority of whoredom to marriage), see Defoe's *Roxana* (1724;
ed. Jane Jack, 1964), 132–133. See also Katharine Rogers' article on Defoe's feminism.

[242] A major complaint against Mandeville's pamphlet from a feminist perspective is the fact that
the needs and rights of women are almost always subordinated to those of the men while the
women themselves are judged by a higher standard of sexual morality. The double standard is
operative in most of this work, and egalitarian love within marriage is far from being Mandeville's
primary concern throughout this pamphlet.

[243] Interestingly, it is precisely this standard of companionate heterosexual monogamy that
prevails at the end of Cleland's *Memoirs of a Woman of Pleasure*, at which point Fanny manages to
marry Charles, the man whom she truly loves.

women who marry imprudently for love and especially in cases where husband and wife are grossly mismatched. In the major example presented in that work, Aurelia, bred in London, disobeys her father by marrying an Irish suitor, Dorante. Her father then ejects her from their comfortable and luxurious house and cuts her out of his will. From that point on, after Dorante takes her to Ireland, she experiences a life of pain and degradation which includes being beaten by her husband, whose bad behavior also causes the death of her young son. Dorante also tries to prostitute her for gain. Eventually this brutish husband is killed in a duel and, luckily for her, she is soon saved by a rich, elderly relative, whose property and wealth she inherits after he dies. In his ironic "Preface" Mandeville separates himself from the anti-marriage bias of the maiden aunt Lucinda, in these words:

> My Design through the whole, is to let young Ladies know whatever is dreadful in Marriage, and this could not be done, but by introducing one that was an Enemy to it. Therefore, tho' *Lucinda* speaks altogether against Matrimony, don't think that I do so too.   (A7r)

The closest he comes to praising marriage in *The Virgin Unmask'd* is to tell us that he does not disapprove of it.

When he speaks of marriage in his other works, he generally aims to reveal its flaws and failures. The chief dereliction in marriages seems to be adultery, though he does not use that word explicitly in *A Modest Defence*. He feelingly depicts the anxieties of a husband, his adulterous wife and her young lover who has intruded into and ruined their marriage. According to Mandeville, the intrusive young lover has an affair with the wife precisely because it would have been more dangerous to engage in private whoring with a street-walker or in a disease-ridden bawdy-house (technically illegal and banned since the mid-sixteenth century). If the proposed new stews, staffed responsibly, had already been available to this young lover, he could have patronized that establishment rather than seeking safe sex with a married woman.

Mandeville continued to illustrate the imperfections of marriage by examining the foibles and immoral behavior of wives at various points in his *Fable of the Bees*. In "Remark (T.)," added in 1723, he inveighed against

> those Base, those wicked Women, who calmly play their Arts and false deluding Charms against our Strength and Prudence, and act the Harlots with their Husbands! Nay, she is worse than Whore, who impiously prophanes and prostitutes the Sacred Rites of Love to vile Ignoble Ends; that first excites to Passion and invites to Joys with seeming Ardour, then racks our Fondness for no other purpose than to extort a Gift, while full of Guile in Counterfeited Transports she watches for the Moment when Men can least deny.[244]

---

[244] *Fable*, ed. Kaye, I, 227–228. This example of female guile can probably be traced at least as far back as the biblical story of Samson and Dalilah, though that tale does not describe the specific means by which she acquired the information she sought. Mandeville probably found this

Whatever incipient feminism he may reveal in *A Virgin Unmask'd* and in his thirty-two papers written for *The Female Tatler* (1709–1710), it is obvious that he also accuses women of behaving foolishly and sometimes even wickedly, as in the above example. Earlier in "Remark (T.)" he shows in different ways that a major flaw in women's characters is their strong and continuing desire for fashionable clothing and other material goods that they believe will enhance their happiness and their reputations. Some husbands who treat their wives as possessions even anticipate their desires for material goods and pamper them, while others who truly love their wives find that they need to restrain and discourage their wives from spending excessively. The marital problem in such cases is not adultery (which would be more serious in corrupting the marriage bed), but the temptation to indulge in conspicuous consumption.

By comparison, his brief description of marriage based on mutual love and respect in *A Modest Defence* will seem like an ideal that is virtually impossible to attain in the real world. It was sanctioned in the Jewish and Christian scriptures, but not as an egalitarian arrangement. It is obvious that the speaker also knew the famous passage commencing with "Hail wedded love" in *Paradise Lost*, Book 3. The marriage debate remained popular over the centuries and Mandeville would not have had to seek far to find writings that support this institution.

One work in particular, *The Praise of Marriage* (*Encomium matrimonii*) is worth considering because it was written by one of his favorite authors, Desiderius Erasmus, and also because, like *A Modest Defence*, it was written in the form of an academic oration or *declamatio*. A recent explication of this work informs us that it is "not . . . a serious treatise" but an informal letter from one lay person to another.[245] Its praises lavished on marriage, however, are said to be exaggerated, "moving beyond the limits of serious credibility." (232) It attacked the celibate life, thus alienating many who had embraced celibacy. In responding to his incensed critics, Erasmus avowed that it was the fictional speaker he created, and not he himself, who wrote against celibacy. As an exercise in declamation it does not claim to be true but is intended rather to be an academic performance. It contains a number of false arguments in order to teach students how to refute them (234).

---

thought in the pornographic tradition, specifically in *The School of Venus* (1680), a series of dialogues between a young woman who eagerly loses her virginity as she is instructed by her more experienced female friend. In this work, an imitation of Aretino's famous dialogues of courtesans called *Ragionamenti*, the more experienced friend tells the novice that "If you have then any Request to make to the man, do it when he is at the height of his Leachery, for then he can deny the Woman nothing. . . ." See pp. 38–39 in *When Flesh Becomes Word*, ed. Bradford K. Mudge.

[245] Walter M. Gordon, *Humanist Play and Belief: The Seriocomic Art of Desiderius Erasmus*, 231. An English translation of the *Encomium matrimonii*, accompanied by Erasmus's "Defense of His Declamation in Praise of Marriage" appears in *Daughters, Wives, and Widows* ed. Joan L. Klein Another translation appears in *Erasmus on Women*, ed. Erika Rummel, 57–77. For an excellent analysis of Erasmus's rhetoric in this work, see Marc van der Poel's essay.

Indeed, Erasmus himself, in responding to an attack on his *Praise of Matrimony*, asks these rhetorical questions:

> Does not the very title *Declamation* sufficiently preserve me from all attack, even if thereafter throughout the entire work I should prefer matrimony to celibacy? For who does not know that declamations are customarily written on artificial topics for the sake of exercising one's talents? [and] Whoever promises a declamation forswears honesty; his talent may be at stake, but not his honesty.[246]

In short, it is quite possible that in composing *A Modest Defence* Mandeville could have been recalling and perhaps emulating Erasmus's literary method in his *Praise of Marriage* and in his defense of that declamation.

Apparently none of Mandeville's readers ever thought to commend him for his having recommended marriage as more delightful and more useful and necessary to society than prostitution. The likeliest explanation for that omission in most later commentaries is the fact that Mandeville placed far more emphasis upon his proposal for state-run brothels. That a loving marriage is much superior to loveless sex was a common opinion in his time, as it is in ours. If one were to ask Mandeville why he did not attempt to do for marriage what he did for the improvement of prostitution, he might well have replied that just as it is impossible to extirpate whoring, so it is impossible to persuade each individual to marry. He would have added, perhaps, that preparing an elaborate and persuasive defense of marriage would be a wasted effort in a society generally convinced that marriage is right and fornication is wrong.[247] But his strongest reason for not undertaking a major defense of marriage was probably the fact that his primary purpose was to improve the system of prostitution in general in order to control the spread of venereal disease.

His account of the superiority of a successful marriage over whoring may be viewed as a merely incidental or minor part of his argument. On the other hand, the fact that his defense of improved public brothels includes

[246] "Defense of His Declamation in Praise of Marriage," pp. 91 and 92 in Joan Larsen Klein, ed., *Daughters, Wives, and Widows*.

[247] By coincidence just such an effort to praise and recommend marriage appeared in the same year in which *A Modest Defence* was published: *A Critical Essay Concerning Marriage . . . By a Gentleman*. The author of this book, Thomas Salmon, agrees with Mandeville that the sexual desires of young adults are irrepressible and should not be stifled. But Salmon differs from Mandeville by regarding marriage as the only legitimate means for fulfilling those desires. Salmon is very attentive to the biblical commandments to marry and multiply, and he cites classical precedents and practices in which a ruler or governing body encouraged marrying by offering tempting rewards and discouraged celibacy by opposite means. Like Mandeville, Salmon asserts that in good marriages the husband and wife will be alike in temper and not forced together by families seeking only to advance their worldly fortunes. For Salmon, prostitution (whoring, fornication) is simply immoral and should not be considered as an option. In fact, he barely alludes to prostitution or whoring throughout his entire book.

an admission that the satisfactions to be had in the companionate model of marriage are superior to those derived from commercial sex is not at all insignificant. Mandeville seems quite serious or earnest in his depiction of marriage here. His assertion of the superiority of marriage has the further effect of reminding the reader that even though the proposed public stews are intended to be more hygienic than they ever had been and far better managed by the government, whoring was still a vice.

It is difficult to imagine a libertine defending this view of the superiority of marriage, but the difficulty vanishes if we imagine that the author is not really a libertine but a physician who wishes to prevent the spread of venereal diseases and who also thinks that marriage is generally superior to casual commercial sex. The interesting twist here is that even while he touts the superiority of marriage from political, social, and personal considerations, he argues that it is dangerous for young males to rush directly into marriage before they have acquired sufficient experience in sexual relations and have learned to control their desires in order to maintain their virility in a state of health. The stews, then, would function, at least in part, as a rite of passage into the marital state: "Whoring, instead of being an Enemy to Matrimony, will advance and promote the Interest of it as much as possible." (1724B, p. 39) This seems tenable, but the number of ways in which commercial sex weakens and threatens the institution of marriage are easily known and tend to cancel out the force and practicality of this pro-marriage argument. Can Mandeville really have it both ways? There seems to be no simple answer to this question. Even in our times one can find published arguments maintaining that one of the positive functions of modern prostitution is to serve as a temporary sexual outlet for husbands or for others in need of such a service.

Contexts of the Law

The law and its concomitant subjects can be found on almost every page of this book. Among the crimes discussed in this work are fornication, adultery, infanticide, theft, sodomy, and rape. Prostitution itself is sometimes presented as criminal, but enacting and implementing Mandeville's proposal for public stews would in effect decriminalize it. Discussion of crime inevitably leads to the subject of punishment which, in this work, consists of shaming, fines, whipping, incarceration, and transportation. Such matters are often decided in the courts of law, which involve trials, judges, lawyers, evidence, testimony, and precedents. This system of justice is founded upon laws and each law is initially a piece of proposed legislation. Other concomitants of the field of justice and the Law are statutes, rules, legislators, and the history of the laws—all of which appear somewhere in this work.

Most of its pages are concerned with the present and the near future, but in a historical coda Mandeville devotes his closing pages to a brief review of specific medieval and early modern laws regulating prostitution and the stew houses. We gradually discover that the speaker is not only attentive to the field of the law throughout but also seems to understand very well how to argue a case before the bar.

In this work and in his next pamphlet (on the frequent executions at Tyburn, 1725) Mandeville attends to matters of law and legal history to a greater degree than he does in any of his other publications. This concern with the statutes and language of the law would seem to reflect the professional interests of his patron Thomas Parker, who was still Britain's Lord Chancellor when *A Modest Defence* was published. Parker and his associates would have been highest on Mandeville's list of preferred readers.

The ideas and images associated with the law in this essay are of two sorts: those directly connected with the proposal that Mandeville offers for legislative approval and enactment, and those that are gratuitously added, usually with some satiric aim. In a famous sentence he expresses his dismay at the frequent arrests and punishments of the common harlot:

> It is very possible, indeed, that leaving a Poor Girl Penny-less, may put her in a Way of living Honestly, tho' the want of Money was the only Reason of her living otherwise; and the Stripping of her Naked, may, for aught I know, contribute to Her Modesty, and put Her in a State of Innocence; but surely, *Gentlemen*, You must all know that Flogging has a quite contrary Effect.   (x–xi)

Suffused with irony, this satirical remark addressed to the members of the SRMs illustrates the hypocrisy of their persecution of streetwalkers who are usually too poor to avoid arrest by offering a bribe. The speaker sounds sympathetic and pities these unfortunates, but he also wishes to drive them off the streets and close the illegal bawdy-houses in which they have been spreading venereal diseases among their customers.

To achieve this end he offers a new proposal and addresses the nation's legislators or "senators" repeatedly in order to persuade them to turn his proposal into law. His ostensible aim, if we accept what he writes uncritically, that is, without attending to the ambiguities of his rhetoric, is to make his proposal the law of the land. That seems to be the central function of the law in this work. A good example of his gratuitous or somewhat peripheral references to the law is his observation (p. [60]) that Pope Sixtus the Fifth "condemned a young Man to the Galleys, only for snatching a Kiss of a Damsel in the Street." Here a Pope and his harsh sentencing are satirized—a sop, perhaps, to Mandeville's Protestant audience? Further gratuitous satire relating to the Law but only loosely related to his proposal occurs in his remark (p. [18]) that "a Lawyer cheats you according to the Law," which he includes (with other examples of professional cheating) merely as a contrast to the courtesan in the new public stews who will certainly be tried and punished if she attempts to cheat or steal from any of her clients.

In a work that is sufficiently pornographic to annoy the guardians of public morality, Mandeville seems to enjoy introducing words and phrases that are charged with sexuality, including that striking piece of old legal Latin, *rem in re*, signifying the penis in the vagina. He introduces this phrase where he discusses the difficulty of proving that any particular episode of sexual penetration really did occur.[248]

In one of the longest continuous stretches involving legal analysis ([52] to [61]), Mandeville tries to prove that neither shame nor monetary fines nor corporal punishment can deter young men from seeking to fulfill their sexual desires. This leads him to conclude that,

> As there is constantly in the Nation, a certain Number of young Men, whose Passions are too strong to brook any Opposition: Our Business is to contrive a Method how they may be gratify'd, with as little Expence of Female Virtue as possible.   (62)

This assumption of the uncontrollable force of the male sex drive is a major pillar supporting his proposal for new public stews. To ensure the success of the new plan for state-regulated prostitution, the new legislation will also require the forceful suppression of "private whoring," punishing both the female and her male clients. If his proposal becomes law it will tell the male that he may indeed have sexual intercourse with a mature unmarried woman, but only on terms stipulated by the state.

In this way, according to the author's logic, the state will direct its irrepressible young males to relieve their "Torrent of Lewdness" in brothels, thus avoiding the greater evils of rape, adultery, and "unnatural" sexual practices. Most commentators on this work, however, have not challenged the author's male-biased assumption that the sex drive of young males is unstoppable. If the state can enact a law directing them to find relief in state-controlled brothels, why can't the state rather find ways to make marriage a more desirable path to sexual satisfaction than "loveless" prostitution? He praises companionate wedded love, but he makes no effort whatever to promote it by eliminating the intermediate stage of promiscuous fornication. As a result, we are led to believe that notwithstanding his high estimation of companionate marriage, he appears to have wanted a controlled form of prostitution to survive.

The work concludes with a brief survey of the laws regulating prostitution in medieval and early modern London, information that Mandeville could have acquired from independent inquiry or (what seems more likely) from a trained barrister conversant with case law and precedents. The closing sentence, however, leaves these early statutes behind and returns to the present, in which the speaker remarks, with a saucy irony, that "we are at

---

[248] The recent development of DNA testing, to be sure, has made that task much easier in our century.

this Writing as bad as we can be," leaving it to the reader to think about which senses of "bad" may be meant here.

★ ★ ★

His essay contains references to all three divisions of the Law—positive, natural, and divine—but it is clear that his major concern is with "positive" or man-made laws, the statutes resulting from legislative action or royal decree. He mentions the Law of Nature once (60), when he refutes the claim made by "some people" that "unlawful Enjoyment is contrary to the Law of *Nature*." Wherever he speaks of the pressures of male sexuality or what we now call the male sex drive, he seems to imply the operation of one of the commonest laws of nature. It is interesting to find, furthermore, that he never mentions Divine Law as such, though he introduces ideas relating to Divine Law in at least two passages: first, when he mentions a verse in the book of Acts (15:29) that urges the reader or hearer to abstain from fornication; and second, when he treats his readers to a flagrantly fallacious line of argument (69) culminating in the statement that "no beneficial Laws can be sinful."

While the terms "law" and its extensions (lawyer, lawful, etc.) appear at least thirty-five times in this work and "crime" and "criminal" appear nineteen times, "divine" and "divinity" are entirely absent—but not the idea of God. When he does refer to God, he does so not with direct reference to prostitution but with the intention of satirizing a deceased supporter of the SRMs, Bishop Burnet. In the only other passage where the idea of God is mentioned, on p. (69), he speaks of "the Lawgivers infinite Wisdom" while refuting the "religious objections" to his own proposal.

There are more instances of the Law in this work that invite analysis and discussion, such as the case of John Felton, who assassinated the Duke of Buckingham with noble intentions and was tried and hanged, or the imagined example of sailors who come ashore from a quarantined ship and are summarily slaughtered by government forces in order to ensure that "the Health and Safety of the Nation" will remain secure (68). Such examples not only support an emergent line of argument involving good intentions combined with evil actions; they also serve as rhetorical embellishments that add dramatic action and expand the human interest of the work as a whole.

If we turn from these fragmentary references to the Law and consider this work as a unitary whole, it is possible to regard it not only as a proposal for reforming the "current" dangerous and corrupt system of satisfying sexual appetites, but also as an indictment, a trial, and a condemnation of that very system. Responding to the evils of the current system, Mandeville emphasizes the need for change, in this case a change from unfettered free trade in sexual services to a supposedly healthier system of legal, highly regulated commercial sex. To what extent his "regulationism" contributed to the wide application of this concept in nineteenth-century France and Britain we do not know, but his plan for regulating the stews became a completely serious matter when its central idea became a practical reality in the next century.

To the regulationism that he seems to recommend we need to add his implicit suggestion that the public stews ought to be legalized. It is difficult to tell whether he was only toying with these two major points involving the Law, or whether he indeed hoped that his public stews would some day materialize. In any event it appears that the broad field of the Law is almost as important in this piece as its main subject, prostitution.

A Note on the *Apologia Pro Lena* by George Buchanan (1506–1582)

Nowhere in *A Modest Defence* does Mandeville mention the title of the elegy, *Apologia pro Lena,* or name the Scottish humanist who wrote it. Yet it is highly probable that he was aware of this Latin poem because it was appended to the French translation of *A Modest Defence* with the title *Vénus la populaire, ou Apologie des maisons de joie* (1727). The translator is unknown, and the fact that Mandeville had published some translations of La Fontaine's fables two decades earlier makes us wonder whether he himself translated his own pamphlet. Whether he did so or not, he would surely have seen a copy of *Vénus la populaire* and thus also Buchanan's poem. In the seventeenth century, editions of Buchanan's poems were published in 1615, 1677, and 1685, and they were reprinted in 1715 and 1716.

The *Pro Lena*, we are told, is a paradoxical praise of the bawd or procuress and thus has some affinities with the most famous paradoxical encomium in the modern world, Erasmus's *The Praise of Folly*.[249] The central fact that most readers remember about Erasmus's speaker, Dame Folly, is that she is completely foolish in praising herself; folly is satirized. But what is sometimes overlooked or forgotten is the fact that Erasmus does seem to praise a higher foolishness associated with Christian mystical devotion. Whether Buchanan wished only to satirize the *lena* or procuress praised in his poem is unclear. According to Barbara Welch, "Buchanan's *pro Lena* displays a steady emphasis on the positive effects of the *lena* on man: she fires the imagination, cures diseases, ensures the continuation of the species, etc."[250] The *lena* or procuress in this poem is sometimes treated as a goddess. Part of the argument in her defense involves a forecast of bad results that would follow if the brothels of Bordeaux were to be prohibited. It is this point above all others, perhaps, that links this elegy to Mandeville's praise of the stews, for Buchanan's poem "purports to be an outraged response to a *bordelais* decree outlawing brothels."[251] Furthermore, it is

---

[249] Philip J. Ford, *George Buchanan: Prince of Poets*, 59; and Charles Platter and Barbara Welch, "The Poetics of Prostitution: Buchanan's 'Ars Lenae,' " 36–38. This article is valuable for anyone studying Buchanan because it contains not only a full transcription of this long Latin poem, but also Platter's useful English translation of it.

[250] Platter and Welch, "The Poetics of Prostitution," p. 37.

[251] Charles Platter, "The Artificial Whore: George Buchanan's *Apologia pro Lena*," 207. Bordelais refers to Bordeaux.

argued in Buchanan's poem that extramarital sex produces greater satisfaction than lawful cohabitation, while chastity is viewed as an impediment to procreation rather than as a positive virtue.[252] The subject in general falls under the heading of the praise of unworthy things, an exercise in the genre of the paradoxical encomium.

It seems quite possible that Mandeville already knew this work when he was composing *A Modest Defence*. If he did know it, then it could have been one of the few most important works to influence, or at least to anticipate, his essay on the stews. It is clear that both works are highly attentive to the traditions of classical rhetoric; but it does not follow that if Buchanan's apology (or praise) for the procuress is ironic, Mandeville's praise of his public stews must also be ironic. In Mandeville's case, there is strong reason to think that he really did want to reduce the incidence of venereal diseases and he might well have believed that male sexual experience prior to marriage would ensure better and more permanent unions. Both writers were dealing with subject matter frowned upon by popular morality or opinion. Buchanan escaped the opprobrium of popular disapproval by writing for the learned in their universal language, Latin. Mandeville, on the other hand, protected himself to a degree by withholding his name.

Buchanan addresses his apology or praise for the procuress to his friend Briandus Vallius of Bordeaux who was connected with a movement to close down the brothels of that city and punish illicit sex. Buchanan as speaker directly urges Vallius not to outlaw the function of the procuress because she really does benefit not only the local city but humanity at large:

> And since the splendid craft of men for evil always finds
> New means for their destruction,
> Can you forbid the trade of Venus? If you destroy the lena
> How great are the services of Venus you forbid!
> Do you dare to forbid the trade of Venus?
> Those which alone can restore the race of humans?
> . . . .
> The lena increases the bed with pleasant children
> Lest the line fail for want of offspring.

To elevate the procuress the speaker denigrates female chastity:

> In addition, a secret brood comes forth more happily
> Than when legal chains and custom bind.
> For truly there is great disdain of customary Venus,
> Nor can what is allowed always be pleasing.[253]

---

[252] Ford, *George* Buchanan p. 59.

[253] "Ad Briandum Vallium Burdegal. Pro Lena Apologia," translated by Charles Platter as "To Briandus Vallius of Bordeaux: A Defense of the Lena," lines 87–92, 103–104, and 151–154, in "The Poetics of Prostitution: Buchanan's 'Ars Lenae,' " by Charles Platter and Barbara Welch, 48–49.

While Mandeville's *Fable* depicts the harlot as a conspicuous consumer who contributes to society by causing a greater circulation of money, Buchanan's poem ignores the contributions of the *lena* to the nation's economy. Curiously, in Mandeville's writings on prostitution the bawd, the procuress, and the pimp are never discussed or examined at any length. And while Mandeville more than once mentions the role of whoring in the spread of the venereal diseases, Buchanan in this elegy simply avoids this subject.

Had Mandeville given us merely a praise of bawds or procuresses, that might have been regarded as a servile imitation. But by proposing a plan for regulated prostitution intended to be widely beneficial, he in a sense "advanced" beyond Buchanan by eliminating the traditional need for the services of the procuress. The likeliest place for a former procuress in the world of Mandeville's stews might well be that of the house mother who oversees the conduct of the twenty whores placed under her charge.

While we may still wonder whether Mandeville was at all involved in producing the 1727 translation of *Venus la populaire*, and whether he knew and was influenced by Buchanan's elegy on the *lena*, it should be apparent that *A Modest Defence* was and remains a major contribution to the pornographic tradition in its earliest sense, writings about prostitutes.

[i] TO THE

GENTLEMEN

OF THE

SOCIETIES

FOR

Reformation of MANNERS.

Gentlemen,

The great Pains and Diligence You have employ'd, in the Defence of Modesty and Virtue, give You an undisputed Title to the Address of this Treatise ; tho' it is with the utmost Concern that I find myself under a Necessity of writing it, and that after so much Reforming, there should be any Thing left to say upon the Subject, besides congratulating You upon Your happy Success. It is no small Addition **[ii]** to my Grief to observe, that Your Endeavours to suppress Lewdness, have only serv'd to promote it ; and that this *Branch* of Immorality has grown under Your Hands, as if it was *prun'd* instead of being *lopp'd*. But however Your ill Success may grieve, it cannot astonish me : What else could we hope for, from Your persecuting of poor stroling Damsels? From Your stopping up those *Drains* and *Sluices* we had to let out Lewdness? From Your demolishing those *Horn-works* and *Breast-works* of Modesty? Those *Ramparts* and *Ditches* within which the Virtue of our Wives and Daughters lay so conveniently *intrench'd*? An Intrenchment so much the safer, by how much the Ditches were harder to be fill'd up. Or what better could we expect, from Your Carting of Bawds, than that the Great Leviathan of Letchery, for Want of these Tubs to play with, should, with one Whisk of his Tail, **[iii]** overset the *Vessel* of Modesty? Which, in her best Trim, we know to be somewhat *Leaky*, and to have a very unsteady *Helm*.

An ancient Philosopher compares Lewdness to a wild, fiery, and head-strong young Colt, which can never be broke till he is rid into a Bog : And *Plato*, on the same Subject, has these Words : *The Gods*, says he, *have given us one disobedient and unruly Member, which, like a greedy and ravenous Animal that wants Food, grows wild and furious till having imbib'd the Fruit of the common Thirst, he has plentifully besprinkl'd and bedew'd the Bottom of the Womb.*

And now I have mention'd the Philosophers, I must beg Your Patience for a Moment, to hear a short Account of their Amours : For nothing will convince us of the irresistable Force of Love, and the Folly of hoping to suppress it, sooner than reflecting, that those venerable *Sages*, those

Standards of Morality, those **[iv]** great *Reformers* of the World, were so sensibly touch'd with this tender Passion.

Socrates confess'd, that, in his old Age, he felt a strange Tickling all over him for five Days, only by a Girl's touching his Shoulder.

Xenophon made open Profession of his passionate Love to *Clineas*.

Aristippus, of *Cyrene*, writ a lewd Book of antient Delights ; he compar'd a Woman to a House or a Ship, that was the better for being used : He asserted, that there was no Crime in Pleasure, but only in being a Slave to it : And often us'd to say, *I enjoy* Lais, *but* Lais *does not enjoy me.*

Theodorus openly maintain'd, that a wise Man might, without Shame or Scandal, keep Company with Common Harlots.

Plato, our great Pattern for Chaste Love, proposes, as the greatest Reward for publick Service, that he who has perform'd a signal Exploit, should **[v]** not be deny'd any amorous Favour. He writ a Description of the Loves of his Time, and several amorous Sonnets upon his own Minions : His chief Favourites were *Asterus, Dio, Phaedrus*, and *Agatho* ; but he had, for Variety, his Female Darling *Archeanassa* ; and was so noted for Wantonness, that *Antisthenes* gave him the Nick-name of *Satho*, i.e. *Well furnish'd.*

Polemo was prosecuted by his Wife for Male Venery.

Crantor made no Secret of his Love to his Pupil *Arcesilaus.*

Arcesilaus made Love to *Demetrius* and *Leocharus* ; the last, he said, he would fain have open'd : Besides, he openly frequented the two *Elean* Courtezans, *Theodota* and *Philæta*, and was himself enjoy'd by *Demochares* and *Pythocles* : He suffer'd the last, he said, for Patience Sake.

Bion was noted for debauching his own Scholars.

[vi]   *Aristotle*, the first *Peripatetick*, had a Son call'd *Nichomacus*, by his Concubine *Herpilis* : He lov'd her so well, that he left her in his Will a Talent of Silver, and the Choice of his Country Houses ; that, as he says, the Damsel might have no Reason to complain : He enjoy'd, beside the Eunuch *Hermias*, others say, only his Concubine *Pythais*, upon whom he writ a Hymn, call'd, *The Inside.*

Demetrius Phalereus, who had 360 Statues in *Athens*, kept *Lamia* for his Concubine, and at the same Time was himself enjoy'd by *Cleo :* He writ a Treatise, call'd, *The Lover*, and was nick-nam'd by the Courtezans, *Charito Blespharus*, i.e. *A Charmer of Ladies* ; and *Lampetes*, i.e. *A great Boaster of his Abilities.*

Diogenes, the *Cynick*, us'd to say, that Women ought to be in Common, and that Marriage was nothing but a Man's getting a Woman in the Mind to be lain with : He often us'd Manual **[vii]** Venery in the Publick Market-place, with this Saying, *Oh! that I [could] asswage my Hunger thus with rubbing of my Stomach!*

But what Wonder if the old *Academicks*, the *Cyrenaicks*, and *Peripateticks*, were so lewdly Wanton, when the very *Stoicks*, who prided themselves in the Conquest of all their other Passions, were forc'd to submit to this?

Zeno, indeed, the Founder of that Sect, was remarkable for his Modesty, because he rarely made Use of Boys, and took but once an ordinary Maid Servant to Bed, that he might not be thought to hate the Sex ; yet, in his Commonwealth, he was for a Community of Women ; and writ a Treatise, wherein he regulated the Motions in getting a Maidenhead, and philosophically prov'd Action and Re-action to be equal.

Chrysippus and *Appollodorus* agree with *Zeno* in a Community of Women, **[viii]** and say, that a wise man may be in Love with handsome Boys.

Erillus, a Scholar of *Zeno's*, was a notorious Debauchee.

I need not mention the *Epicureans* that were remarkable for their Obscenity.

Epicurus used to make a Pandar of his own Brother ; and his Scholar, the Great *Metrodorus*, visited all the noted Courtezans in *Athens*, and publickly kept the famous *Leontium*, his Master's *Quondam* Mistress. Yet, if You will believe *Laertius*, he was every Way a good Man.

But what shall we say of our Favourite *Seneca*, who, with all his Morals, could never acquire the Reputation of Chastity? He was indeed somewhat Nice in his Amours, like the Famous *Flora*, who was never enjoy'd by any Thing less than a Dictator or a Consul ; for he scorn'd to intrigue with any Thing less than the Empress.

[ix] Now, if those Reverend School-Masters, of Antiquity, were so Loose in their Seminals, shall we, of this Age, set up for Chastity? Have our *Oxford Students* more Command of their Passions than the *Stoicks*? Are our Young *Templars* less Amorous than *Plato*? Or, is an *Officer* of the Army less Ticklish in the Shoulder than *Socrates*?

But I need not waste any Rhetorick upon so evident a Truth ; for plain and clear Propositions, like Windows painted, are only the more Obscure the more they are adorn'd.

I will now suppose, that You have given up the Men as Incorrigible ; since You are convinc'd, by Experience, that even Matrimony is not able to reclaim them. Marriage, indeed, is just such a Cure for Lewdness, as a Surfeit is for Gluttony ; it gives a Man's Fancy a Distaste to the particular Dish, but leaves his Palate as Luxurious as ever ; for this Reason **[x]** we find so many Marry'd Men that, like *Sampson's* Foxes, only do more Mischief for having their Tails Ty'd. But the Women, You say, are weaker Vessels, and You are resolv'd to make them submit ; rightly judging, if You could make all the Females Modest, it would put a considerable Stop to Fornication. It is great Pity, no doubt, so Fine a Project should Miscarry : And I would willingly entertain Hopes of seeing one of these *Bridewell* Converts. In the mean Time it would not be Amiss, if You chang'd somewhat your present Method of Conversion, especially in the Article of Whipping. It is very possible, indeed, that leaving a Poor Girl Pennyless, may put her in a Way of living Honestly, tho' the Want of Money was the only Reason of her living otherwise ; and the Stripping of her Naked, may, for ought I know, contribute to Her Modesty, and put Her in a State of **[xi]** Innocence ; but surely, *Gentlemen*, You must all know, that Flogging has a quite contrary Effect. This Project of pulling down Bawdy-houses to prevent Uncleanness, puts me in Mind of a certain Over-nice Gentleman, who could never Fancy his Garden look'd Sweet, till he had demolish'd a Bog-house that Offended his Eye, in one Corner of it ; but it was not Long before every Nose in the Family was convinc'd of His Mistake. If Reason fails to Convince, let us profit by Example : Observe the Policy of a Modern Butcher, persecuted with a Swarm of Carnivorous Flies ; when all his Engines and Fly-flaps have prov'd ineffectual to defend his Stall against the Greedy Assiduity of those Carnal Insects, he very Judiciously cuts off a Fragment, already blown, which serves to hang up for a Cure ; and thus, by Sacrificing a Small Part, already Tainted, and not worth Keeping, he **[xii]** wisely secures the Safety of the Rest. Or, let us go higher for Instruction, and take Example by the Grazier, who far from denying his Herd the Accustom'd Privilege of Rubbing, when their Sides are Stimulated with Sharp Humours, very Industriously fixes a Stake in the Center of the Field ; not so much, You may imagine, to Regale the Salacious Hides of his Cattle, as to preserve his Young Trees from Suffering by the Violence of their Friction.

I could give You more Examples of this Kind, equally full of Instruction, but that I'm loth to detain You from the Perusal of the following Treatise ; and at the same Time Impatient to have the Honour of Subscribing Myself

Your Fellow-Reformer,

and Devoted Servant,

PHIL-PORNEY.

THE PREFACE.

L EST *any inquisitive Reader should puzzle his Brains to find out why this Foundling is thus clandestinely dropt at his Door, let it suffice him, that the Midwife of a Printer was unwilling to help bring it into the World, but upon that Condition or a much harder, that of my openly* Fathering *it. I could make many other reasonable Apologies if requisite : For, besides my having follow'd the modest Example of several other pious* Authors, *such as that of* ʹΕικὼν Βασιλικὴ, *of the* Whole Duty of Man, &c. *who have studied rather their Country's Publick Good, than their own Private Fame. I think, I have also play'd the Politick Part ; for should my* Off-spring *be defective, why, let it fall upon the Parish : On the other Hand, if* [*xiv*] *acci-|dentally it prove hopeful, 'tis certain I need be at no farther Trouble : There will then be* Parents *enough ready to own the* Babe, *and take it upon themselves. Adoption amongst the* Machiavillian *Laws of the* Muses, *is strictly kept up, and every Day put in Practice : How few of our now bright* Noblemen *would otherwise have* Wit? *How many of our present thriving* Poets *would else want a* Dinner? *'Tis a vulgar Errour to imagine Men live upon their own Wits, when generally it is upon other's Follies ; a Fund that carries by much the best Interest, and is by far upon the most certain Security of any : The* Exchequer *has been shut up, the* Bank *has stopt* Payment, South-Sea *has been demolish'd, but* Whites *was never known to fail ; and indeed how should it, when almost every Wind blows to* Dover, *or* Holyhead, *some fresh* Proprietor *amply qualified with sufficient* Stock.

I am in some pain for the Event of this Scheme, *hoping the* Wicked *will find it too* Grave, *and fearing the* Godly *will scarce venture beyond the Title-Page : And should they even, I know they'll object, 'tis here and there interwoven with too ludicrous Expressions, not considering that a dry Argument has occasion for the larding of Gaiety to make it the better Relish and go down. Besides, finding by the exact Account tack'd to* [*xv*] *that most edifying* Ante-Heidegger ★ *Discourse, that eighty six Thousand Offenders have been lately punish'd, and that four hundred Thousand religious Books have been distributed about* Gratis (*not to mention the numberless Three-penny Jobs daily Publish'd to no Ends, or Purpose, but the* Author's) ; *I say, finding all these Measures have been taken, and that Lewdness still so much prevails, I thought it highly proper to try this Experiment, being fully convinc'd that opposite Methods often take place.* Own Preferment-Hunter! *when sailing on with the Tide avails nothing, does not tacking about steer you sometimes into that snug Harbour, an Employment? Speak* Hibernian Stallion! *When a meek fawning Adoration turns to no Account, does not a pert assuming Arrogance frequently forward, nay, gain the critical Minute? And say* † Mesobin! *Where a Purge fails, is not a Vomit an infallible* Recipe *for a Looseness?*

★ A Sermon lately Preach'd against Masquerades.
† An able Member of the College of Physicians.

To conclude, when my Arguments are impartially examin'd, I doubt not but my Readers will joyn with me, that as long as it is the Nature of Man (and Naturam expellas furcâ licet usq ; recurret) *to have a Salt* **[xvi]** Itch *in the Breeches, the* Brimstone *under the Petticoat will be a necessary Remedy to* lay *it ; and let him be ever so sly in the Application, it will still be found out : What avails it then to affect to conceal that which cannot be conceal'd, and that which if carried on openly and above board, would become only less detrimental and of consequence more justifiable.*

Be the Success of this Treatise as it happens, the Good of Mankind is my only Aim ; nor am I less hearty or zealous in the Publick Welfare of my Country, than that Noble ‡ *Pattern of Sincerity, who finishes his Preface with the following Paragraph.* And now, O my G-d, the G-d of my Life, and of all my Mercies, I offer this Work to Thee, to whose Honour it is chiefly intended ; that thereby I may awaken the World to just Reflections on their own Errours and Follies, and call on them to acknowledge thy Providence, to adore it, and ever to depend on it.

[1] A Modest Defence, &c.

T HERE is nothing more idle, or shows a greater Affectation of Wit, than the modern Custom of Treating the most grave Subjects with Burlesque and Ridicule. The present Subject of *Whoring*, was I dispos'd, would furnish me sufficiently in this kind, and might possibly, if so handled, excite Mirth in those who are only capable of such low Impressions. But, as the chief Design of this Treatise is to promote the general Welfare and Happiness of Mankind, I hope to be excus'd, if I make no farther Attempts to please, than are consistent with that Design. The Practice of *Whoring* has, of late Years, become so universal, and its Effects so prejudicial to Mankind, that several Attempts have been made to put a Stop to it ; and a certain *Society* of Worthy *Gentlemen* have undertaken that Affair with a Zeal truly commendable, tho' the Success does but too plainly make it appear, that they were mistaken in their **[2]** Mea-|sures, and had not rightly consider'd the Nature of this Evil, which we are all equally sollicitous to prevent, however, we may differ in our Opinions as to the Manner. And tho' the Method I intend to propose, of erecting *Publick Stews* for that purpose, may seem at first sight somewhat ludicrous, I shall, nevertheless, make it appear to be the only Means we have now left for redressing this Grievance. As this Redress is the whole Scope and Design of this Treatise, I hope to be acquitted of my Design, when I have prov'd the following Proposition ; That publick Whoring is neither so criminal in itself, nor so

---

‡ B——p B——t.

Detrimental to the *Society* as private Whoring ; and that the encouraging of publick Whoring, by erecting *Stews*, will not only prevent most of the ill Consequences of this Vice, but even lessen the Quantity of Whoring in general, and reduce it to the narrowest Bounds which it can possibly be contain'd in. But before we proceed, it is requisite that we examine what those mischievous Effects are which Whoring naturally produces, that we may the better judge whether or no they will be prevented by this Scheme.

The greatest Evil that attends this Vice, or could well befal Mankind, is the Propagation of that infectious Disease, called the *French-Pox*, which in two Centuries, has made such incredible Havock all over *Europe*. **[3]** In these Kingdoms it so seldom fails to attend Whoring, now a days mistaken for Gallantry and Politeness, that a hale, robust Constitution is esteem'd a Mark of Ungentility ; and a healthy young Fellow is look'd upon with the same View, as if he had spent his Life in a Cottage. Our Gentlemen of the Army, whose unsettled way of Life makes it inconvenient for them to marry, are hereby very much weaken'd and enervated and render'd unfit to undergo such Hardships as are necessary for defending and supporting the Honour of their Country : And our Gentry in general seem to distinguish themselves by an ill State of Health, in all Probability the Effect of this pernicious Distemper ; for the Secresy which most People are oblig'd to in this Disease, makes the Cure of it often ineffectual ; and tho' the Infection itself may possibly be remov'd, yet for want of taking proper Methods, it generally leaves such an ill Habit of Body as is not easily recover'd. 'Tis to this we seem to owe the Rise of that Distemper, the *King's-Evil*, never known till the *French Disease* began to prevail here. But what makes this Mischief the more intolerable, is that the Innocent must suffer by it as well as the Guilty : Men give it to their Wives, Women to their Husbands, or perhaps their Children ; they to their Nurses, and the Nurses again to **[4]** other Children ; so that no Age, Sex or Condition can be entirely safe from the Infection.

Another ill Effect of this Vice is, its making People profuse, and tempting them to live beyond what their Circumstances will admit of ; for if once Men suffer their Minds to be led astray by this unruly Passion, no worldly Consideration whatever will be able to stop it ; and Wenching as it is very expensive in itself, without the ordinary Charges of Physick or Children, often leads Men into a thousand other Vices to support its Extravagance : Besides, after the Mind has once got this extravagant Turn, there naturally follows a Neglect and Contempt of Business ; and Whoring of itself disposes the Mind to such a sort of Indolence, as is quite inconsistent with Industry, the main Support of any, especially a Trading Nation.

The Murdering of Bastard Infants is another Consequence of this Vice, by much worse than the Vice itself ; and tho' the Law is justly severe in this Particular, as rightly judging that a Mind capable of divesting itself so intirely of Humanity, is not fit to live in a civiliz'd Nation ; yet there are so many ways of evading it, either by destroying the Infants before their Birth, or suffering them afterwards to die by willful Neglect, that there appears but little Hope of putting any Stop to this Practice, which, besides the Barbarity of it, tends very much to dispeople the [5] Country : And since the Prosperity of any Country is allow'd to depend in a great Measure, on the Number of its Inhabitants, the *Government* ought, if it were possible, to prevent any Whoring at all, as it evidently hinders the Propagation of the Species : How many thousand young Men in this Nation would turn their Thoughts towards Matrimony, if they were not constantly destroying that Passion, which is the only Foundation of it? And tho' most of them, sooner or later, find the Inconvenience of this irregular Life, and think fit to confine themselves to one, yet their Bodies are so much enervated, by the untimely or immoderate Encrease of this Passion, together with the Relicks of Venereal Cures, that they beget a most wretched, feeble, and sickly Offspring : We can attribute it to nothing else but this, that so many of our ancient Families of Nobles are of late extinct.

There is one thing more we ought to consider in this Vice, and that is the Injury it does to particular Persons and Families ; either by alienating the Affections of Wives form [sic] their Husband [sic], which often proves prejudicial to both, and sometimes fatal to whole Families ; or else by debauching the Minds of young Women, to their utter Ruin and Destruction ; for the Reproach they must undergo, when a Slip of this Nature is discover'd, prevents their marrying in any Degree [6] suitable to their Fortune, and by Degrees hardens them to all Sense of Shame ; and when they have once overcome that, the present View of Interest as well as Pleasure, sways them to continue in the same Course, till at length they become common Prostitutes.

These are the several bad Effects of Whoring ; and it is an unhappy Thing, that a Practice so universal as this is, and always will be, should be attended with such mischievous Consequences : But since few or none of them are the necessary Effects of Whoring, consider'd in itself, but only proceed from the Abuse and ill Management of it ; our Business is certainly to regulate this Affair in such sort as may best prevent these Mischiefs. And I must here beg pardon of those worthy *Gentlemen* of the *Society*, if I can't conceive how the Discouragement they have given, or rather attempted to give, to publick Whoring, could possibly have the desired Effect. If this was a Vice acquir'd by Habit or Custom, or depended upon Education, as most other Vices, there might be some Hopes of suppressing it ; and then it would, no doubt, be commendable to attack it without Distinction, in whatever Form or Disguise it should appear : But alas, this violent Love for Women is born and bred with us ; nay, it is absolutely necessary to our being born at all : And however [7] some People may pretend, that unlawful Enjoyment is contrary to the Law of *Nature* ; this is certain, that Nature never fails to furnish us largely with this Passion, tho' she is often sparing to bestow upon us such a Portion of Reason and Reflection as is necessary to curb it.

That long Course of Experience which most of these *Gentlemen* have had in the World, and which is of such great Use in other Cases, may probably occasion their Mistake in this ; for Age is very liable to forget the violence of youthful Passions, and, consequently, apt to think them easier curb'd ; whereas if we consider the true Source of Whoring, and the strong Impulse of Nature that way, we shall find, it is a Thing not to be too violently restrain'd ; lest, like a Stream diverted out of its proper Channel, it should break in and overflow the neighbouring *Enclosures*.

History affords us several Instances of this Truth ; I shall mention but one, and that is of Pope *Sixtus* the 5th, who was so strictly severe in the Execution of Justice, if such Severity may be call'd Justice, and particularly, against Offenders of this kind, that he condemned a young Man to the Galleys, only for snatching a Kiss of a Damsel in the Street ; yet notwithstanding this his *Holiness's* Zeal, he never attempted once to exterpate Whoring intirely. But **[8]** like a true *Pastor* seperated the clean Sheep from the unclean, and confin'd all the Courtezans to one Quarter of the City : It is true, he did attempt to moderate this Vice, and banish'd as many Courtezans as he thought exceeded the necessary Number ; but he was soon convinc'd of the Error of his Computation, for *Sodomy*, and a thousand other unnatural Vices sprung up, which forced him soon to recall them, and has left us a remarkable Instance of the Vanity of such Attempts.

Let us now proceed to the Proof of our Proposition, in the first Part of which it was asserted, that publick Whoring is neither so Criminal in itself, nor so Detrimental to the *Society* as private Whoring.

Publick Whoring consists in lying with a certain Set of Women, who have shook off all Pretence to Modesty ; and for such a Sum of Money, more or less, profess themselves always in a Readiness to be enjoy'd. The Mischief a Man does in this Case is entirely to himself, for with respect to the Woman he does a laudable Action, in furnishing her with the Means of Subsistance, in the only, or at least most innocent way that she is capable of procuring of it. The Dammage he does to himself is either with regard to his Health, or the Expence of Money, and may be consider'd under the same View as Drinking with this considerable Advantage, that it restores us to that cool Exercise of our Reason, **[9]** which Drinking tends to deprive us of. Indeed was there a Probability of a Woman's Amendment, and of her gaining a Livelihood by some honester Method, there might be some Crime in encouraging her to follow such a Profession : But the Minds of Women are observ'd to be so much corrupted by the Loss of Chastity, or rather by the Reproach they suffer upon that Loss, that they seldom or never change that Course of Life for the better ; and if they should, they can never recover that good Name, which is so absolutely necessary to their getting a Maintenance in any honest Way whatever ; and that nothing but meer Necessity obliges them to continue in that Course, is plain from this ; that they themselves in Reality utterly abhor it : And indeed there appears nothing in it so very alluring and bewitching, especially to People who have that Inclination to Lewdness entirely extinguish'd, which is the only thing could possibly make it supportable.

The other Branch of Whoring, viz. *Private*, is of much worse Consequence ; and a Man's Crime in this Case, increases in proportion to the different Degree of Mischief done, if you consider his Crime with regard to the *Society* ; for as to personal Guilt, Allowance ought to be made for the Encrease of Temptation, which is very considerable in the Case of debauching *Married Women* ; **[10]** upon account of the Safety to the Aggressor, either with Respect to his Health, or the Charge, and, if that affects him, the Scandal of having a Bastard. On the other Hand, the Injury done, is very considerable, as such an Action tends to corrupt a Woman's Mind, and destroys that mutual Love and Affection between Man and Wife, which is so necessary to both their Happiness. Besides, the Risque run of a Discovery, which at least ruins a Woman's Reputation, and destroys the Husbands quiet ; nay, where Virtue does not entirely give way, if it Warps but ever so little, the Consequence is shockingly fatal ; for tho' the good Man, suspicious of the Wife's Chastity, the Wife of the Gallant's Constancy, and the Gallant of the Husband's Watchfulness, by being a Check upon each other, may keep the Gate of Virtue shut ; yet then even all Parties must be attended with a never ceasing Misery not to be imagin'd, but by those who too fatally *feel it.*

The Crime of debauching young *Virgins* will appear much greater, if we consider that there is much more Mischief done, and the Temptation to do it much lessen'd by the fear of getting Children ; which, in most Circumstances of Life, does a Man a deal of Prejudice, and keeps at least three Parts in four of our sober Youth from gratifying this violent Passion. Besides, the Methods that are **[11]** Necessa-|ry to be taken, before a Man can have such an Action in his Power, are in themselves Criminal ; and it shows a certain Baseness of Mind to persuade a Woman, by a thousand solemn Vows and Protestations, into such a good Opinion of you, and Assurance of your Love to her, that she trusts you with all that is dear and near to her, and this with no other View but the Gratification of a present Passion, which might be otherwise vented, than at the certain Expence of her Ruin, and putting her under the Necessity of leading the Life of a *Publick Courtezan.*

From this general Consideration of Whoring it is evident, that tho' all the several Species of it proceed from the same Cause, our natural Love and Passion for Women, yet they are very different in their Natures, and fully as distinct Crimes as those which proceed from our Love to Money, such as Murder, Shoplifting, *&c.* And I hope I have said enough to prove, that the publick Part of it is by far the least Criminal, and least Detrimental to the *Society* ; which of itself is a sufficient Motive for the *Legislature* to confine it to that Channel. I shall now proceed farther, and show, as I before propos'd, that the incouraging of publick Whoring, will not only prevent most of the mischievous Effects of this Vice, but even lessen the Quantity of Whoring in general, and reduce it to **[12]** the narrowest Bounds which it can possibly be contain'd in.

When I talk'd of encouraging publick Whoring, I would be understood to mean, not only the erecting *Publick Stews*, as I at first hinted, but also the endowing them with such Privileges and Immunities, and at the same time giving such Discouragement to private Whoring, as may be most effectual to turn the general Stream of Lewdness into this common Channel.

I shall here lay down a Plan for this Purpose, which, tho' it may well serve to illustrate this Point, and make good the Proof of my present Argument, would doubtless receive infinite Improvement by coming through the Hands of a *National Senate*, whose august Body, being compos'd of *Spirituals* as well as *Temporals*, will, I hope, take into Consideration this important Affair, which so nearly concerns both.

The Plan I would propose is this : Let a hundred or more Houses be provided in some convenient Quarter of the City, and proportionably in every Country Town, sufficient to contain two thousand Women : If a hundred are thought sufficient, let a hundred *Matrons* be appointed, one to each House, of Abilities and Experience enough to take upon them the Management of twenty Courtezans each, to see that they keep themselves neat and decent, and entertain Gentlemen after a **[13]** civil and obliging Manner. For the encouragement of such *Matrons*, each House must be allow'd a certain Quantity of all sorts of Liquor, Custom and Excise free ; by which Means they will be enabled to accommodate Gentlemen handsomely, without that Imposition so frequently met with in such Houses. Besides the hundred above mention'd, there must be a very large House set apart for an Infirmary, and Provision made for two able Physicians, and four Surgeons at least. Lastly, there must be three Commissioners appointed to superintend the whole, to hear and redress Complaints, and to see that each House punctually observes such Rules and Orders as shall be thought Necessary for the good Government of this Community. For the better Entertainment of all Ranks and Degrees of Gentlemen, we shall divide the twenty Women of each House into four Classes, who for their Beauty, or other Qualifications may justly Challenge different Prices.

The first Class is to consist of eight, who may legally demand from each Visitant Half a Crown. The second Class to consist of six, whose fix'd Price may be a Crown. The third Class of four at half a Guinea each. The remaining two make up the fourth Class, and are design'd for Persons of the first Rank, who can afford to Pay a Guinea for the Elegancy of their Taste. To defray the Charges of this Establishment, **[14]** will require but a very moderate Tax : For if the first Class pays but forty Shillings Yearly, and the rest in Proportion, it will amount to above ten thousand Pounds a Year, which will not only pay the Commissioners Salaries, Surgeons Chests, and other Contingencies, but likewise Establish a good Fund for the Maintenance of Bastard-Orphans and superannuated Courtezans.

For the better Government of this *Society*, it will be necessary that the Mistress have an absolute Command in her own House, and that no Woman be suffer'd to go Abroad without her Leave. No Woman must be suffer'd to lye in within the House, nor any young Children admitted under any Pretence. No Musick or Revelling to be allow'd in any Room to the Disturbance of the rest. No Gentlemen disorderly or drunk to be admitted at an unseasonable Hour, without the Consent of the Mistress : And, in Case of Violence, she must be impower'd to call the Civil Aid.

For the *Society's* Security in Point of Health, it must be order'd, That if any Gentleman complains of receiving an Injury, and the Woman, upon Search, be found tainted, without having discover'd it to the Mistress, she shall be stripp'd and cashier'd. But if a Woman discovers her Misfortune before any Complaint is made against her, she shall be sent to the **[15]** *Infir-|mary*, and cur'd at the Publick Charge. No Woman that has been twice pox'd shall ever be re-admitted. *Note*, That three Claps shall be reckon'd equivalent to one Pox.

But as no *Society* ever fram'd a compleat Body of Laws at once, till unforeseen Accidents had taught them Foresight, we shall refer the farther Regulation of these Laws, with whatever new ones shall be thought necessary to the *Wisdom* of the *Legislature*.

The *Publick Stews* being thus erected and govern'd by good and wholesome Laws, there remains nothing to compleat this project, but that proper Measures be taken effectually to discourage all other Kinds of Whoring whatsoever. And here it is to be hop'd, that those worthy *Gentlemen* of the *Society* who have hitherto distinguish'd their *Zeal* to so little Purpose, will now exert themselves where they have so good a Prospect of Success ; for altho' a poor Itinerant Courtezan could not by any Means be persuaded to starve at the Instigation of a *Reforming* Constable, yet a little *Bridewell* Rhetorick, or the Terrors of a Transportation, will soon convince her that she may live more comfortably and honestly in a *Publick Stew*. If there are any so foolish as to love Rambling better, or who are not qualify'd to please Gentlemen according to Law, they ought to be transported ; for *Bridewell*, as it is now manag'd, only makes them **[16]** poor-|er, and consequently lays them under a greater Necessity than ever of continuing Whores.

Let us now suppose, for Brevity Sake, that the *Publick Stews* are as much as possible favour'd and encourag'd, and that all the other Branches of this Vice have the utmost Rigour of the Laws exerted against them.

It now remains for me to show what Benefit the *Nation* would receive thereby, and how this Project would prevent or in any Degree alleviate those Mischiefs which I have mention'd to be the necessary Consequences of this Vice. As for any Objections that may be rais'd against me, either *Christian* or *Moral*, I shall refer them to the Close of this Discourse.

First then, I say, the *Nation* would receive a general Benefit by having such a considerable Number of its most disorderly Inhabitants brought to live after a regular civiliz'd Manner. There is, one Year with another, a certain Number of young Women who arrive gradually, Step by Step, at the highest Degree of Impudence and Lewdness. These Women, besides their Incontinence, are commonly guilty of almost the whole Catalogue of immoral Actions : The Reason is evident : They are utterly abandon'd by their Parents, and thereby reduc'd to the last **[17]** De-|gree of Shifting-poverty ; if their Lewdness cannot supply their Wants, they must have Recourse to Methods more criminal, such as *Lying, Cheating, open Theft, &c.*

Not that these are the necessary Concomitants of Lewdness, or have the least Relation to it, as all *lewd Men of Honour* can testify ; but the Treatment such Women meet with in the World, is the Occasion of it.

Those Females, who either by the Frigidity of their Constitutions, a lucky Want of Temptation, or any other Cause, have preserv'd their Chastity, and the Men, in general, Chaste or Unchaste, are so outrageous against these Delinquents, that they make no Distinction ; all of them are branded with the same opprobrious Title, they are all treated with the same Contempt, all equally despis'd ; so that let them be guilty of what other Crimes they please, they cannot add one Jot to the Shame they already undergo. Having thus remov'd the Fear of worldly Reproach, which is justly esteem'd the greatest *Bulwark* of *Morality*, it is no Wonder if these Women, insensible of Shame, and prick'd on by Want, commit any Crimes, where they are not deterr'd by the Fear of corporal Punishments. But the Case now will be quite alter'd ; these Women, as soon as they have attain'd a competent Share of Assurance, and before they are pinch'd with [18] the Extreme of Poverty, will enter themselves in some of the above-mention'd Classes of profess'd Courtezans ; where, instead of being necessarily dishonest, they will have more Inducements to Honesty than any other Profession whatsoever. The same Money defends as well as it corrupts a *Prime Minister* : A *Churchman* takes Sanctuary in a Gown, and who dare accuse a Mitre of *Simony*? Accuse a *Colonel* of Injustice, he is try'd by his Board of *Peers*, and your Information is false, scandalous, and malicious : A *Lawyer* cheats you according to Law ; and you may thank the *Physician*, if you live to complain of him : *Over-reaching* in Trade, is *prudent Dealing* ; and *Mechanick Cunning* is styl'd *Handicraft*. Not so fares the poor Courtezan ; if she commits but one ill Action, if for Instance, she should circumvent a Gentleman in a *Snuff-Box*, she can hardly escape Detection ; and the first Discovery ruins her ; she is banish'd the *Publick Stews*, mark'd out for Infamy, and can have no better Prospect than a Transportation. On the other Hand, the Motives to Honesty will be as great here as any where : It is natural for Mankind to regard chiefly the good Opinion of those with whom they converse, and to neglect that of Strangers ; now in this Community, Lewdness not being esteem'd a Reproach, but rather [19] a Commendation, they will set a Value on their good Name, and stand as much upon the Puncto of Honour as the rest of Mankind ; being mov'd by the same commendable Emulation, and deterr'd by greater, or at least more certain Punishments. Besides this Reformation in Point of Honesty, the Publick will receive another Benefit in being freed from those nocturnal Disorders, Quarrels, and Brawlings, which are occasion'd by vagrant Punks, and the Number of private Brothels dispers'd throughout the City, to the great Disturbance of its sober Inhabitants.

We have already mention'd the *French Disease* as one of the worst Attendants upon Lewdness, and with good Reason ; for in the Enjoyment of this Life, Health is the *sine qua non* ; and this Distemper has one Thing in it peculiarly inveterate, as if it came out of *Pandora*'s worst Box : there is no other Disorder, but what at some Age, or in some particular Constitution, will abate of itself without the Application of Medicines ; but this is such a busy restless Enemy, that unless resisted, he is never at a Stand, but gathers Strength every Day, to the utter Disquiet of the Patient. Now it is so evident that the *Publick Stews*, when well regulated, will prevent the Spreading of this Plague, that a prolix and tedious **[20]** Proof of it would look like Declaiming. As this Disease has its Spring and Source entirely from publick Whoring, and from thence creeps into private Families ; so it likewise receives continual Supplies and Recruits thro' the same Channel : When this Source is once dry'd up, the Nation will naturally recover its pristine Health and Vigour : And this cannot fail to happen, if due Care be taken to keep the *Stews* free from Infection ; for what young Fellow will be so industriously mad as to take Pains to run his Head into an Apothecary's Shop, when he may with so much Ease and Conveniency, and without the Fear of a *Reforming Officer*, both secure his Health and gratify his Fancy with such a Variety of Mistresses.

'Tis true, the keeping of the *Publick Stews* so very safe will appear a difficult Task, at first Sight, but not so if we consider the Case a little nearer. This Disease is propagated reciprocally from the Woman to the Man, and from the Man to the Woman ; but the first is the most common for several Reasons : We are not like Cocks or Town-Bulls, who have a whole Seraglio of Females entirely and solely at their Devotion ; on the contrary, one industrious pains-taking Woman, that lays herself out that Way, is capable of satisfying several **[21]** rampant Males ; insomuch, that a select Number of Women get a handsome Livelihood by being able to oblige such a Number of Customers. Now, if but a few of these Women are unsound, they can infect a great many Men ; whereas these Men have neither Power nor Inclination to infect the like Number of Women. I say, Inclination ; for a Woman, to raise Money for the Surgeon's Fee, may counterfeit Pleasure when she really receives Pain ; nay, she may even venture to complain of being hurt ; for the Man will attribute the Pain he gives her either to her Chastity or his own Vigour ; not dreaming, perhaps, that he has molested a *Shanker*. This a Female may do, as being only passive in the Affair, but a Man must have real Fancy and Inclination before he is qualify'd to enter upon Action : And how far this Fancy to Woman may be cool'd by a stinging *Gonorrhœa*, I leave the experienc'd Reader to judge ; and whether a Man won't rather employ his Thoughts upon his *round Diet*, how to digest two at Night, and three in the Morning ; what Conveyance to find out, when poach'd Eggs grow Nauseous, and how to preserve his Linnen from being speckled, with a Thousand other Particulars that occur to a Man in this Distress ; but these are sufficient, with the Assistance of **[22]** a *Cordee*, to *bridle* any moderate Passion. So that from the whole we may safely draw this Conclusion ; that since the Men are so seldom guilty of transgressing in this Kind, the spreading of this Distemper must be owing to the Neglect of Cure in the Women. Now the *Publick Stews* will be so regulated, that a Woman cannot possibly conceal her Misfortune long ; nay it will be highly her Interest to make the first Discovery ; so that whatever Dammage the *Society* may sustain at first, when Claps are most current, it will be soon repair'd, and this Distemper, in Time, entirely rooted out. But of this enough.

The next Thing that comes to be consider'd in this Vice, is the Expence it occasions, and the Neglect of worldly Business, by employing so much of our Time and Thoughts ; for let a Man have ever so much Business, it can't stop the Circulation of his Blood, or prevent the Seminal Secretion ; for Sleeping or Waking, the *Spermaticks* will do their Office, tho' a Man's Thoughts may be so much employ'd about other Affairs that he cannot attend to every minute Titillation. A Man of Pleasure, indeed, may make this copulative Science his whole Study ; and, by Idleness and Luxury, may prompt Nature that Way, and spur up the Spirits to Wantonness ; but then his **[23]** Constitution will be the sooner tir'd ; for, the Animal Spirits being exhausted by this Anticipation, his Body must be weaken'd, and his Nerves relax'd ; neither will his irregular effeminate Life assist them in recovering their former Force. Besides, those Parts which more particularly suffer the Violence of this Exercise, are liable to many Accidents ; and Men of Pleasure, thought otherwise pretty healthy, are often troubled with Gleets and Weaknesses, either by a former Ulceration of the *Prostrates*, or else some violent Over-straining, which occasions this Relaxation. These Men, tis true, will talk very lusciously of Women ; but, pretend what they please, they can never have that burning Desire which they had formerly, when their Vessels were in full Vigour. The Truth is, their Lust lies chiefly in their Brain, kept alive by the Impression of former Ideas, which are not so easily rubb'd out as the Titillation which created them ; and this Passion comes to be so diminish'd, that, in time, it changes its Residence from the *Glans Penis* to the *Glandula Penealis*. A Man of Business, on the contrary, or one who leads a sober regular Life, will seldomer be attack'd by these wanton Fits, but then they will come with double the Violence ; for tho' it is a **[24]** common receiv'd Opinion, that the longer a Man refrains, the better he is able to refrain, yet it is only true in one Sense, and amounts to no more than this : That if a Man has been able, for such and such Reasons, to curb this Passion, for Instance, a Month, he will, if the same Reasons hold and without an additional Temptation, be able to curb it a Month longer ; but nevertheless, he may have Desires much stronger than a Man who, for Want of these Motives to Abstinence, gratifies them every Day. If there are some Men of a particular Constitution, whose puny Desires may be easily block'd up with the Assistance of *three small Buttons*, or else endow'd with such an extraordinary Strength of Reason, that they can master the most *rampant* Sallies of this raging Passion, I heartily congratulate their happy Conquest, but have nothing more to do with them at present, the *Publick Stews* not being design'd for such : I am here speaking of those Men of Business who, notwithstanding their Abstinence or the Regularity of their Lives, are sometimes prevail'd upon to quench these amorous Heats ; and

I say in such Men, the Passion is much stronger than in Men of Pleasure, and that their Abstinence contributes to heighten the Violence of the Desire, and make it the more irresistable ; **[25]** for the Fancy not being cloy'd with too frequent Enjoyment, presently takes Fire ; and the *Spermaticks*, not being weaken'd with forc'd Evacuations, are in their full Vigour, and give the Nerves a most exquisite Sensation ; so that upon the least Toying with an alluring Wench, the Blood-Vessels are ready to start ; and, to use *Othello*'s Words, *The very Sense aches at her.*

Now what shall this Man do, when he has once taken the Resolution to make himself Easy? He must either venture upon the Publick, where, it is Odds, he may meet with a Mischance that will either drain his Pocket and make him unfit for any Business, at least without Doors ; or else he must employ both his Time and Rhetorick, and perhaps too his Purse, in deluding some modest Girl ; which, besides the Loss of Time in carrying on such an Intrigue, is apt to give the Head such an amorous Turn as is quite inconsistent with Business, and may probably lead a Man into after Expences, which at first he never dream'd of.

Now, to remedy all these Inconveniencies, the *Publick Stews* will be always ready and open, where a Man may regulate his Expences according to his Ability, from Half a Crown to a Guinea ; and that too without endangering his Health : And besides, which is chiefly to be consider'd, if **[26]** a Man should be overtaken with a sudden Gust of Lechery, it will be no Hinderance to him even in the greatest Hurry of Business, for a ready and willing Mistress will ease him in the Twinkling of an Eye, and he may prosecute his Affairs with more Attention than ever, by having his Mind entirely freed and disengag'd from those troublesome Ideas which always accompany a wanton Disposition of the Body. But to proceed :

Another ill Consequence of Whoring, is the Tendency it has to dispeople a Nation ; and that both by the Destruction of Bastard Infants, and by ruining young Men's Constitutions so much, that, when they marry, they either beget no Children, or such as are sickly and short–liv'd. The first of these, indeed, is almost unavoidable, especially in modest Women, who will be guilty of this Cruelty as long as Female Chastity carries that high Reputation along with it, which it really deserves : However, in common Women, it may and will be, in a great Measure, prevented by this Scheme ; for every profess'd Courtezan, that is legally licens'd, will have an Apartment allotted her in the Infirmary when she is ready to lye in, and will be oblig'd to take Care of her Child ; by which Means a considerable number of Infants will be rear'd up, that **[27]** otherwise might probably have perish'd. Besides, there are a great many ordinary Girls, such as Servant-Maids, who are chiefly mov'd to this Action, by the Fear of losing their Services and wanting Bread ; now this handsome Provision that is made for them, will be a great Inducement for such to enter themselves in the *Stews*, rather than commit such an unnatural Action, especially when the Discovery is Death.

Let us now consider the Affair of Matrimony. Since the World is now no longer in a State of Nature, but form'd into several Societies independent of one another, and these Societies again divided into several Ranks and Degrees of Men, distinguish'd by their Titles and Possessions, which descend from Father to Son, it is very certain that Marriage is absolutely necessary, not only for the regular Propagation of the *Species*, and their careful Education, but likewise for preserving that Distinction of Rank among Mankind, which otherwise would be utterly lost and confounded by doubtful Successions. And it is no less certain and indisputable, that all Sorts and Kinds of Debauchery whatever are Enemies to this State, in so far as they impair the natural Vigour of the Constitution, and weaken the very Springs of Love.

[28]   This necessary Passion is, indeed, of such a Ticklish Nature, that either too much or too little of it is equally prejudicial, and the *Medium* is so hard to hit, that we are apt to fall into one of the Extremes. We are naturally *furnish'd* with an extraordinary *Stock* of Love ; and, by the *Largeness* of the Provision, it looks as if Nature had made some Allowance for *Wear and Tear*. If young Men were to live entirely Chaste and Sober, without blunting the Edge of their Passions, the first Fit of Love would turn their Brains Topsyturvy, and we should have the Nation Pester'd with Love Adventures and Feats of Chivalry : By the Time a *Peer*'s Son came to be Sixteen, he would be in Danger of turning Knight-errant, and might possibly take a Cobler's Daughter for his *Dulcinea* ; and who knows but a sprightly young *Tailor* might turn an *Orlando Furioso*, and venture his Neck to carry off a Lady of Birth and Fortune. In short, there are so many Instances, every Day, of these ruinous disproportion'd Matches, notwith-standing our present Intemperance, that we may justly conclude, if the Nation was in a State of perfect Sobriety, no Man could answer for the Conduct of his Children.

It must, indeed, be confess'd, as Matters now stand, the Excess of Chastity is not so [29] much to be fear'd as the other Extreme of Lewdness, tho' there are Instances of both ; and many Fathers, now living, would gladly have seen their Sons Fifty Times in a *Stew* rather than see them so unfortunately marry'd. The other Extreme is equally, or rather more dan-gerous, as it is more common ; for most young Men give too great a Loose to their Passions, and either quite destroy their Inclination to Matrimony, or make their Constitutions incapable of answering the Ends of that State.

To avoid therefore these two dangerous Extremes, we have erected the *Publick Stews*, which every considerate Man must allow to be that Golden Mean so much desired ; For, in the first Place, we avoid the Inconvenience of too strict a Chastity : When a Man has gained some Experience by his Commerce in the *Stews*, he is able to form a pretty good comparative Judgment of what he may expect from the highest Gratifications of Love ; he finds his Ideas of Beauty strangely alter'd after Enjoyment, and will not be hurry'd into an unsuitable Match by those romantick chimerical Notions of Love, which possess the Minds of unexperienced Youth, and make them fancy that Love alone can compleat the Happiness of a Marry'd State. But this [30] will be so readily granted, that I shan't insist upon it further.

In the next Place, the *Publick Stews* will prevent the ill Effects of excessive Lewdness, by preserving Men's Constitutions so well, that altho' they may defer Matrimony some Time for their special Advantage, yet they will have a sufficient Stock of Desire left to persuade them, one Time or other, to quit the Gaiety of a Single Life : And when they do marry, they will be able to answer all the Ends and Purposes of that State as well, and rather better, than if they had liv'd perfectly Chaste.

This may seem a bold Proposition, but the Proof of it is nevertheless obvious. However, to proceed Methodically, there are three Ways by which lewd young Men destroy their natural Vigour, and render themselves Impotent : First, By Manufriction, *alias* Masturbation. Secondly, by too frequent and immoderate Enjoyment. And, lastly, by contracting Venereal Disorders, as Claps or Poxes.

The first lewd Trick that Boys learn, is this Manual Diversion ; and when they have once got the Knack of it, they seldom quit it till they come to have actual Commerce with Women : The Safety, Privacy, Convenience, and Cheapness of this Gratification, are very strong Motives, and chiefly **[31]** persuade young Men to continue the Practice of it.

If these *Onanites* were so abstemious as to wait the ordinary Calls of Nature, this Action, however unnatural, would be no more prejudicial when prudently manag'd, than Common Copulation ; but, instead of this, they are every Day committing *Rapes* upon their own Bodies ; and tho' they have neither real Inclination nor Ability to attack a Woman, yet they can attack themselves, and supply all these Defects by the Agility of their Wrists ; by which Means they so weaken their Genitals, and accustom them to this violent Friction, that, tho' they have frequently Evacuations without an Erection, yet the common and ordinary Sensation which Females afford to those Parts, is not able of itself to promote this Evacuation ; so that they are impotent to all Intents and Purposes of Generation.

To put a Stop therefore to these clandestine Practises, and prevent young Men from *laying violent Hands* upon themselves, we must have Recourse to the *Publick Stews*, which cannot fail to have the desir'd Effect : For which of these private Practitioners can be so brutish, as to prefer this boyish, solitary Amusement before the actual Embraces of a fine Woman, when they can **[32]** proceed with the same Convenience, Safety, and Privacy, in the one, as well as the other.

In the next Place, Men are often weaken'd, and sometimes contract almost incurable Gleets, by too frequent and immoderate Enjoyment : This seldom or never happens but in private Whoring, when some particular Mistress has made such a strong Impression upon a Man's Fancy, that he exerts himself in an extraordinary Manner beyond his natural Ability, and thereby contracts a Seminal Weakness, which is generally more difficult to cure than a virulent Running. Now this Danger will be pretty well remov'd by the Encouragement given to *Publick Whoring*, which, as I shall show more particularly hereafter, will divert Mens Minds, and turn their Thoughts very much from private Intrigues : And it will be readily granted me, that no such Excess is to be fear'd in *Publick Stews* ; where a Man only acting out of a general Principle of Love to the whole Sex, will be in no Danger of proceeding any farther than he is prompted by Nature and the particular Disposition of his Body at that time.

As for the third Cause of Impotency, the Venereal Disease, we have already prov'd, that this Institution of the *Stews* **[33]** is the best and surest Remedy against it ; and shall only observe here how happily this Project provides against the various ill Effects of Lewdness, in whatever Light we consider them.

Thus, I think, the first Part of my Proposition pretty well clear'd, *viz.* That the *Publick Stews* will preserve Men's Constitutions so well, that they will have a sufficient Stock of corporal Ability, and consequently Inclination left to persuade them, sooner or later, to enter into the Marriage State.

I say further, that these Men, having thus preserv'd their Constitution, will answer all the Intents and Purposes of that State, rather better than if they had liv'd perfectly Chaste.

When a Man and a Woman select one another out of the whole Species, it is not merely for Propagation ; nay, that is generally the least in their Thoughts : What they chiefly have in View, is to pass the Remainder of their Lives happily together, to enjoy the soft Embraces and mutual Endearments of Love ; to divide their Joys and Griefs ; to share their Pleasures and Afflictions ; and, in short, to make one another as happy as possible. As for Children, they come of Course, and of **[34]** Course are educated according to their Parents Abilities.

Now all these Enjoyments depending upon the mutual Affection of these two, Man and Wife ; when ever this Affection fails, either in the Woman or the Man, that Marriage is unhappy, and all the good Ends and Designs of this State entirely frustrated. To give the Women their Due, they must have the Preference in Point of Constancy ; their Passions are not so easily rais'd, nor so suddenly fix'd upon any particular Object ; but when this Passion is once rooted in Women, it is much stronger and more durable than in Men, and rather increases than diminishes, by enjoying the Person belov'd. Whether it is that Women receive as much Love as they part with, and that the Love they receive is not entirely lost, but takes Root again by Conception ; whereas what a Man parts with never affects him farther, than just the Pleasure he receives at the Time of parting with it, or whether this Difference is owing to the different Turn of Men's Fancies, which are more susceptible of fresh Impressions from every handsome Face they meet, or perhaps that their Heads are so much employ'd in worldly Affairs, that they only take Love *en passant* to get rid of a present Uneasiness, whereas Women **[35]** make it the whole Business of their Lives. Whatever the Reason is, I say, it is experimentally true, that a Woman has but a very *slippery Hold* of a Man's Affections after Enjoyment. Let us see therefore which of these two, the Chaste or the experienc'd Man, will be least liable to this Failure of Affection, and consequently which of the Two will make the best marry'd Man.

The first great Cooler of a Man's Affections, after Marriage, is the Disparity of the Match. When a Man has marry'd entirely for Love, and to the apparent Detriment of his worldly Affairs, as soon as the first Flash of it is over, he can't help reflecting upon this Woman as the Cause, and, in some Sense, the Author of his Misfortunes : This naturally begets a Coldness and Indifference, which, by Degrees, turns to an open Dislike. Now, it is these Sort of Marriages that Chaste Men are always in Danger of falling into, as I have already prov'd ; neither is there any effectual Way to convince a Man of this Folly and secure him against it, but by giving him some Experience in Love Affairs. Again, as chaste Men seldom marry for any Thing but sheer Love, so they have fram'd to themselves such high extravagant Notions of the Raptures they expect to possess in the Marriage Bed, that they are **[36]** mightily shock'd at the Disappointment. A Chaste unexperienc'd Man is strangely surpriz'd, that those bewitching Charms should make such a faint Impression upon him after a thorough Perusal ; he can scarce believe that the Woman is still possess'd of the same Charms which transported him formerly ; he fancies he has discover'd abundance of little Faults and Imperfections, and attributes his growing Dislike to this Discovery, not dreaming that this Alteration is entirely in himself, and not in the Object of Desire, which remains still the same. The Truth is, when a Man is full fraught with Love, and that his Pulse beats high for Enjoyment, this peccant Love-Humour falls down upon the Eye, which may be observ'd at such a Time to be full brisk and sparkling : 'Tis then the Beauty of every Feature is magnify'd by coming thro' this false Perspective, and *Parthenope* is no less than a Goddess. But when this dazling Humour is drawn downwards by a Revulsion, as in the Case of Marriage, a Man's Eyes are perfectly open'd ; and tho' they may look languid, sunk, and environ'd with blewish Circles, yet he actually sees much better than before ; for *Parthenope* will now appear to him a Mortal, such as she really is, divested of all those false Glosses and Appearances.

[37]   The Chaste Man is supriz'd at this Change ; he is apt to lay the Fault upon the Woman, and generally fixes his Affections on some other Female, who, he imagines, is free from those Faults ; then farewel happy Wedlock. The experienc'd Man, on the contrary, has try'd several Women ; he finds they all agree in one Particular, and that after a Storm of Love there always succeeds a Calm : When he enters into Matrimony, he is prepar'd against any Disappointments of that Nature, and is ready to make Allowance for those Faults and Imperfections which are inseparable from human Kind. This is so true, that Women have establish'd a Maxim, that Rakes make the best Husbands ; for they are very sensible how difficult it is to monopolize a Man's Affections ; that he will have his Curiosity about those Affairs sat-isfy'd one Time or other : And tho' this Experience is useful before Marriage, it is very dangerous afterwards.

Besides, to compleat the Happiness of the Marriage State, or indeed to make it tolerable easy, there must be some Agreement in the Temper, Humour, and Disposition of the two Parties concern'd. If, for Instance, the

Man can't endure the Sight of a *Metropolis*, and the Woman can't enjoy herself out of it ; if the Man is grave, serious, [38] and an Enemy to all jocular Merriment, when his Wife is a profess'd Lover of Mirth and Gaiety ; these Two can never agree ; Differences will arise every Day ; and Differences in Wedlock are as hard to reconcile as those in Religion : We may guess at the Reason from a parallel Instance.

After the Revocation of the Edict of *Nantz*, several Protestant Gentlemen were shut up in the *Bastile* at *Paris*, where they liv'd constantly together for a considerable Time : They made an Observation, during their Stay there, That whenever the least Difference or Dispute happen'd amongst them, it was never reconcil'd till some Time after their Enlargement ; because, said they, altho' we were Yoke-Fellows in Affliction, yet never being out of one another's Company, our Animosities were always kept up warm, for Want of a little Absence to cool them : It is the same Case with Matrimony ; and People ought to be particularly careful to chuse a Wife as nearly of their own Temper as possible.

Now this Consideration never enters into the Head of a Chaste unexperienc'd Man ; he is so infatuated with personal Love, that he imagines his whole future Happiness depends upon the Possession of such a Shape, or such a Composition of Features ; when he is disappointed in this, how much will [39] it add to his Chagrin, to find himself yok'd for Life to a Woman whose Temper is quite opposite to his own, and consequently whose Satisfaction is quite inconsistent with his? We may guess the Sequel ; separate Beds, separate Maintenance, and all the whole Train of Conjugal Misfortunes. In short, let us consider Matrimony under what View we please, we shall still find that the experienc'd Man will make the best Husband, and answer all the Ends of Marriage much better than a Man who lives perfectly Chaste to his Wedding-Day.

Thus we see, by this happy Regulation of the *Publick Stews*, that Whoring, instead of being an Enemy to Matrimony, will advance and promote the Interest of it as much as possible.

We come now to the last great Point propos'd, *viz*. that this Project of the *Publick Stews* will prevent, as much as possible, the Debauching of Modest Women, and thereby reduce Whoring to the narrowest Bounds in which it can possibly be contain'd.

To illustrate this Matter, we must slip a little back to consider the Constitution of Females, while they are in a State of Innocence ; and when we have taken a View of the Fortifications, which Nature has made to preserve their Chastity, we shall [40] find out the Reason why it is so often surrender'd, and be the better able to provide for its Defence.

Every Woman, who is capable of Conception, must have those Parts which officiate, so fram'd, that they may be able to perform whatever is necessary at that Juncture. Now, to have those Parts so rightly adapted for the Use which Nature design'd them, it is requisite that they should have a very quick Sensation, and, upon the Application of the *Male Organ*, afford the Woman an exquisite Pleasure ; for, without this extravagant Pleasure in

Fruition, the recipient Organs could never exert themselves to promote Conception as they now do, in such an extraordinary Manner : The whole *Vagina*, as one continu'd *Sphincter*, contracting and embracing the *Penis*, while the *Nymphæ* and adjacent Islands have their particular Emissions at that Critical Minute, either as a Vehicle to lubricate the Passage, or else to incorporate with the Masculine Injection : Add to this, that the *Fallopiantubes* [*sic*] put themselves in a proper Posture to receive the impregnating Fluid, and convey it, as is suppos'd, to the *Ovaria*. Now it is hard to imagine, that so many alert Members, who can exert themselves in such a lively Manner on this Occasion, should be at all **[41]** other Times in a State of perfect Tranquillity ; for, besides, that Experience teaches us the contrary, this handsome Disposition would be entirely useless, if Nature had not provided a prior Titillation, to provoke Women at first to enter upon Action ; and all our late Discoveries, in Anatomy, can find out no other Use for the *Clitoris*, but to whet the Female Desire by its frequent Erections ; which are, doubtless, as provoking as those of the *Penis*, of which it is a perfect Copy, tho' in Miniature.

In short, there requires no more to convince us of the Violence of Female Desire, when rais'd to proper Height, but only to consider, what a terrible Risque a Woman runs to gratify it. Shame and Poverty are look'd upon as Trifles, when they come in Competition with this predominating Passion. But altho' it must be allow'd, that all Women are liable to these amorous Desires, yet, the Variety of Constitutions will make a considerable Difference ; for as in some Men the *Olfactory, Auditory*, or *Optick* Nerves, are not so brisk and lively as in others, so there are some Women who have the Nerves of their *Pudenda* more lively, and endow'd with a much quicker Sensation than others. Now, whether this Difference is owing to the Formation of the Nerves, or to the different **[42]** Velocity of the Blood circulating thro' those Parts, or whether it is owing to the different Quantity, or perhaps Acrimony, of that Fluid which is separated from the Blood by the *Nymphæ*, and other titillating Glands : I say, from whence soever this Difference proceeds, according to the Degree of this Sensation, we may venture to pronounce a Woman more or less in her own Nature Chaste.

To counterballance this violent natural Desire, all young Women have strong Notions of Honour carefully inculcated into them from their Infancy. Young Girls are taught to hate a *Whore*, before they know what the Word means ; and when they grow up, they find their worldly Interest entirely depending upon the Reputation of their Chastity. This Sense of Honour and Interest, is what we may call artificial Chastity ; and it is upon this Compound of natural and artificial Chastity, that every Woman's real actual Chastity depends.

As for Instance, Some Women are naturally more Chaste, or rather, to speak properly, less Amorous than others, and at the same Time have very strict Notions of Honour. Such Women are almost impregnable, and may be compar'd to Towns strongly fortify'd both by Art and Nature, **[43]** which, without Treachery, are safe from any sudden Attacks, and must be reduc'd by long and regular Sieges, such as few Men have the Patience or Resolution to go thro' with.

Other Women, again, have the same Value for their Reputation, and stand as much upon the Puncto of Honour ; but then they are naturally of a very sanguine amorous Disposition. A Woman of this Class may not unjustly be compar'd to a Town well garrison'd, but whose mutinous unruly *Inhabitants* are strongly inclin'd to revolt and *let in* the Enemy. Such Women, it's true, by extraordinary Care and Vigilance may suppress these Mutinies ; and Honour may for a long While keep Inclination under, but yet they are never perfectly safe ; there are certain Times and Seasons, certain unguarded Hours, when Honour and Interest are lull'd asleep, and Love has got the entire Ascendant. Besides, altho' we allow Love and Honour to be pretty equal Combatants, nay even granting that, in a *Pitch'd Battel*, when they have muster'd up all their Forces, Honour will have the Advantage, and quell Inclination ; yet, in the Course of a long *Civil War*, it is Odds but Love one Time or other obtains a Victory, which is sure to be decisive : for Inclination has this unluckly [*sic*] Advantage over **[44]** Honour, that, instead of being weaken'd, it grows stronger by Subjection ; and, like *Camomile*, the more it is press'd down and kept under, the Sturdier it grows ; or, like *Antæus*, it receives fresh Vigour from every Defeat, and rises the Brisker the oftener its thrown. Whereas Honour once routed never rallies ; nay, the least *Breach* in Female Reputation is irreparable ; and a *Gap* in Chastity, like a *Casm* in a young Tree, is every Day a *Widening*. Besides, Honour and Interest require a a long Chain of solid Reasoning before they can be set in Battel-Array ; whereas Inclination is presently under Arms the Moment Love has pitch'd his *Standard :* For, as we find that the least wanton Glance of a Lady's Eye quickly alarms a Man's Animal Spirits, and puts the whole Body Corporate into an unruly Ferment ; so, doubtless, the Female Imagination is at least equally alert ; and in such a sudden Scuffle betwixt Love and Honour, it's ten to one but the Enemy *enters* ; for the *Gate* of Chastity, like the *Temple* of *Janus*, always stands *open* during these Conflicts. It must indeed be granted, that if the Loss of Honour was immediately to succeed the Loss of Chastity, the Virtue of these Women would be much stronger than it is ; but they flatter themselves with the Hopes of Secrecy, and fancy that they have **[45]** found out an Expedient to purchase Pleasure without the Expence of Reputation ; by this means Honour is reconcil'd to Inclination, or at best made to stand Neuter ; and then the Consequence is very obvious. In short, a wanton Woman of Honour may withstand a great many Attacks, and possibly defend her Chastity to the very last ; but yet she is every Day in danger of being surpriz'd, and at best will make but a very precarious Defence.

A third Sort of Women, the very Reverse of the Preceding, have neither Honour nor Inclination ; that is to say, they have neither the one nor the other to an equal Degree with the rest of the Sex. These Kind of Women who put a slighter Value than ordinary upon their Characters, are generally, in their Circumstances, either above the World or below it ; for when a

Woman has her Interest and Fortune depending upon her Reputation, as all the middle Rank of Womankind have, she is a Woman of Honour of Course. Interest, indeed, is inseparable from Female Honour, nay it is the very Foundation of it ; and Honour and Interest, when they are consider'd as Guardians to Chastity, are synonimous Terms. The bare Puncto of Honour, when abstracted from Interest, would prove but a small Rub to Women in their eager [46] Pur-|suit of Pleasure : Thus we see the Conduct of a Maiden Lady, how much more Circumspect it is whilst her Fortune in Marriage is depending, than afterwards, when that Point of Interest is secur'd by a Husband ; for all marry'd Women are above the World in so far as they are out of the Reach of any Suspicions or Surmises, or even a Probability of Incontinence ; and since they are not liable to be detected by Pregnancy, there's no other Sort of Conviction able to prejudice them, but downright ocular Demonstration : Which seems to be the Reason why so many of them take such Liberties, as if they were of *Falstaff*'s Opinion, when he said, *Nothing but Eyes confutes me.* Female Honour, therefore, being so nearly ally'd and closely annex'd to worldly Interest, we must continue [confine] this Class of Women to two Sorts : First, those whose Fortunes are independent, and above being influenc'd by the Censure of the World, and, secondly, those who are so far below the World, that they either escape its Censure, or else are incapable of being hurt by it. The first Sort lie under this Disadvantage, that let their natural Chastity be ever so great, the smallest Spark of Desire is capable of being blown up and rais'd to a considerable Pitch ; whereas, when a Woman is once arriv'd to [47] Ma-|turity, that Portion of Honour which she has acquir'd, as [is] with Difficulty preserv'd, and at best is incapable of any Improvement. The second Sort are equally liable to have their Passions rais'd, however low they may be naturally, and besides lie under this farther Disadvantage, that tho' they can't promote their Interest by preserving their Chastity, yet, if they have the least Spark of Beauty, they will find their Account sufficiently in parting with it. The Virtue, indeed, of this Class of Women, seems chiefly to depend upon the Degree of Beauty which they stand possess'd of ; for, if they have Charms sufficient to pro-voke young Men to be at any tolerable Pains and Cost, their Chastity can never hold out long, but must infallibly surrender.

The fourth and last Kind of Women we shall mention, are those who have a very moderate Share of Honour, join'd to a very amorous Constitution.

The Virtue of these Women is entirely Defenceless ; and, as soon as a Man has remov'd that little timorous Coyness, which is natural to young Women in their first Attempts, he may proceed with Confidence, and conclude the Breach to be practicable ; for, whatever Resistance he meets with afterwards, will only enhance the Pleasure of Conquest. Most Women, indeed, let [48] them be ever so fully resolv'd to comply, make as great a Shew of Resistance as they can conveniently counterfeit ; and this the Sex would pass upon the World for a Kind of innate Modesty ; but it is very easily accounted for.

As soon as Women have entertain'd any Degree of Love, they make it their whole Study to raise and maintain an equal Degree of Passion in the Men ; and they are very sensible how far the bare Appearance of Modesty will prevail to render them amiable. The Pain they suffer in smothering their Desires, is fully recompenc'd by that secret Pleasure which a Lover's Eagerness gives them, because they esteem it a Proof both of the Sincerity and Violence of his Passion. A Woman is not, without some Reason, afraid, lest a Man's Love should diminish after Enjoyment, and would gladly bribe his After-Love, by the great Value she seems to put upon her Chastity before she makes him a Present of it.

Besides, not to mention the actual Pleasure a Woman receives in Strugling, it is a Justification of her in the Eye of the Man, and a Kind of *Salvo* to her Honour and Conscience, that she never did fully comply, but was in a Manner forc'd into it. This is the plain natural Reason why most Women refuse, to *surrender* upon **[49]** Trea-|ty, and why they delight so much in being *storm'd*.

Having thus taken a cursory View of the Sex, in their several Classes, and according to their several Circumstances, we may conclude, preferring Truth to Complaisance, that by far the greater Part of Womenkind hold their Virtue very precariously ; and that Female Chastity is, in its own Nature, built upon a very *Ticklish* Foundation.

Hudibras has ludicrously plac'd the Seat of Male-Honour in the Posteriours, whereby it is secur'd from any Attack in Front ; but Female-Honour, notwithstanding the apparent Safety of the Situation, like a Debtor's House upon the Verge of two Counties, is liable to be attack'd both Ways ; *a parte ante, & a parte post.*

That the Seat of Honour in Females has this double Aspect, like *Janus bifrons*, and consequently, that it is two Ways accessible, has already been taken Notice of by almost all the *Writers* upon this Subject ; but it is worth remarking here, that *Licurgus* had an Eye to it when he modell'd the *Spartan* Petticoat ; for tho' the Warmth of the Climate oblig'd the Women to be very open in that Part of their Dress, insomuch that, if we believe *Plutarch* in his Comparison of *Numa* and *Licurgus*, the **[50]** Habit which the Maidens of *Laconia* wore, came but to their Knees, and was open on both Sides, so that as they walk'd their Thighs appear'd bare ; yet this wise *Lawgiver* would not permit them to make the least Aperture, either in the fore or hind Part of that Garment ; rightly judging, that those two sacred *Avenues* to a Maid's Honour ought to be guarded with the utmost Caution.

For this same Reason the upright Posture of the Body has always been esteem'd the most decent ; and it has ever been the Mode, in all Countries, for Ladies to Cursey instead of Bowing ; for tho' a Female-Bow might seem a modest and coy Reclension of the Body, with Regard to the Person saluted, yet it would occasion a very indecent Projection to those who should happen to be behind ; especially since that dangerous Fashion of *Postern Plackets* has crept into the *European* Petticoat.

But to return to our present Argument, the Design of which was to prove the following *Syllogism.*

The only Way to preserve Female Chastity, is to prevent the Men from laying Siege to it : But this Project of the *Publick Stews* is the only Way to prevent Men's **[51]** lay-|ing Siege to it : Therefore this Project is the only Way to preserve Female Chastity.

The former Part of the Proposition is, I hope, sufficiently prov'd. It is, indeed, evident, from the bare Consideration of the Nature of Females, that if the Men are suffer'd to go on, as they now do, in the Pursuit of Pleasure, there is no possible Way can be found out, effectually, to secure the Virtue of any one Woman of any Rank, or in any Station of Life. If a Woman is handsome, she has the more Tryals to undergo ; if homely, and for that Reason seldom attack'd, the Novelty of the Address makes the greater Impression : If she is marry'd, it is Odds but there's a Failure at Home ; and habitual Pleasures are not easily foregone, especially when they may be enjoy'd with Safety : If a Maid, her unexperienc'd Virgin Heart is capable of any Impression : If she is rich, Ease and Luxury make the Blood run mad ; and Love, if high-dieted, is ungovernable : If poor, she will be the easier brib'd, when Love and Avarice jointly must be gratify'd.

In short, to sum up all, there is in the Passion of Love a certain fatal *Crisis*, to which all Womenkind are capable of being wrought up : The Difference of Virtue consisting only in this, that it is very hard to work a virtuous Woman up to this **[52]** *Crisis*, and requires a very unlucky Concurrence of Circumstances : Whereas a Woman without a good Stock of Virtue, must have an unaccountable Series of good Fortune if she escapes. But, virtuous or not virtuous, when this Passion is once rais'd to the *critical* Height, it is absolutely irresistable.

Since therefore Female Virtue cannot effectually be secur'd, but by preventing the Men from laying Siege to it, it remains for us to examine, if this Prevention can be effected by any other Method than that of erecting the *Publick Stews* ; and whether or no the *Publick Stews*, when erected, will have the desir'd Effect.

That young Men, in a good State of Health, have their Desires towards Women much stronger, and more violent, than for the Enjoyment of any Thing else in this Life, is a Truth not to be contested. And it is likewise as certain, that young Men will gratify these Desires, unless the *Legislature* can affix such a Penalty to the Commission of the Fact, that the Apprehension of the Penalty may give their Minds more Uneasiness, than refraining from the Gratification.

Now, there are but three Things which Men fear in this Life, *viz.* Shame, Poverty, and bodily Pain, and consequently but three **[53]** Sorts of Punishments which the *Legislature* can inflict. The first of these, indeed, might be omitted ; for Shame is so very little in the Power of the Laws, that it hardly deserves the Name of a Penalty. If the Pillory, and such like infamous Punishments, are more terrible for the Shame that attends them, than for the bodily Pain, it is not because such a Posture of a Man's Body, with his Neck through a Hole, is in itself ignominious, or that any Law can make it so, but because it publishes to the World that a Man has been prov'd to commit such a certain Action, in its own Nature scandalous, which he is asham'd to have thus publickly made known. The Truth is, Honour and Dishonour being only the different Opinions of Mankind, as to the Good or Evil of any Action ; and these Opinions in the Mind arising, as Dr. *Cl——ke* well observes, from the natural Fitness or Unfitness of the Actions them-selves, cannot be alter'd or determin'd by any *secular Force*. And that they are entirely out of the Power of the *Legislature*, is evident in the Instance of Duelling ; where a Man often receives Honour for a Breach of the Law, nay is forc'd to break it in Defence of his Honour.

[54]   The utmost Scandal, therefore, which the Laws can affix to any Action, is to make a full and open Publication of the Fact : Now it is evident that this Publication cannot have a sufficient Influence over Men's Minds to deter them from Wenching, a Crime which meets with so favourable a Reception in the Eye of the World, that young Men are not asham'd to boast of it.

We must have Recourse then to [a] Fine or Corporal Punishment, or perhaps both. If it is a Fine, it must be one of these three Sorts ; either a certain determinate Sum for every Offence, or, to make it fall more equally, such a certain Portion of a Man's whole Substance, or else it must be such a Sum as the Jury shall think sufficient to repair the Woman's Dammages. The first is impracticable because of its Inequality, with Regard to Men's different Fortunes. The second, would punish none but Men of Fortune. And the third, in many Cases, would be impossible ; for Women are often ruin'd by such as have it not in their Power to make them Amends. But granting that a Fine could be so happily contriv'd as to affect all Men equally in their several Stations of Life ; and let us suppose this Fine considerable enough, for so it must be, to deter any moderate spirited Man ; yet still we lye under a manifest Dilemma as to the Point of [55] Proof ; for if the Proof is to depend upon the Evidence of Eye-Witnesses, none but Fools will be convicted ; and let a Man be ever so indiscreet, he that swears to *rem in re* must have good Eyes, and be a good Swearer withal. If, on the other Hand, a Man is to be convicted upon the sole Evidence of the Woman, we run into greater Inconveniencies ; for either a Woman is to be recompenc'd for the Injury she has receiv'd, or not ; if not, there is no modest Woman of common Sense but will chuse much rather to conceal her Weakness than expose it in publick Court so much to her own Prejudice ; and this too upon the sole Motive of doing Prejudice to a Man, for whom in all Probability she still retains an Affection : So that no Man would be accus'd, but by such Sort of Women as the Law can never intend to favour or countenance.

And if the Woman is to receive this Fine, either in Part or the Whole, by Way of Reparation, not to mention its being an actual Encouragement to transgress, this Recompence would only be a Means to promote a Multitude of false Accusations ; for what Man could live with so much

Circumspection, that a Woman might not often have an Opportunity to accuse him of such a Fact, with very probable Circumstances, when there is no Opportunity of detecting the Fallacy. **[56]** This Difficulty, indeed, is not to be got over ; and the Objection lyes equally strong against all Sorts of Corporal Punishment, Death itself not excepted. For if there are so many false Indictments for *Rapes*, where a Woman receives no Benefit by the Prosecution, where she is liable to such cross Examinations, and where the Possibility of the Fact is so much doubted, that a Woman is generally discountenanc'd, and must bring a Number of probable concurrent Circumstances before she can gain Credit ; I say, if notwithstanding these Discouragements, there are so many malicious Prosecutions for *Rapes*, that the Benefit of the Law in general is much disputed, what may we expect in the present Case, where a Woman has nothing to do but acknowledge that she was overpersuaded, and then all Difficulties vanish? Besides, if such a Law was made, setting aside that the Remedy would be worse than the Disease, it is much to be question'd if it prov'd any Remedy at all : For what Fine can we propose as sufficient to deter Men, when there are so many that squander away their whole Fortunes upon this sole Gratification? And what Corporal Punishment, on this Side Death, can we find out equivalent to a *Pox*, which they every day run the Risque of?

[57] But no such Law, as yet, has been so much as propos'd, altho' Whoring has been a very obvious Mischief ever since Laws were in Being ; therefore, without farther Argument, considering the Wisdom of our *Legislature*, that such a Law never has been made, ought to be sufficient Reason for us to judge it impracticable.

Since the Torrent of Lewdness, then, is too strong to be oppos'd by open Force, let us see if we can find out an Expedient to divert it by Policy, and prevent the Mischief tho' we can't prevent the Crime.

Most *Authors*, who have writ of Government, have chose to express their Sentiments by comparing the Publick Body with the Body Natural ; and Mr. *Hobbs*, in his *Leviathan*, has carry'd the *Allegory* as far as it will go. To make use of it in the present Instance, we may look upon *Whoring* as a Kind of Peccant Humour in the Body-Politick, which, in order to its Discharge, naturally seizes upon such external Members as are most liable to Infection, and at the same Time most proper to carry off the Malignity. If this Discharge is promoted by a Licence for *Publick Stews*, which is a Kind of legal Evacuative, the Constitution will certainly be preserv'd : Whereas, if we apply Penal Laws, like violent Astringents, they will only drive the Disease back into **[58]** the Blood ; where, gathering Strength, and at last assimilating the whole Mass, it will break out with the utmost Virulence, to the apparent Hazard of those sound Members, which otherwise might have escap'd the Contagion. As we may observe in a *Clap*, where Nature of her own Accord expels the noxious Humour thro' the same Passages by which it was at first receiv'd ; but if we resist Nature in this Discharge, and repel the Venom by too hasty an Application of *Stypticks*, the Disease, then, turns to a *Pox*, seizes the Vitals, and, to use *Solomon*'s Words, *like a Dart, strikes* *thro' the Liver.* But, leaving *Allegory* as more proper for *Rhetorick* or *Poetry*, than such serious Debates, since this Project of the *Publick Stews* is the only Expedient now left for the Preservation of Female Chastity, the Question is, Whether or no this Expedient will really answer the End propos'd.

To prove the affirmative, requires no more but that we look into ourselves, and examine our own Passions ; for Love ever was and will be the same in all Men, and in all Ages. The first amorous Emotions that young Men feel are violent ; they are plagued with a Stimulation which raises a vehement Desire : The Passion is strong, but then it is General : It is Lust, not Love : And therefore the natural Impatience of *Lust* will prompt them [59] to take the speediest way for present Gratification, and make them prefer the ready and willing Embraces of a Courtezan, before the doubtful and distant Prospect of enjoying a modest Damsel, whose Coyness will cost so much Pains as, well as Time, to overcome ; and, when over-come, may probably occasion a future Uneasiness, and give them more Trouble after Enjoyment than they had before.

Besides this, if their first Affections should happen to be engaged to a particular Object, which is very rare ; and that this particular Object was in their Power to Compass, which is still rarer ; yet there is naturally in Young-men a certain secret Shame, which attends their first Sallies, and prevents their declaring a private Passion, 'till it grows so violent, that they are forced to give it vent upon the Publick ; and by that Means get into a regular Method of making themselves easy, without doing their Modesty any Violence.

But tho' the natural Bent of Men's Minds inclines them to an easy Purchase of Pleasure in their first Amours ; yet publick Whoring lies at pres-ent under so many Disadvantages, the publick Women, for want of good Regulation, are so infamous in the Principles and Practice, the Places of Resort so vile, and so scandalously imposing in the common Expence, and, lying under the Lash of the [60] *Ci-|vil* Power, so pester'd with the merce-nary Officiousness of *Reforming Constables* and, which is worst of all, the Plague of *Claps* and *Poxes* is so inevitable, that Men contrary to their Inclinations are often forced to enter upon private Intrigues ; either without trying the Publick, or after meeting with some Misfortunes in the Tryal.

Now if we see daily so many Young Men who prefer the publick Commerce under all these Disadvantages, what Success may we not expect from this happy Establishment of the *Stews*, when the Young Women's Behaviour will be regulated after a civil decent Manner ; when the Houses of Entertainment will be so Commodious, and the Expence of Accommodation so reasonable ; when the horrid dread of *Claps* is entirely removed ; and when the Laws, instead of disturbing such Assemblies, will be employ'd in their Protection, to give them the greater Countenance and Encouragement? Surely we may hope for a thorough Reformation.

But if these Considerations should not prove fully effectual, and some Men should be so obstinate as to persist in private Whoring, notwithstand-ing these Inducements to the contrary, we must then have Recourse to

Legal Force, and drive those who are too resty to be led : For tho' the Laws can't prevent Whoring, they may yet regulate it ; **[61]** the *Quid* is not in their Power, but the *Quomodo* is. A Man must Eat, but he may be directed how to Eat. The strongest Curb can't stop an unruly Horse, but the weakest will serve to turn him : And the smallest Stream is not to be obstructed, tho' we can change the Course of the greatest River. So Love, tho' ever so unruly and headstrong in the general, changes the particular Object of its Passion with the smallest Circumstance ; and legal Penalties are no trifling dissuasives when the Laws don't command Impossibilities.

This Argument indeed, of Compulsion is in a manner Supernumerary, and thrown in, as it were, *ex abundanti :* For the *Publick Stews* under this regular Oeconomy, will have so much the Advantage of private Whoring, whether we regard the Ease and Conveniency of Enjoyment, or the Beauty and Variety of Mistresses, that Men's natural Inclinations will sway them sufficiently without this Superfluous Constraint. If there is any Fear of Success, the Danger lies on the other Side ; and indeed we have some Colour of Reason to apprehend, least the whole Body of Lewdness being turn'd upon the Publick, there should want a sufficient Supply of young Women to recruit the *Stews* ; which, by that Means, may run into a sudden Dis-repute, and lose a **[62]** Cha-|racter that will be difficult to retrieve. But however plausible this Objection may seem at first Sight, we shall find, upon a nearer View, that it only serves to make the Excellence of this Scheme the more manifest.

As there is constantly in the Nation a certain Number of young Men, whose Passions are too strong to brook any Opposition : Our Business is to contrive a Method how they may be gratify'd, with as little Expence of Female Virtue as possible. But the Difficulty lies in adjusting this Matter and gaging our young Men's Affections so exactly, that the Modesty of one Woman may not be sacrific'd, more than is absolutely necessary for the Preservation of the rest.

The Gallants of this Age, indeed, are not quite so sturdy as that Rampant *Roman* Emperor who deflour'd ten *Sarmatian* Virgins in one Night ; but what we want in Constitution, we make up in the Nicety of our Palates ; as a squeamish Stomach requires the greatest Variety of Dishes : And some of our Youth are grown such perfect *Epicures* in Venery, that they can relish nothing but *Virgins :* They destroy, its true, a great deal of Beauty, by browsing only upon the Buds :

But we ought not to judge of these Men's Abilities by the Number of Women they **[63]** de-|bauch, no more than we should measure the Goodness of a certain curious Gentleman's Appetite by his bespeaking several Dozen of young Pigeons, when he only regal'd upon the Rumps : Neither is it intirely from a Wantonness of Fancy, or a Luxurious Taste of Pleasure, that Men indulge themselves in making this Havock, but chiefly for their own personal Safety. Young Girls are so giddy, thoughtless, and unexperienc'd, and withal so fond of the Sport, at their first setting out, that they seldom escape a Taint ; and a Man is not safe in being constant : Nay, some Men are afraid of venturing even after themselves : By this Means several likely Women, that might do the Publick signal Service, are in a short Time render'd useless : And, by a modest Computation, we are put to the Expence of as many virtuous Women, in one Year, as might reasonably serve the Nation six.

Now, the *Publick Stews* will regulate this Affair so precisely, and with such critical Exactness, that, one Year with another, we shall not have one Woman employ'd in the Publick Service more than is absolutely necessary, nor one less than is fully sufficient.

When this Project is first set on foot, the vast Choice and Variety there is at present of these Women, will give us an **[64]** Op-|portunity of making a very beautiful Collection ; and will, doubtless, for some Time, occasion a considerable Run upon the Publick ; so that *Private Whoring*, the only Nursery of our Courtezans, may probably remain too long neglected : For the whole Body of our incontinent Youth, like a standing Army, being employ'd in constant Action, there cannot well be spar'd a sufficient Detachment to raise the necessary Recruits.

But however true this may be, we shall thereby suffer no Inconvenience ; for if the Supplies of young Women, which we may reasonably expect from the Northern and Western Parts of these Kingdoms, or from such Places as are remote and out of the Influence of this *Scheme* : I say, if these Supplies should not prove sufficient to answer the greatness of the Demand, and that the Reputation of the *Stews,* upon this Account, should begin to flag, why then the worst Accident that can befall, is a gradual Relapse into our former State of *Private Whoring* ; and this no farther than is just necessary to recruit the *Stews*, and thereby make them retrieve their former Character ; For every Woman that is debauch'd more than is barely necessary, only brings so much additional Credit and Reputation to the *Stews*, and in some Measure attones for the Loss of her own Chastity, by being a Means **[65]** to preserve that of others ; so that whenever the Tide of private Lewdness runs too high, and exceeds the just and ordinary Bounds, it must of Course, by encouraging the *Publick Stews*, immediately suffer a proportionable Ebb : That is to say, it must be reduc'd again so low, that there will remain but just a sufficient Quantity to supply the *Stews* ; which is as low as, in the Nature of the Thing, is possible.

I might here lavish out Encomiums, and take Occasion to dwell upon those many Advantages that will accrue to the *Nation* by this admirable Scheme, but shall only take Notice of this peculiar Excellence, which it has above all other Schemes, that it necessarily executes itself.

But since the Necessity of debauching a certain Number of young Women, is entirely owing to the Necessity of supplying the *Publick Stews* ; a Question may very reasonably arise, whether this Project might not be vastly improv'd, even to the total Extirpation of *Private Whoring*, by an Act *for encouraging the Importation of Foreign Women*. This, I must confess, deserves a serious Debate ; for, besides the Honour of our Females, which would be preserv'd by such an Act, it might bring this farther Advantage ;

that whereas most of our estated Youth spend a great Part of their **[66]** Time
and Fortunes in travelling Abroad, for no other End, as it seems by most of
them, but to be inform'd in the *French* and *Italian* Gallantry ; they would then
have an Opportunity of satisfying their Curiosity in foreign Amours, without
stirring out of *London*. But I shall leave the Decision of this Matter to abler
Pens, well knowing, that a Truth of this Nature, which carries so much the
Air of Novelty, will require much better Authority than mine to warrant it.

Let it suffice for the present, that I have fully prov'd what I at first propos'd in this Treatise : That *Publick Whoring* is neither so criminal in itself,
nor so detrimental to the *Society* as *Private Whoring* ; and that the encouraging of *Publick Whoring*, by erecting *Stews* for that Purpose, will not only
prevent most of the mischievous Consequences of this Vice, but even
lessen the Quantity of *Whoring* in general, and reduce it to the narrowest
Bounds which it can possibly be contain'd in.

After what has been said, it may perhaps appear somewhat odd to talk of
religious Objections, as if either Christianity or Morality could possibly object
against a *Scheme*, which is entirely calculated for the Welfare and Happiness of
Mankind. But since a **[67]** great many Men amongst us have entertain'd such
whimsical Notions of Religion, as to imagine that, in some Cases, a Law may
be unjust and wicked, tho' it evidently promotes the Publick Good ; as if the
right Enjoyment of this Life was inconsistent with our Happiness in the next :
I say, since many Men of Understanding have suffer'd themselves to be
possess'd with this mistaken Principle, I shall, as briefly as may be, answer such
objections as can with any Colour of Reason be offer'd.

First, then, I expect to be attack'd with that old moral Precept, of *Not
doing Evil that Good may come of it*. This may be answer'd with another old
Saying, equally authentick, and more applicable to the present Purpose,
that *of two Evils we ought to chuse the least*. The Case is this : A private
Member of a *Society*, may, doubtless, commit a Crime, with a Design to
promote the Good of that *Society*, which was partly the Case of *Felton*
against the Duke of *Buckingham* ; and this Evil Action may possibly answer
the Goodness of the Intention, but is universally condemn'd as an unwarrantable Presumption ; and falls justly under the Censure of doing a certain
Evil, for the Prospect of an uncertain Good. But as to the *Legislature*, there
is a wide Difference ; for they, and they only, are entrusted with **[68]** the
Welfare of the *Society* : This Publick Welfare is, or ought to be, the whole
End and Scope of their Actions ; and they are fully impower'd to do whatever they judge conducive to that End. If their Intentions come up to this,
they are certainly in their Consciences acquitted : But as to the World, their
Actions, that is, their Laws, are judg'd good or bad, just or unjust, according as they actually prove beneficial or detrimental to the *Society* in general :
And therefore it is the grossest Absurdity, and a perfect Contradiction, in
Terms, to assert, that a *Government* may not commit Evil that Good
may come of it ; for, if a Publick Act, taking in all its Consequences, really
produces a greater Quantity of Good, it must, and ought to be term'd a

good Act ; altho' the bare Act, consider'd in itself, without the consequent Good, should be in the highest Degree wicked and unjust.

As for Instance : A Ship performing Quarantine, and known to be infected, is sunk by a Storm ; some of the Crew, half drown'd, recover the Shore ; but the Moment they land, the *Government* orders them to be shot to Death. This Action, in itself, is no less than a downright unchristian and inhuman Murther ; but since the Health and Safety of the Nation is secur'd by this severe Precaution, it is no Wonder, if we allow **[69]** the Action to be not only justifiable, but in the strictest Sense of Morality Just.

Another Objection, or rather the same set in a stronger Light, is, that altho' the Welfare and Happiness of the Community is, or ought to be, the only End of all Law and Government, yet, since our spiritual Welfare is the *summum bonum* which all Christians should aim at, no Christian Government ought to authorize the Commission of the least known Sin, tho' for the greatest temporal Advantage.

To this Objection, I answer, That it is universally allow'd as one of the greatest Perfections of the Christian Religion, that its Precepts are calculated to promote the Happiness of Mankind in this World as well as the next ; if so, then it is a direct Arraignment of the Lawgivers infinite Wisdom, *i.e.* a Contradiction, to assert that, in Matters of Law and Government, the Publick Breach of any Gospel-Precept can possibly be for the temporal Good of any *Society* whatever : And therefore we may with Confidence affirm, that no sinful Laws can be beneficial, and *vice versa*, that no beneficial Laws can be sinful. Now we have already given sufficient Proof of the Benefit the *Publick* would receive by licensing the *Stews*, and therefore ought to conclude such Licence lawful ; but, least the apparent Wickedness of the *Stews* **[70]** should be objected against this general Reasoning, it is fit that we examine this Matter a little nearer.

Fornication is, no doubt, a direct Breach of a *Gospel*-Precept, and is therefore a Sin ; but this Sin, barely as such, concerns the *Government* no more than the Eating of Black-puddings, equally prohibited in the same ⋆ Text. The Reason is this : The Sin consists in a full Intention to gratify a lustful Desire ; which Intention the *Legislature* cannot possibly prevent : Penalties indeed may deter Men from gratifying their Desires, at the Expence of the Publick, but will rather encrease than lessen the Desires themselves. If it is argu'd, that the Sin of the Intention is aggravated by being put in Execution, so much the better for our Purpose ; for then the Argument stands thus :

Since the Sin of the Intention is entirely out of the *Legislature's* Power, the utmost they can do, with Regard to this Sin is, to prevent its being aggravated by actual Commission.

[71] But the *Publick Stews*, as we have already prov'd, will prevent as much as possible this actual Commission.

Therefore the *Publick Stews* will prevent as much as possible this S ɪ N.

⋆ Acts, c.15 v.29. *That ye abstain from Meats offer'd to Idols, and from Blood, and from Things strangled and from Fornication : from which if ye keep yourselves, ye do well. Fare ye well.*

Another Branch of this Objection, without which the Objection itself would be of no Force, is, that the authorizing of *Publick Stews* is a Publick Encouragement for People to Whore.

If by People are meant those in the *Stews*, I hope it will be thought no Crime to encourage such People, rather to confine themselves to the Practise of one Vice, than live by committing a Thousand ; especially when that one Vice is what they would really practise, whether they were encourag'd or not.

But if any imagine that this particular Licence would be a general Encouragement to the whole *Nation*, they are certainly mistaken. For, as to the Men, they are already as bad as they can be ; if any Thing cures them, it must be *Satiety :* Let them have full and free Leave to take a Surfeit of unlawful Love, and they will soon learn to prefer the Chaste Embraces of Innocence before the bought Smile of Harlots loveless, joyless, unindear'd casual Fruition. **[72]** It is a right Observation, that Restraint does but whet a Man's Passions instead of curing them.————*Exuperat magis, ægrescitque medendo.* Æn.12. And a late ingenious *Author,* who study'd Mankind, speaking on this Subject, has these Words : *To put down* Publick Stews, *is not only to disperse Fornication into all Parts, but, by the Difficulty, to excite wild and wanton People to this Vice.*

It was observ'd at *Rome,* that in the full Liberty of Divorces, there was not a single Instance of one in fifty Years : And that *Cato* long'd for his Wife again as soon as she was in another's Possession.

The Master of Love says positively, *Quod licet ingratum est quod non licet Acrius urit.* And *Martial* speaking to a married Rake, *B. 3. Ep.* 68. says,

> *Cur aliena placet tibi, quæ tua non placet uxor?*
> *Nunquid Securus non potes arrigere?*

> I prithee tell me why a Wife
>   Thy am'rous Fancy never warms?
> What! without Danger o'thy Life,
>   Cannot thy Cod-piece stand to Arms?

[73]   And again, *B.* I. *Ep.*74.

> *Nullus in urbe fuit tota, qui tangere vellet*
> *Uxorem gratis, Cæciliane tuam*
> *Dum licuit : sed nunc, positis custodibus, ingens*
> *Turba fututorum est. Ingeniosus homo es.*

> There's no Man, *Cæcil,* in the Town,
>   Would, *gratis,* have enjoy'd thy Spouse ;
> But now thou art so jealous grown,
>   Lord! what a Croud about the House.
> You've lock'd her up t'increase her Value.
>   In short, you are a cunning Fellow.

The *Publick Stews* will not encourage Men to be lewd, but they will encourage them to exercise their Lewdness in a proper Place, without disturbing the Peace of the *Society*, and with as little Detriment to themselves as possible. And, as to the Women, there's not the least Shadow of Encouragement : For no modest Woman ever lost her Maiden-head with the dismal Prospect of becoming a *Publick* **[74]** *Cour-|tezan* : And if a Woman is not modest, the Licensing of the *Publick Stews* is no more an Encouragement for her to practise, than the allowing a certain Number of Hackney-Coaches every *Sunday*, is an Encouragement for the rest to Ply ; when the very Licence, to some, expresly implies a Prohibition of the rest.

Having now sufficiently prov'd the Institution of the *Publick Stews* to be a Political Good, and answer'd all the religious Objections against it, I shall conclude, with observing, That I have the Authority of *Italy*, the most Politick Nation in the World, to back me in the first Part of my Argument ; and the Opinion of *Holland*, one of the strictest Reform'd Churches, to vindicate me in the Second ; and that we ourselves enjoy'd the Benefit of this Institution till we were depriv'd of it by the over-hasty Zeal of our first Reformers in the Sixteenth Century.

The *Publick Stews* were anciently kept in *Southwark*, if not by an express Licence from the Government, at least by an open Permission ; though we have most Reason to believe the first, since they paid regular Taxes, both to the *Lord-Mayor* of the City, and to the Bishop of the See. **[75]** We do not find that they were ever molested 'till the 25th of *Edward* the Third, when, in the Parliament at *Westminster*, at the Request of the *Londoners*, says *Daniel*, an Act pass'd, obliging all Common Whores to distinguish themselves by wearing Hoods strip'd with divers Colours, or Furs, and their Gowns turn'd Inside out.

This, indeed, was but a Trifle to what they suffer'd thirty Years after, by *Wat Tyler's* Rebellion.

In the fifth of *Richard* the Second, *Wat* march'd up from *Dartmouth*, with a true Spirit of Reformation, fully resolv'd to burn and destroy every Thing that oppos'd him : If the Archbishop's Palace at *Lambeth* could not escape, there was little Mercy to be expected for the *Stews* : Besides, Whoring was not the least of *Wat's* Grievances : He began his Rebellion by killing a Collector of the Poll-Tax for being a little too Brisk upon his Daughter : And his Antipathy to the *Stews* was still encreas'd, by the *Lord-Mayor's* shutting the City Gates, and denying him Entrance ; for he could not revenge the Affront more effectually than by cutting off so large a Branch of his Lordship's Revenue. **[76]** In short, every Thing concurr'd to the Destruction of the *Stews*, and demolish'd they were.

This Action, however, lost *Tyler* his Life ; for *Will. Walworth*, the then Lord-Mayor, was the very Man that struck him first off his Horse in *Smithfield :* For which, the King Knighted him, gave him a Hundred Pounds Pension, and added the Dagger to the City Arms.

Whilst Whoring was in this unsettled Condition, the *Bishop* thought it a good Opportunity to ingross the whole Profit of licensing Courtezans, which occasion'd them fresh Trouble ; for *John Northampton*, who succeeded *Walworth*, either piqu'd at the Bishop's invading his Right, or out of a real reforming Principle, for he was a Follower of *Wickliff*, commenc'd a severe Persecution. He had his Spies and Constables in every Street to apprehend Strollers ; and such Women as were neither handsome nor rich enough to bribe his Officers, were carry'd thro' the Streets in great Pomp, with their Hair Shorn, and Trumpets, and Pipes Playing before them. All this he did contrary to the express Commands of the Bishop, who had several Bickerings with him upon that Head.

This great Reformer *John Northampton* was from his troublesome Temper **[77]** Nick-|nam'd *Cumber-Town* ; and as he succeeded *Tyler* in the Work of Reformation, so he had like to have met with as bad a Fate : For two Years after he was found Guilty of High Treason, without making the least Defence ; had his Goods confiscated, and was condemn'd to perpetual Imprisonment, a hundred Miles from *London :* Accordingly he was sent to *Tentagil Castle* in *Cornwall*.

This dreadful *Cumber-Town* being remov'd, the Stews had leasure to re-settle themselves under the Protection of the Church ; and enjoy'd an almost uninterrupted Tranquillity for a hundred and fifty Years.

We find, indeed, an Act passed at *Westminster*, in the 11th of *Hen*. 6th, that no Keepers of *Stews*, or *Whore-Houses*, in *Southwark* should be impannel'd upon any Jury ; or keep a Tavern in any other Place.

But the most sensible Blow they ever felt was the Invasion of the *French-Pox*. The *Spaniards* had brought it from the Islands of *Florida* to *Naples* ; and the Army of *Charles* the 8th, when he conquer'd that Kingdom in the Year 1495, transmitted it into *France*, from whence it had a very quick Passage into *England* ; for there was an Act passed in the latter end of *Hen*. the 7*th*'s Reign, for expelling out of the *Stews* **[78]** all such Women as had the Faculty of burning Men.

However, we find they still continued in good Repute in the Reign of *Henry* the 8*th*, and yielded a considerable Revenue to the *Bishop* of *London* ; for *Bucer*, in one of his Books against *Gardiner* taxes him with it as an heinous Crime, that he should receive most of his Rents out of the Publick *Stews*.

After this terrible Accusation, we may easily guess what Quarter our *Stews* met with at the Reformation. But now *Bucer* has got his ends ; the *Stews* are destroyed ; those publick Nusances are demolished ; Whoring is attack'd on all Hands without Mercy ; and what then? Why, truely, by meer dint of Reforming, we have reduced Lewdness to that pass, that hardly one Batchelor in the Kingdom will lye with a Woman, if he is sure that she's not Sound ; and very few modest Women will suffer a Man to get them with Child, unless he makes a promise to Marry. In short, the Truth is, we are at this present Writing as bad as we can be ; and I hope I have fairly shown how we may be better.

F I N I S.

BIBLIOGRAPHY

Early Works and Translations

Editions of *A Modest Defence*, in chronological order:

[1724A] *A Modest Defence of Publick Stews: Or, an Essay upon Whoring. As it is now Practis'd in these Kingdoms. Written by a Laymam.* London: Printed by A. Moore, 1724. ESTC N4820. The Dedication in this and in later editions is signed "Phil-Porney." This appears to be the true first edition of this work. The typographical error on the title page was corrected promptly in the second edition, published in the same year.

[1724B] *A Modest Defence of Publick Stews: Or, an Essay upon Whoring. As it is now Practis'd in these Kingdoms. Written by a Layman.* London: Printed by A. Moore, 1724. ESTC T114402. A facsimile reprint of this edition was published by the Augustan Reprint Society, Publication no. 162, with an Introduction by Richard I. Cook, Los Angeles: Clark Library, University of California, 1973.

A Modest Defence of Publick Stews: Or, an Essay upon Whoring, As it is now Practis'd in these Kingdoms. Written by a Layman. Answer'd. London: printed by A. Bussy, 1725. ESTC T144291.

Mordaunt, Harry, Colonel [pseud.]. *A Modest Defence of the Publick Stews; Or, an Essay upon Whoring, As it is now Practis'd in these Kingdoms. By the late Colonel Harry Mordaunt.* Glasgow: Printed for J. Moral, and sold by Jocolo Itinerant, [1730?]. ESTC T147388.

———. *A Modest Defence of Publick Stews: Or, an Essay upon Whoring. As it is now Practis'd in these Kingdoms. By the late Colonel Harry Mordaunt.* London: Printed for T. Read, 1740. ESTC T130482.

———. (Another imprint for the preceding edition is: London: Printed for S. Scott and T. Browne, [1740?], as recorded in the *National Union Catalogue, Pre-1956 Imprints*, vol. 358, p. 460.)

Ogle, Luke [pseud.]. *The Natural Secret History of Both Sexes, Or, a Modest Defence of Publick Stews. With an Account of the Present State of Whoring in these Kingdoms. By Luke Ogle, Esq; The fourth edition.* London: Printed in the year 1740. ESTC T114930.

———. *The Natural Secret History of Both Sexes; or, A Modest Defence of Publick Stews*, in William Beckett, *A Collection of Chirurgical Tracts. . . .* London: Printed for E. Curll, and sold by C. Rivington, Mess. Birt, Ware, Longman, Hitch, Wood, and Company, J. Clark, and J. Hodges, 1740. ESTC T30482.

A Modest Defence of Publick Stews: Or, an Essay upon Whoring, as it is now Practis'd in these Kingdoms. Written by a Layman. London: Printed by A. Bussy, 1745.

Translations

Venus la Populaire, ou Apologie des Maisons de Joye. A Londres, Chez A. Moore, 1727. (Translator unknown.) ESTC T115816. Reprinted, Paris: Chez Mercier, 1796; and Bruxelles (Brussels): Gay and Doucé, 1881.

Venere Popolare ovvero Apologia delle Case di Piacere. Cosmopoli: All' Insegna della Riforma. Nel Secolo della Dissolutezza. (Translator unknown), n.d. (17–?).

Modesta difesa delle pubbliche case di piacere. A cura di Kate Singleton. Milano: Electa, 1979.

Modesta difesa delle pubbliche case di piacere. A cura di Dario Castiglione. Palermo: S.F. Flaccovio, 1989.

Una modesta difesa delle case di piacere. Translated by Giacinto Borelli. Soveria Mannelli: Rubbettino, 1995.

Modesta difesa delle pubbliche case di piacere. Translated with notes by Francesca Bandel Dragone. Series: Le lettere, no. 85. Firenze [Florence]: Passigli, 1998; latest edition, 2003.

Eine Bescheidene Streitschrift für Öffentliche Freudenhäuser oder ein Versuch über die Hurerei wie sie jetzt im Vereinigten Königreich praktiziert wird. Translated and annotated with an essay by Ursula Pia Jauch. München [Munich] and Wien [Vienna]: Carl Hanser Verlag, 2001.

Relevant Classical and Early Modern Works
(in chronological order)

[Cicero]. *Ad C. Herennium de Ratione Dicendi (Rhetorica ad Herennium)*, trans. Harry Caplan. Loeb Classical Library, no. 403. Cambridge: Harvard University Press, 1954; first published in Venice, 1470.

Aretino, Pietro. *Ragionamenti.* [1534–1536.] Translated as *Aretino's Dialogues* by Raymond Rosenthal. New York: Stein and Day, 1971.

Stow, John. *A Survey of London* [1603], ed. Charles Lethbridge Kingsford. Oxford: Clarendon, 1908; reprinted 1971.

Burton, Robert. *The Anatomy of Melancholy* [1621], ed. by Floyd Dell and Paul Jordan-Smith. New York: Tudor Publishing Co., 1927, 1955.

Rare Verities: The Cabinet of Venus Unlocked, and Her Secrets Laid Open. London: P. Briggs, 1657. (Roy Porter and Lesley Hall [1995, p. 298] report that this work is a partial translation of Giovanni Sinibaldus's *Geneanthropeiae, sive de Hominis Generatione Decateuchon.* Rome, 1642.)

The Practical Part of Love. Extracted out of the Extravagant and Lascivious Life of a Fair but Subtle female. London, 1660. (Wing Catalog, second edition, P3154; Thomason collection, E.1793).

Chorier, Nicholas. *Satyra Sotadica.* 1660. Translated as *A Dialogue between a Married Lady and a Maid.* London, 1740; reprinted in Mudge, *When Flesh Becomes Word*, listed below. Contains dialogues attributed to Aloisia or Luisa Sigea of Toledo.

Aretino, Pietro. *The wandring-whores complaint for want of trading. Wherein the cabinet of her iniquity is unlockt and all her secrets laid open, in a merry discourse.* . . . London: J. Iones, 1663. (Selections translated from Aretino's *Ragionamenti*, 1534–1536.)

The Wandering Whore. 1660–1663.

The wandring whore continued. A dialogue between Magdalena a crafty bawd, Julietta an exquisite whore, Francion a lascivious gallant, and Gusman a pimping Hector. London: Printed in the year 1660 [and later]. ESTC P1076. (A pornographic weekly, published irregularly between 1660 and 1663).

[Oldys, Alexander.] *The London Jilt, or, The Politick Whore. The Second and Last Part. Shewing, All the Artifices and Stratagems which the Ladies of Pleasure make use of for the Intreaguing and Decoying of Men; Interwoven with several Pleasant stories of the Misses Iingenious Performances.* London: Printed for Hen. Rhodes . . . , 1683.

The Whore's Rhetoric. London: George Shell, 1683. (Based upon Ferrante Pallavicino's *La retorica delle putane*, 1642).

The Parliament of Women, or, A compleat history of the proceedings and debates, of a particular Junto, of ladies and gentlewomen, with a design to alter the government of the world. London: Printed for John Holford . . . , 1684. An earlier edition is dated 1656: Wing Catalogue, second edition / P506.

Sodom, Or the Quintessence of Debauchery. 1684. Attributed to John Wilmot, Earl of Rochester.

Aristotle's master-piece: or, The secrets of generation display'd in all the parts thereof. London: Printed by F.L. for J. How, 1690. This work, first published in 1684, was continually reprinted, with variations, into the nineteenth century.

[Drake, Judith]. *An Essay in Defence of the Female Sex.* London: Printed for A. Roper and E. Wilkinson . . . and R. Clavel, 1696. Reprinted, New York: Source Book Press, 1970.

Dunton, John. *The Night-walker, or Evening Rambles in Search after Lewd Women, with the various conferences held with them, dedicated to the whores and whoremasters of London and Westminster.* Two volumes. London: J. Orme, 1696–1697.

Anon. *An essay towards a general history of whoring From the creation of the world, to the reign of Augustulus, (which, according to common computation, is 5190 years) and from thence down to the present year 1697. Being a collection of the most remarkable instances of uncleanness, that are to be found in sacred or prophane history during that time. With observations thereon.* London: Printed for Richard Baldwin, at the Oxford Arms in Warwick-Lane, 1697.

Mandeville, Bernard. *Æsop Dress'd; or a Collection of Fables Writ in Familiar Verse.* London, 1704. (An expanded edition of Mandeville's first publication in English, *Some Fables after the Easie and Familiar Method of Monsieur de la Fontaine*, 1703.)

Venette, Nicolas. *The Mysteries of Conjugal Love Reveal'd. Written in French by Nicholas de Venette.* The second edition corrected. London: Printed in the year, 1707.

———. *Le Tableau de l'amour conjugal.* New York: Garland, 1984; translated as *The Mysteries of Conjugal Love Reveal'd.* London: S.N., 1712.

———. *Conjugal Love Reveal'd, In the Nightly Pleasure of the Marriage Bed and the Advantages of that Happy State, in an Essay Concerning Humane Generation, done from the French of Monsieur Venette, by a Physician.* Seventh edition. London: Printed for the author, and sold by Tho. Hinton, at the White Horse, in Water Lane, Blackfryars, c. 1720.

Marten, John. *Gonosologium Novum: Or, A New System of all the Secret Infirmities and Diseases, Natural, Accidental, and Venereal in Men and Women.* London: Printed for and sold by N. Crouch et al., 1709.

The Fable of the Bees [1714–1729], ed. F.B. Kaye. 2 vols. Oxford: Clarendon Press, 1924; reprinted 1957; reprinted 1998 by the Liberty Fund, Indianapolis, IN.

The Ladies Diary or Woman's Almanack. London, 1715.

[Meibomius, John Henry; i.e., Meibom, Johann Heinrich]. *A Treatise of the Use of Flogging in Venereal Affairs.* London: Printed for E. Curll, 1718.

Defoe, Daniel. *The Poor Man's Plea To all the Proclamations, Declarations, Acts of Parliament, &c. which have been, or shall be made, or publish'd, for a Reformation of Manners, and suppressing Immorality in the Nation.* London: A. Baldwin, 1698.

———. *The Fortunes and Misfortunes of the Famous Moll Flanders, &c.* London, 1722.

———. *The Fortunate Mistress: Or, . . . Roxana.* London, 1724.

———. *Conjugal Lewdness; or, Matrimonial Whoredom. A Treatise concerning the Use and Abuse of the Marriage Bed* (1727), ed. M. Novak. Gainesville, FL: Scholars' Facsimiles and Reprints, 1967.

[Salmon, Thomas]. *A Critical Essay Concerning Marriage . . . By a Gentleman.* London: Printed for Charles Rivington, 1724.

Venus in the Cloister: Or, The Nun in her Smock. Translated from the French by a Person of Honour. London: [published by E. Curll], 1724. A translation of Jean Barrin's *Vénus dans le cloître, ou la Religieuse en chemise, entretiens curieux par l'abbé du Prat,* 1683. An English translation appeared in the same year, 1683. Reprinted in *When Flesh Becomes Word,* ed. Bradford K. Mudge, 2004.

Bluet (or Blewitt), George. *An enquiry whether a general practice of virtue tends to the wealth or poverty, benefit or disadvantage of a people? In which the pleas offered by the author of The fable of the bees, . . . are considered. With some thoughts concerning a toleration of publick stews.* London: printed for R. Wilkin, 1725. (Probably the ablest and most comprehensive attack on Mandeville's writings by one of his contemporaries.)

A Conference about Whoring. London: J. Downing, 1725.

A New Canting Dictionary. London, 1725.

A Modest Defence of Chastity. London: A. Bettesworth, 1726.

[Tindal, Matthew]. *An address to the inhabitants [sic] of the two great cities of London and Westminster: in relation to a pastoral letter, said to be written by the Bishop of London. . . .* London: J. Peele, 1728 (and 1729; second ed., 1730). After the 1728 edition, "inhabitants" is corrected to "inhabitants."

Disney, John. *A View of Ancient Laws against Immorality and Profaneness. . . .* Cambridge and London, 1729.

Hell upon Earth: Or the Town in an Uproar. Occasion'd by the late horrible Scenes of Forgery, Perjury, Street-Robbery, Murder, Sodomy, and other shocking Impieties. London, 1729.

Pretty Doings in a Protestant Nation. Being a view of the present state of fornication, whorecraft, and adultery, in Great-Britain . . . Written originally in French by Father Poussin. London: Printed for J. Roberts et al., 1734. (In the Yale Library catalogue, attributed to B. Mandeville, supposed author. This work is based in part on *A Modest Defence.* Roberts had previously published other works by Mandeville.)

Satan's Harvest Home: Or the Present State of Whorecraft, Adultery, Fornication, Procuring, Pimping, Sodomy, and the Game at Flatts. London, 1749. (The anonymous compiler of this piece of hackwork patched it together from various pieces. Whole paragraphs are lifted directly from *A Modest Defence* and the entire work is devoted to the sensational exposure of vices.)

Welch, Saunders. *A Proposal to render effectual a Plan, to remove the Nuisance of Common Prostitutes from the Streets of this Metropolis; to prevent the Innocent from being seduced; to provide a decent and comfortable Maintenance for those whom Necessity or Vice hath already forced into that infamous Course of Life. . . .* London, 1758; reprinted in *Prostitution Reform: Four Documents,* New York and London: Garland, 1985.

Restif, Nicolas-Edmé, called Restif de la Bretonne. *Le pornographe; ou, Idées d'un honnête homme sur un projet de règlement pour les prostituées, propre à prévenir les malheurs qu'occasionne le publicisme des femmes.* Bruxelles [Brussels]: Gay and Doucé, 1879 [first edition, 1769].

Matthews, A.G. *Calamy Revised: Being a Revision of Edmund Calamy's Account of the Ministers and others Ejected and Silenced, 1660–1662.* Oxford: Clarendon Press, 1934. (Has information on Ogle.)

Mudge, Bradford K., ed. *When Flesh Becomes Word: An Anthology of Early Eighteenth-Century Libertine Literature.* Oxford and New York: Oxford University Press, 2004.

Modern Studies

Because readers might well find it annoying to search through a half-dozen alphabetized lists in order to find a particular author or title, all of the entries have been arranged in a single list from A to Z. The subjects or topics represented here include bibliography and textual studies, Bernard Mandeville, history of sexuality, marriage, prostitution, pornography, masturbation, bastardy, infanticide, the Societies for Reformation of Manners, rhetoric, paradox, and other literary topics.

Anderson, Scott A."Prostitution and Sexual Autonomy: Making Sense of the Prohibition of Prostitution," *Ethics* 112 (July 2002): 748–780.

Anselment, Raymond A. *"Between Jest and Earnest": Marprelate, Milton, Marvell, Swift and the Decorum of Religious Ridicule.* Toronto: University of Toronto Press, 1979.

Arrizabalaga, Jon, John Henderson, and Roger French. *The Great Pox: The French Disease in Renaissance Europe.* New Haven: Yale University Press, 1997.

Backscheider, Paula R. *Daniel Defoe: His Life.* Baltimore: Johns Hopkins University Press, 1989.

Bahlman, Dudley W.R. *The Moral Revolution of 1688.* New Haven: Yale University Press, 1957.

Barker-Benfield, G.J. *The Culture of Sensibility: Sex and Society in Eighteenth-Century Britain.* Chicago: University of Chicago Press, 1992.

Barry, Kathleen. *Female Sexual Slavery.* New York: New York University Press, 1979.

———. *The Prostitution of Sexuality.* New York: New York University Press, 1995.

Bennett, Paula, and Vernon A. Rosario II, eds. *Solitary Pleasures: The Historical, Literary and Artistic Discourses of Autoeroticism.* New York: Routledge, 1995.

Bloch, I. *Sexual Life in England Past and Present.* Trans. W.H. Forstern. London: Francis Aldor, 1938.

Boehrer, Bruce Thomas. "Early Modern Syphilis." *Journal of the History of Sexuality* 1.2 (October, 1990): 197–214; reprinted in Fout (below) pp. 11–28.

Bogel, Fredric V. "Dulness Unbound: Rhetoric and Pope's Dunciad." *PMLA* 97 (October 1982): 844–855.

Booth, Wayne. *A Rhetoric of Irony.* Chicago: University of Chicago Press, 1974.

Bowen, Barbara. *The Age of Bluff: Paradox and Ambiguity in Rabelais and Montaigne.* Studies in Language and Literature, 62. Urbana: University of Illinois Press, 1972.

Bristow, Edward J. *Vice and Vigilance: Purity Movements in Britain since 1700.* Dublin: Gill and Macmillan; Totowa, NJ: Rowman and Littlefield, 1977.

Brundage, James A. *Law, Sex, and Christian Society in Medieval Europe.* Chicago: University of Chicago Press, 1987.

Bullough, Vern, ed. *A Bibliography of Prostitution.* New York: Garland, 1977.

———. "Prostitution and Reform in Eighteenth-Century England." *Eighteenth-Century Life* 9 (1985): 61–74; also in Maccubbin, below.

———. *Science in the Bedroom: A History of Sex Research.* New York: Basic Books, 1994.

Bullough, Vern and Bonnie Bullough. *Women and Prostitution: A Social History.* Buffalo, NY: Prometheus Books, 1987. (Revised edition of *Prostitution: an Illustrated Social History*, New York: Crown Publishers, 1978.)

Buret, F. *Syphilis in the Middle Ages and in Modern Times.* Trans. A.H. Ohmann- Dumesnil. Philadelphia: F.A. Davis, 1895.

Burford, E.J., *Bawds and Lodgings: A History of the London Bankside Brothels, c. 100–1675.* London: Peter Owen, 1976.

Burtt, Shelley. "The Societies for the Reformation of Manners: Between John Locke and the Devil in Augustan England," pp. 149–169 in *The Margins of Orthodoxy: Heterodox Writing and Cultural Response, 1660–1750*, ed. Roger D. Lund. Cambridge: Cambridge University Press, 1995.

Carlin, Martha. *Medieval Southwark.* London and Rio Grande, OH: Hambledon Press, 1996.

Carrive, Paulette. *La Philosophie des Passions chez Bernard Mandeville.* (Dissertation), 2 vols. Lille and Paris, 1983.

Chapman, Antony J., and Nicholas J. Gadfield. "Is Sexual Humor Sexist?" *Journal of Communication* 26 (1976): 141–153.

Cheek, Pamela. *Sexual Antipodes: Enlightenment Globalization and the Placing of Sex.* Stanford: Stanford University Press, 2003.

Chernaik, Warren. *Sexual Freedom in Restoration Literature.* Cambridge: Cambridge University Press, 1995.

Colie, Rosalie. *Paradoxia Epidemica.* Princeton: Princeton University Press, 1966.

Cook, Richard I. *Bernard Mandeville*, TEAS 170. New York: Twayne, 1974.

———. " 'The Great Leviathan of Leachery': Mandeville's *Modest Defence of Publick Stews* (1724)," pp. 22–33 in *Mandeville Studies: New Explorations in the Art and Thought of Dr. Bernard Mandeville 1670–1733*, ed. I. Primer. The Hague: Martinus Nijhoff, 1975.

Corbin, Alain. *Les Filles de noce: Misère sexuelle et prostitution aux 19e et les 20e siècles* (Paris, 1978), translated as *Women for Hire: Prostitution and Sexuality in France after 1850.* Cambridge: Harvard University Press, 1990.

Crane, Ronald S. "Bernard de Mandeville." *Philological Quarterly* 13 (1934): 122–123. (A rebuttal to Harder's essay, below.)

Curtis, T.C. and W.A. Speck. "The Societies for the Reformation of Manners: A Case Study of the Theory and Practice of Moral Reform." *Literature and History* 3 (1976): 45–64.

Dabhoiwala, Faramerz. "The Pattern of Sexual Immorality in Seventeenth and Eighteenth-Century London," pp. 86–106 in *Londinopolis: Essays in the Cultural and Social History of Modern London*, ed. by Paul Griffiths and Mark S.R. Jenner. Manchester and New York: Manchester University Press, 2000.

———. "Sex, Social Relations and the Law in Seventeenth- and Eighteenth-Century London," pp. 85–101 in *Negotiating Power in Early Modern Society: Order, Hierarchy and Subordination in Britain and Ireland*, ed. by Michael J. Braddick and John Walter. Cambridge: Cambridge University Press, 2001.

Davidson, Julia O'Connell. "The Rights and Wrongs of Prostitution." *Hypatia* 17.2 (2002): 84–98.

Davison, Lee et al., eds. *Stilling the Grumbling Hive: The Response to Social and Economic Problems in England, 1689–1750.* New York: St. Martin's Press, 1992.

Davenport-Hines, Richard. *Sex, Death and Punishment: Attitudes to Sex and Sexuality in Britain since the Renaissance.* London: Collins, 1990.

DeJean, Joan, *The Reinvention of Obscenity: Sex, Lies, and Tabloids in Early Modern France.* Chicago: University of Chicago Press, 2002.

Dufour, Pierre (pen name of Paul Lacroix). *Histoire de la Prostitution chez tous les peuples du monde . . .* 6 vols., Paris: Sere, Editeur, 1851–1853.

Dworkin, Andrea. *Pornography: Men Possessing Women.* New York: Perigee, 1981; with a new introduction, Penguin, 1989.

Ellis, Havelock. *Studies in the Psychology of Sex.* Vol. II. New York: Random House, 1936 [1906]. (In this volume, chapter 6 of Part III deals with prostitution, and chapter 7 addresses venereal diseases.)

Foucault, Michel. *The History of Sexuality: An Introduction.* Vol. I. New York: Pantheon, 1978; Vintage Books, 1980.

Fout, John C., ed. *Forbidden History: The State, Society, and the Regulation of Sexuality in Modern Europe* (Essays from the *Journal of the History of Sexuality*). Chicago and London: University of Chicago Press, 1992.

Fowler, Patsy, ed. *Launching Fanny Hill: Essays on the Novel and its Influence.* New York: AMS Press, 2003.

Foxon, David. *Libertine Literature in England, 1660–1745.* New Hyde Park, NY: University Books, 1965.

Frantz, David O. *Festum Voluptatis: A Study of Renaissance Erotica*. Columbus, OH: Ohio State University Press, 1989.

———. *A Critical Bibliography of Daniel Defoe*. London: Pickering and Chatto, 1998.

Furbank, P.N. and W.R. Owens. *Defoe De-attributions: A Critique of J.R. Moore's Checklist*. London and Rio Grande, Ohio: Hambledon Press, 1994.

Gaskell, Philip. *A New Introduction to Bibliography*. New York and Oxford: Oxford University Press, 1972.

Gilfoyle, Thomas J. "Prostitutes in History: From Parables of Pornography to Metaphors of Modernity [a review essay]," *American Historical Review* 104.1 (February 1999): 117–141.

Gillis, John R. *For Better, for Worse: British Marriages, 1600 to the Present*. Oxford and New York: Oxford University Press, 1985.

Goldsmith, M.M. *Private Vices, Public Benefits: Bernard Mandeville's Social and Political Thought*. Cambridge: Cambridge University Press, 1985.

———. " 'The Treacherous Arts of Mankind': Bernard Mandeville and Female Virtue." *History of Political Thought* 7.1 (1986): 93–114.

Gould, Stephen J. "Syphilis and the Shepherd of Atlantis," in *Natural History* (October 2000); reprinted in his last collection of essays, *I Have Landed*. New York: Harmony House, 2002.

Gregg, Stephen H. " 'A Truly Christian hero'; Religion, Effeminacy and Nation in the Writings of the Societies for the Reformation of Manners." *Eighteenth-Century Life* vol. 25 Ns, no. 1 (Winter 2001): 17–28.

Griffin, Robert J. "Anonymity and Authorship." *New Literary History* 30.4 (1999): 877–895.

———, ed. *The Faces of Anonymity: Anonymous and Pseudonymous Publication from the Sixteenth to the Twentieth Century*. New York and Houndmills: Palgrave Macmillan, 2003.

Griffiths, Paul, and Mark S.R. Jenner, eds. *Londinopolis: Essays in the Cultural and Social History of Early Modern London*. Manchester: Manchester University Press; and New York: St. Martin's Press, 2000.

Gunn, J.A.W. *Beyond Liberty and Property; The Process of Self-Recognition in Eighteenth-Century Political Thought*. Kingston and Montreal: McGill-Queen's University Press, 1983. (See chapter 3.)

Harder, Johannes Hendrik. "The Authorship of *A Modest Defence of Public Stews, etc.*" *Neophilologus* 18 (1933): 200–203.

———. *Observations on some Tendencies of Sentiment and Ethics chiefly in . . .* New York: Haskell House, 1966 [1933].

Harvey, A.D. *Sex in Georgian England: Attitudes and Prejudices from the 1720s to the 1820s*. New York: St. Martin's Press, 1994.

Hawkins, Gordon and Franklin E. Zimring. *Pornography in a Free Society*. Cambridge and New York: Cambridge University Press, 1988.

Henderson, Tony. *Disorderly Women in Eighteenth-Century London*. London and New York: Longman, 1999.

Henriques, Fernando. *Prostitution and Society: A Survey*. 3 vols. London: MacGibbon & Kee, 1962–1968.

Hind, George. "Mandeville's *Fable of the Bees* as Menippean Satire." *Genre* I (1968): 307–315.

Hitchcock, Tim. *English Sexualities, 1700–1800*. New York: St. Martin's Press, 1997.

———. "Redefining Sex in Eighteenth-Century England," *History Workshop Journal* 41 (1996): 73–90; reprinted in *Sexualities in History: A Reader*, ed. by Kim M. Phillips and Barry Reay. New York and London: Routledge, 2002; pp. 185–202.

Hoffbrand, Barry. "John Misaubin, Hogarth's Quack: A Case for Rehabilitation," *Journal of the Royal Society of Medicine*. 94.3 (March 2001): 143–147.

Hoffer, P.C. and N.E.H. Hull. *Murdering Mothers: Infanticide in England and New England, 1558–1803.* New York: New York University Press, 1981.

Horne, Thomas A. *The Social Thought of Bernard Mandeville: Virtue and Commerce in Early Eighteenth-Century England.* New York: Columbia University Press, 1978.

Hundert, E.J. *The Enlightenment's Fable: Bernard Mandeville and the Discovery of Society.* Cambridge and New York: Cambridge University Press, 1994.

Hunt, Alan. *Governing Morals: A Social History of Moral Regulation.* Cambridge and New York: Cambridge University Press, 1999. See pp. 45–56.

Hunt, Lynn. *The Invention of Pornography: Obscenity and the Origins of Modernity.* New York: Zone Books, 1993.

Hurl-Eamon, Jennine. "Policing Male Heterosexuality: The Reformation of Manners Societies' Campaign against the Brothels in Westminster, 1690–1720." *Journal of Social History,* 37.4 (Summer, 2004): 1017–1035.

Ingram, Martin. "Reformation of Manners in Early Modern England," pp. 47–88 in *The Experience of Authority in Early Modern England,* ed. by Paul Griffiths et al. New York: St. Martin's Press, 1996.

Isaacs, Tina. "The Anglican Hierarchy and the Reformation of Manners, 1688–1738." *Journal of Ecclesiastical History* 33.3 (1982): 391–411.

Jack, Malcolm. *The Social and Political Thought of Bernard Mandeville.* New York: Garland Publishing Co., 1987.

———. *Corruption and Progress: The Eighteenth-Century Debate.* New York: AMS Press, 1989.

Jackson, Mark, ed. *Infanticide: Historical Perspectives on Child Murder and Concealment, 1550–2000.* Aldershot, England; Burlington, Vermont: Ashgate, 2002.

Jeffreys, Sheila. *The Idea of Prostitution.* North Melbourne, Victoria, Australia: Spinifex, 1997.

Karras, Ruth Mazo. "The Regulation of Brothels in Late Medieval England." *Signs: Journal of Women in Culture and Society* 14 (1989): 399–433.

———. *Common Women: Prostitution and Sexuality in Medieval England.* New York: Oxford University Press, 1996.

Kaye, F.B. "The Influence of Bernard Mandeville." *Studies in Philology* 19 (1922): 83–108.

———. "The Writings of Bernard Mandeville: A Bibliographical Survey," *Journal of English and Germanic Philology,* 20 (1921): 419–467. (Makes the strongest case for attributing *A Modest Defence* to Mandeville.)

Kearney, Patrick J. *The Private Case: An Annotated Bibliography of the Private Case Erotica Collection in the British (Museum) Library.* Compiled by P.J. Kearney; with an Introduction by G. Legman. London: J. Landesman; Atlantic Highlands, NJ: Humanities Press, 1981.

Kendrick, Walter. *The Secret Museum: Pornography in Modern Culture.* New York: Penguin Books, 1988.

Kent, Gerard, and Gert Hekman, eds. *The Pursuit of Sodomy: Male Homosexuality in Renaissance and Enlightenment Europe.* New York and London: Harrington Park, 1989.

Klein, Joan Larsen, ed. *Daughters, Wives, and Widows: Writings by Men about Women and Marriage in England, 1500–1640.* Urbana and Chicago: University of Illinois Press, 1992.

Kowaleski-Wallace, Elizabeth. *Consuming Subjects: Women, Shopping, and Business in the Eighteenth Century.* New York: Columbia University Press, 1996. (See the eighth chapter, "Prostitutes.")

Kurzel-Runtscheiner, Monica. *Töchter der Venus: die Kurtisanen Roms in 16. Jahrhundert.* München [Munich]: C.H. Beck, 1995.

Lacroix, Paul. (See Dufour, above.)

Lanham, Richard A. *A Handlist of Rhetorical Terms: A Guide for Students of English Literature.* Berkeley and Los Angles: University of California Press, 1969.

Laqueur, Thomas W. *Making Sex: Body and Gender from the Greeks to Freud*. Cambridge: Harvard University Press, 1990.

————. *Solitary Sex: A Cultural History of Masturbation*. New York: Zone Books, 2003.

Laslett, Peter. *Family Life and Illicit Love in Earlier Generations: Essays in Historical Sociology*. Cambridge: Cambridge University Press, 1977.

Leemans, Inger. *Het woord is aan de onderkant. Radicale ideeën in Nederlandse pornografische romans, 1670–1700*. (Dissertation) Leiden, Netherlands: Vantilt, 2002. (English translation of title, supplied by Dr. Leemans: *Bottom takes the floor. Radical ideas in Dutch pornographic novels, 1670–1700*. She discusses Mandeville on pp. 267–273, 301.)

Maccubbin, R.P., ed. *'Tis Nature's Fault: Unauthorized Sexuality during the Enlightenment*. Cambridge and New York: Cambridge University Press, 1987.

MacDonald, R.H. "The Frightful Consequences of Onanism: Notes on the History of a Delusion." *Journal of the History of Ideas*, 28.3 (1967): 423–431.

Macfarlane, Alan. Review of *The Family, Sex and Marriage in England, 1500–1800* by Lawrence Stone, in *History and Theory* 18 (1979): 103–326.

————. *Marriage and Love in England: Modes of Reproduction, 1300–1840*. Oxford and New York: B. Blackwell, 1986.

MacKinnon, Catharine A. "Not a Moral Issue," pp. 146–162 in her *Feminism Unmodified: Discourses on Life and Law*. Cambridge, MA: Harvard University Press, 1987; reprinted in *Feminism and Pornography*, ed. by Drucilla Cornell, Oxford and New York: Oxford University Press, 2000; pp. 169–197.

————. *Only Words*. Cambridge: Harvard University Press, 1993.

McElroy, Wendy. "An Overview of 'Solutions' to Prostitution." Available at: http://www.zetetics.com/mac/articles/prostsol.html.

————. *XXX: A Woman's Right to Pornography*. New York: St. Martin's Press, 1995.

McGinn, Thomas A.J. *The Economy of Prostitution in the Roman World: A Study of Social History and the Brothel*. Ann Arbor: University of Michigan Press, 2004.

Malcolmson, Robert W. "Infanticide in the Eighteenth Century," pp. 187–211 in *Crime in England, 1550–1800*, ed. by J.S. Cockburn. Princeton: Princeton University Press, 1977.

Mandell, Laura. "Bawds and Merchants: Engendering Capitalist Desires." *ELH* 59.1 (1992): 107–123.

————. *Misogynous Economies: The Business of Literature in Eighteenth-Century Britain*. Lexington, KY: University Press of Kentucky, 1999. (See especially chapter 3, based largely on her article above.)

Marcus, Irwin and John Francis, eds. *Masturbation: From Infancy to Senescence*. New York: International University, 1975.

Merians, Linda E., ed. *The Secret Malady: Venereal Disease in Eighteenth-Century Britain and France*. Lexington, KY: University Press of KY, 1996.

Miller, Henry Knight. "The Paradoxical Encomium," *Modern Philology* 53 (1956): 145–178.

Monro, Hector. *The Ambivalence of Bernard Mandeville*. Oxford: Clarendon Press, 1975.

Moore, John Robert. *A Checklist of the Writings of Daniel Defoe*. Second edition. Hamden, CT: Archon Books, 1971 (first edition, Indiana University Press, 1960, 1962).

Moulton, Ian Frederick. *Before Pornography: Erotic Writing in Early Modern England*. New York and Oxford: Oxford University Press, 2000.

Mudge, Bradford K. *The Whore's Story: Women, Pornography, and the British Novel, 1684–1830*. New York and Oxford: Oxford University Press, 2000.

Nash, S.D. *Prostitution in Great Britain, 1485–1901: An Annotated Bibliography*. Metuchen, NJ: Scarecrow Press, 1994.

Nelson, T.G.A. "Women of Pleasure." *Studies in the Eighteenth Century* vol. 6. Papers presented at the D. Nichol Smith Memorial Seminar. Ed. by Colin Duckworth and Homer

Le Grand. (Special issue of *Eighteenth-Century Life* vol. 11 Ns, no. 1 [February 1987]: pp. 181–198.)

Norberg, Kathryn. "Prostitutes," Chapter 15 in *A History of Women in the West, III. Renaissance and Enlightenment Paradoxes*, ed. by Natalie Zemon Davis and Arlette Farge. Cambridge, MA: Belknap Press, 1993.

Norton, Rictor. *Mother Clap's Molly House: The Gay Subculture in England 1700–1830*. London: GMP Publishers Ltd, 1992.

Novak, Macimillan E. "The Unmentionable and the Ineffable in Defoe's Fiction." *Studies in the Literary Imagination* 15.2 (1982): 85–102.

———. *Daniel Defoe: Master of Fictions. His Life and Ideas*. London and New York: Oxford University Press, 2001.

Nussbaum, Felicity A. *Torrid Zones: Maternity, Sexuality, and Empire in Eighteenth-Century English Narratives*. Baltimore: The Johns Hopkins University Press, 1995.

Nussbaum, Martha C. *Sex and Social Justice*. New York: Oxford University Press, 1999.

Oriel, J.D. *Scars of Venus: A History of Venereology*. London and New York: Springer-Verlag, 1994.

Parker, Todd C. *Sexing the Text: The Rhetoric of Sexual Difference in British Literature, 1700–1750*. Albany, NY: State University of New York Press, 2000.

Pateman, Carol. *The Sexual Contract*. Stanford: Stanford University Press, 1988.

Paulson, Ronald. *Hogarth's Harlot: Sacred Parody in Enlightenment England*. Baltimore: Johns Hopkins University Press, 2003.

Peakman, Julie. *Mighty Lewd Books: The Development of Pornography in Eighteenth-Century England*. Houndmills, England and New York: Palgrave Macmillan, 2003.

Pheterson, Gail, ed. *A Vindication of the Rights of Whores*. Seattle, WA: Seal Press, 1989.

———. *The Prostitution Prism*. Amsterdam: Amsterdam University Press, 1996.

Platter, Charles. "The Artificial Whore: George Buchanan's *Apologia Pro Lena*," pp. 207–222 in *Sex and Gender in Medieval and Renaissance Texts: The Latin Tradition*, ed. by Barbara K. Gold, Paul Allen Miller, and Charles Platter. Albany: State University of New York Press, 1997.

Platter, Charles and Barbara Welch. "The Poetics of Prostitution: Buchanan's 'Ars Lenae.'" *Celestinesca* 16.1 (1992): 35–81.

Plomer, H.R. *Dictionary of the Printers and Booksellers Who Were at Work in England, Scotland and Ireland from 1726 to 1775*. Oxford: Oxford University Press, 1932.

Poel, Marc van der. "Erasmus, Rhetoric and Theology: The *Encomium Matrimonii*," pp. 207–227 in *Myricae: Essays on Neo-Latin Literature in Honour of Jozef Ijsewijn*, ed. by Dirk Sacré and Gilbert Tornoy. Leuven: Leuven University Press, 2000.

Pol, Lotte C. van de. *Het Amsterdams hoerdom: Prostitutie in de zeventiende en achttiende eeuw*. Amsterdam: Wereldbibliotheek bv, 1996.

Porter, Roy. "Mixed feelings: The Enlightenment and Sexuality in Eighteenth-Century Britain," pp. 1–27 in *Sexuality in Eighteenth-Century Britain*, ed. by P.G. Boucé. Totowa, NJ: Barnes & Noble, 1982.

———. "Spreading Carnal Knowledge or Selling Dirt Cheap? Nicolas Venette's *Tableau de l'Amour Conjugal* in Eighteenth Century England." *Journal of European Studies* 14 (1984): 233–255.

———. " 'The Secrets of Generation Display'd': Aristotle's Master-Piece in Eighteenth-Century England," pp. 1–21 in *'Tis Nature's Fault Unatuthorized Sexuality during the Enlightenment*, ed. by R.P. Maccubbin (see above).

———. "A Touch of Danger: The Man-Midwife as Sexual Predator," pp. 206–232 in *Sexual Underworlds of the Enlightenment*, ed. by G.S. Rousseau and Roy Porter cited below.

————. "Is Foucault Useful for Understanding Eighteenth- and Nineteenth-Century Sexuality?" *Contention: Debates in Society, Culture and Science*, 1.1 (1991): 62–81.

———— and Mikulas Teich, eds., *Sexual Knowledge, Sexual Science: The History of Attitudes to Sexuality*. Cambridge: Cambridge University Press, 1994.

———— and Lesley Hall. *The Facts of Life: The Creation of Sexual Knowledge in Britain, 1650–1950*. New Haven and London: Yale University Press, 1995.

Primer, Irwin, ed. *Mandeville Studies: New Explorations in the Art and Thought of Dr. Bernard Mandeville 1670–1733*. The Hague: Martinus Nijhoff, 1975.

————. "Erasmus and Bernard Mandeville: A Reconsideration," *Philological Quarterly* 72 (1993): 313–335.

Primoratz, Igor. "What's Wrong with Prostitution?" *Philosophy* 68 (1993): 159–182; reprinted in *The Philosophy of Sex: Contemporary Readings*, fourth edition, ed. by Alan Soble. Lanham, MD: Rowman and Littlefield, 2002; pp. 451–473.

Prior, Charles W.A., ed. *Mandeville and Augustan Ideas: New Essays*. ELS Monograph Series, 83. University of Victoria, 2000.

Quétel, Claude. *History of Syphilis*. (*Mal de Naples* [1990], translated by Judith Braddock and Brian Pike.) Baltimore: Johns Hopkins University Press, 1992.

Rawson, Claude. "Mandeville and Swift," pp. 60–80 in *Eighteenth-Century Contexts: Historical Inquiries in Honor of Phillip Harth* ed. by Howard D. Weinbrot et al. Madison, WI: University of Wisconsin Press, 2001; pp. 60–80.

Redfern, Walter. *Puns*. Oxford and New York: Blackwell, 1984.

Reiman, Donald H. " 'Versioning': The Presentation of Multiple Texts," pp. 167–180 in *Romantic Texts and Contexts*. Columbia: University of Missouri Press, 1987.

Roberts, Nickie. *Whores in History: Prostitution in Western Society*. Hammersmith, London: HarperCollins, 1992.

Robertson, J.M. "Mandeville," in his *Essays towards a Critical Method*. London, 1889; reprinted in his *Pioneer Humanists*, London, 1907.

Rocke, Michael. "Gender and Sexual Culture in Renaissance Italy," pp. 150–170 in *Gender and Society in Renaissance Italy*, ed. by Judith C. Brown and Robert C. Davis. London and New York: Longman, 1998.

Rogal, Samuel J. "The Selling of Sex: Mandeville's *Modest Defence of Publick Stews*." *Studies in Eighteenth-Century Culture*, vol. 5, pp. 141–150. Madison, WI: University of Wisconsin Press, 1976.

Rogers, Katharine. "The Feminism of Daniel Defoe," pp. 3–24 in *Woman in the Eighteenth Century and Other Essays*, ed. by Paul Fritz and Richard Morton. Toronto: Hakkert, 1976.

Rossiaud, Jacques. *Medieval Prostitution*. Trans. Lydia Cochrane. London: Blackwell, 1988.

Rousseau, G.S. and Roy Porter, eds. *Sexual Underworlds of the Enlightenment*. Chapel Hill: University of North Carolina Press, 1988.

Rummel, Erika, ed. *Erasmus on Women*. Toronto: University of Toronto Press, 1986.

Sanger, William W. *The History of Prostitution: Its Extent, Causes, and Effects throughout the World. Being an official report to the Board of Alms-house Governors of the City of New York*. New York: Harper, 1858; reprinted in New York 1939; AMS Press, 1974.

Schneider, Louis. *Paradox and Society: The Work of Bernard Mandeville* New Brunswick, NJ: Transaction Books, 1987.

Schwarzenbach, Sybil. "Contractarians and Feminists Debate Prostitution." *Review of Law and Social Change* 18 (1990–1991): 103–130.

Schwoerer, Lois G. *"No Standing Armies!": The Antiarmy Ideology in Seventeenth-Century England*. Baltimore: Johns Hopkins University Press, 1974.

Scribano, Maria E. *Natura Umana e Società Competitiva: Studio su Mandeville* Milan: Feltrinelli, 1980.

Shoemaker, Robert B. *Prosecution and Punishment: Petty Crime and the Law in London and Rural Middlesex, c. 1660–1725*. Cambridge: Cambridge University Press, 1991. (For the SRMs, see pp. 238–272.)

———. "Reforming the City: The Reformation of Manners Campaign in London, 1690–1738," pp. 99–120 in *Stilling the Grumbling Hive*, ed. by Lee Davison et al. New York: St. Martin's Press, 1992.

Shrage, Laurie. "Should Feminists Oppose Prostitution?" *Ethics* 99.2 (1989): 347–361; reprinted in Soble (2002), below, 435–450.

———. *Moral Dilemmas of Feminism: Prostitution, Adultery, and Abortion*. New York: Routledge, 1994.

———. "Feminist Perspectives on Sex Markets." *The Stanford Encyclopedia of Philosophy* (Spring 2004 edition), ed. by Edward N. Zalta. (This encyclopedia has its own web site.)

Shugg, Wallace. "Prostitution in Shakespeare's London." *Shakespeare Studies* 10 (1977): 291–313.

Siena, Kevin P. "Pollution, Promiscuity, and the Pox: English Venereology and the Early Modern Medical Discourse on Social and Sexual Danger." *Journal of the History of Sexuality* 8.4 (1998): 553–574.

Simpson, Anthony. " 'The Mouth of Strange Women is a Deep Pit:' Male Guilt and Legal Attitudes Toward Prostitution in Georgian London." *Journal of Criminal Justice and Popular Culture* 4.3 (1996): 50–79.

Soble, Alan, ed. *The Philosophy of Sex: Contemporary Readings*. Fourth edition. Lanham, MD: Rowman and Littlefield, 2002.

Sommerville, Margaret R. *Sex and Subjection: Attitudes to Women in Early Modern England*. London: Edward Arnold, 1995.

Speck, W.A. "Mandeville and the Eutopia Seated in the Brain," pp. 66–79 in *Mandeville Studies*, ed. by I. Primer. The Hague: Martinus Nijhoff, 1975.

———. "Bernard Mandeville and the Middlesex Grand Jury," *Eighteenth-Century Studies* 11 (1978): 362–374.

———. "The Harlot's Progress in Eighteenth-Century England." *British Journal for Eighteenth-Century Studies* 3 (1980): 127–139.

Stafford, J. Martin, ed. *Private Vices, Publick Benefits? The Contemporary Reception of Bernard Mandeville* Solihull, England: Ismeron, 1997. (Excellent collection of most texts in the eighteenth-century Mandeville controversy.)

Stengers, Jean and Anne van Neck. *Masturbation: The History of a Great Terror*. New York and Houndmills: Palgrave, 2001.

Stephanson, Raymond. *The Yard of Wit: Male Creativity and Sexuality, 1650–1750*. Philadelphia: University of Pennsylvania Press, 2004.

Stewart, Philip. "Définir la pornographie?" pp. 86–98 in *Du genre libertin au XVIIIe siècle*, ed. by Jean-François Perrin and Philip Stewart. Paris: Desjonquères, coll. "L'esprit des lettres," 2004.

Stolberg, Michael. "Self-Pollution, Moral Reform and the Venereal Trade: Notes on the Sources and Historical Context of the *Onania* (1716)." *Journal of the History of Sexuality* 9.1/2 (January–April 2000).

———. "An Unmanly Vice: Self-pollution, Anxiety, and the Body in the Eighteenth Century." *Social History of Medicine*, 13.1 (2000): 1–21.

———. "The Crime of Onan and the Laws of Nature. Religious and Medical Discourses on Masturbation in the Late Seventeenth and Early Eighteenth Centuries." *Pedagogica Historica* 39.6 (2003): 701–717.

Stone, Lawrence, *The Family, Sex and Marriage in England (1500–1800)*. New York: Harper & Row, 1977.

————. *Uncertain Unions: marriage in England, 1660–1753*. Oxford: Oxford University Press, 1992.

Strossen, Nadine. *Defending Pornography: Free Speech, Sex, and the Fight for Women's Rights*. New York: New York University Press, 2000.

Thomas, Keith. "The Double Standard." *Journal of the History of Ideas* 20 (1959): 195–216.

Thompson, Roger. *Unfit for Modest Ears: A Study of the Pornographic, Obscene and Bawdy Works Written or Published in England in the Second Half of the Seventeenth Century*. Totowa, NJ: Rowman and Littlefield, 1979.

Thorn, Jennifer, ed. *Writing British infanticide: child-murder, gender, and print, 1722–1859*. Cranbury, NJ: University of Delaware Press; Associated University Presses, 2003.

Treadwell, Michael. "On False and Misleading Imprints in the London Book Trade, 1660–1750," pp. 29–46 in *Fakes and Frauds: Varieties of Deception in Print & Manuscript*, ed. by Robin Myers and Michael Harris. Winchester: St Paul's Bibliographies, and Detroit: Omnigraphics Inc., 1989.

Trumbach, Randolph. "Sex, Gender, and Sexual Identity in Modern Culture: Male Sodomy and Female Prostitution in Enlightenment London." *Journal of the History of Sexuality* 2.2 (1991) 186–203.

————. *Sex and the Gender Revolution: Volume One: Heterosexuality and the Third Gender in Enlightenment London*. Chicago: University of Chicago Press, 1998.

Turner, James Grantham. *Sexuality and Gender in Early Modern Europe: Institutions, Texts, Images*. Cambridge and New York: Cambridge University Press, 1995.

————. "Pictorial Prostitution: Visual Culture, Vigilantism, and 'Pornography' in Dunton's *Night Walker*." *Studies in Eighteenth-Century Culture*, vol. 28. Baltimore: Johns Hopkins University Press, 1999.

————. *Libertines and Radicals in Early Modern London: Sexuality, Politics and Literary Culture, 1630–1685*. Cambridge and New York: Cambridge University Press, 2002.

————. *Schooling Sex: Libertine Literature and Erotic Education in Italy, France, and England, 1534–1685*. Oxford: Oxford University Press, 2003.

Vichert, Gordon S. *A Critical Study of the English Works of Bernard Mandeville (1670–1733)*. (Dissertation) University of London, June 1964.

Wagner, Peter. *Eros Revived: Erotica of the Enlightenment in England and America*. London: Secker & Warburg, 1988.

————, ed. *Erotica and the Enlightenment*. Series: Britannia, vol. 2. Frankfurt am Main and New York: P. Lang, 1990.

Walkowitz, Judith R. *Prostitution and Victorian Society: Women, Class, and the State*. Cambridge: Cambridge University Press, 1980.

Weber, Harold. "The Jester and the Orator: A Re-examination of the Comic and the Tragic Satirist." *Genre* 13 (1980): 171–185.

Wiesner-Hanks, Merry E. *Christianity and Sexuality in the Early Modern World: Regulating Desire, Reforming Practice*. New York: Routledge, 2000.

Yeazell, Ruth Bernard. *Fictions of Modesty: Women and Courtship in the English Novel*. Chicago: University of Chicago Press, 1991.

INDEX